UNRAVELING
THE MYSTERIES OF
The Big Bang Theory

OTHER SMART POP TELEVISION TITLES

Seven Seasons of Buffy

Five Seasons of Angel

What Would Sipowicz Do?

Stepping through the Stargate

Finding Serenity

Alias Assumed

Farscape Forever!

Totally Charmed

Welcome to Wisteria Lane

Boarding the Enterprise

Getting Lost

So Say We All

Investigating CSI

Neptune Noir

Coffee at Luke's

Grey's Anatomy 101

Serenity Found

House Unauthorized

In the Hunt

A Taste of True Blood

Inside Joss' Dollhouse

A Visitor's Guide to Mystic Falls

Filled with Glee

Fringe Science

A Friday Night Lights Companion

Triumph of The Walking Dead

OTHER BOOKS BY GEORGE BEAHM

The Stephen King Companion

War of Words: The Censorship Debate

Muggles and Magic: An Unofficial Guide to J.K. Rowling
and the Harry Potter Phenomenon

Caribbean Pirates: A Treasure Chest of Facts, Fiction, and Folklore

Twilight Tours: An Illustrated Guide to the Real Forks

UNRAVELING
≡ MYSTERIES OF
The Big Bang Theory
AN UNABASHEDLY UNAUTHORIZED TV SHOW COMPANION

GEORGE BEAHM

AN IMPRINT OF BENBELLA BOOKS, INC.
DALLAS, TEXAS

Smart Pop is an Imprint of BenBella Books, Inc.
10300 N. Central Expressway, Suite 400
Dallas, TX 75231

www.benbellabooks.com
www.smartpopbooks.com

Send feedback to feedback@benbellabooks.com
Printed in the United States of America

Printed in the United States of America
10 9 8 7 6 5 4 3 2 1

Library of Congress Cataloging-in-Publication Data is available for this title.
ISBN 978-1-936661-14-5

Copyediting by Oriana Leckert
Proofreading by Michael Fedison
Cover design by Faceout Studio
Text design and composition by Elyse Strongin, Neuwirth & Associates, Inc.
Printed by Bang Printing

Distributed by Perseus Distribution
http://www.perseusdistribution.com/

Significant discounts for bulk sales are available. Please contact Glenn Yeffeth
at glenn@benbellabooks.com or (214) 750-3628.

for Scott, who shaped the book proposal;

and for Leah, who shaped the book

"I'm meant for greater things, like unraveling the mysteries of the universe . . ."

—Dr. Sheldon Cooper, in a conversation with
Dr. Leonard Hofstadter, explaining why he doesn't drive,
in "The Euclid Alternative" (2-5)

CONTENTS

Introduction: "Excuse Me, But Do You Speak Klingon?"   xiii

PART 1: A BRIEF HISTORY OF TIME   1

Intelligent Designers: Cocreators Chuck Lorre and Bill Prady,
    and the Genesis of *The Big Bang Theory*   3
To Badly Go Where No One Has Gone Before: The 2006 Pilot   7
The Successful Reboot: The 2007 Pilot   16

PART 2: THE STARS' TREKS   21

A Night to Remember: "And the Golden Globe Goes to . . ."   23
The Search for Spock: The Evolution of Dr. Sheldon Cooper   26
Great Expectations: Dr. Leonard Hofstadter   46
Lust in Space: Mr. Howard Wolowitz   54
The Invisible Man: Dr. Rajesh Koothrappali   65
The Voyage Home: Penny   75
Shooting Stars: The Supporting Cast   87

PART 3: BEAMING DOWN TO PASADENA   101

The Sheldonian Universe: From the Couch to the Cosmos   103
    1. Home Sweet Home   103
    2. Dining   108
    3. Shopping   112
    4. Comic Book Stores   115
    5. Movies   118

6. Miscellaneous Pasadena Locations 119

7. California Institute of Technology (Caltech) 122

8. Greater Los Angeles 127

9. Greater California 133

10. The United States 136

11. International Locations 140

12. Space 143

PART 4: FANDOM 147

The Newcomer's Guide to Fandom 149

Exploring Your Inner Geek 155

The Insider's Guide to Getting In for a Live Taping of
The Big Bang Theory 161

The Warner Bros. Studio VIP Tour 166

Getting Your Geek On in Public: A Convention Primer
for Muggles 171

The Noob's Gaming Guide 181

PART 5: RELIANCE ON SCIENCE 185

A Condensed History of the Universe, from the Big Bang to
the Twenty-First Century 187

Science Matters 191

Stellar Scientists Star on *The Big Bang Theory* 195

The Science of *The Big Bang Theory:* A Primer for the
Science-Impaired, Perpetually Perplexed, but Sufficiently
Intelligent Person 200

PART 6: THE EPISODE TITLE EXPLICATION 209

Season One 211

Season Two 216

Season Three 223

Season Four 228

PART 7: SHEDDING LIGHT ON DARK MATTER   235

Afterword: "All Good Things . . ."   311

Acknowledgments   313
About the Author   315

INTRODUCTION

"Excuse Me, But Do You Speak Klingon?"

"We have a perfect life. We go to the lab, we do our research, we eat, we watch Lord of the Rings. Who has a better life than us?"

—Dr. Sheldon Cooper, to Dr. Leonard Hofstadter, in the 2006 pilot

Movies and television shows about geeks are nothing new. In fact, the premise of *The Big Bang Theory* is simple: geeky guys meet beautiful girl. This premise has proven to be profitable through the years, but most often at the geeks' expense: we laugh *at* them, not *with* them. For instance, in *Revenge of the Nerds*, the geeks/nerds are portrayed as physically unappealing and socially awkward, and thus ripe for abuse at the hands of the beauties (cheerleaders) and the beasts (football players). It's little wonder, then, that when CBS announced yet another show about geeks, the media was skeptical. What could be said about one more show about geeks gawking at gorgeous girls as muscular goons look on and laugh?

It depends, of course, on the show. *The Big Bang Theory* didn't simply serve warmed-up leftovers, but instead gave viewers new, tasty fare. Although we have geeks and girls aplenty, the critical difference is that *The Big Bang Theory* is a celebration, not a denigration, of cerebration. The good-natured humor can be found in the show's situations, not in lampooning the characters themselves.

The tried-and-true formula of mocking geeks is so pervasive that in the 2006 pilot of the show, the cocreators took the path more traveled: they, too, made fun of the geeks. Wisely, and despite this misstep, CBS saw the potential in the pilot and, after retooling, came up with a new twist that would eventually propel *The Big Bang Theory* high into the ratings stratosphere.

Set in Pasadena, California, the show focuses on four friends who work at Caltech: Dr. Sheldon Cooper, Dr. Leonard Hofstadter, Dr. Rajesh Koothrappali, and *Mr.* Howard Wolowitz. For years their lives have followed predictable orbits, until the presence of a new heavenly body, in the form of a beautiful young woman, fortuitously changes all their lives.

In the inevitable collision between the geek world and the real world, hilarity ensues, especially in the form of its presumed leader, Dr. Cooper, who stands apart from and above them all. Like his hero Mr. Spock, Sheldon Cooper is at war with himself. Though he wishes to live a life free of the petty biological distractions, like sex, that plague carbon-based life forms, he finds himself flummoxed by *la comédie humaine*—the human comedy—at every turn. What's even funnier is that he doesn't see himself as part of the proceedings; he sees himself as an aloof, disinterested observer, though he's often at the center of the maelstrom.

Based on its own merits as a comedy, the sitcom can hold its own; however, the cocreators chose to enrich it with verisimilitude by taking pains to ensure that the show, which is laden with scientific references, is vetted by a physicist from California State University. By doing so, the show celebrates real science, among the scientific community and students alike. In its own way, just as *Star Trek* led many young people into related fields, *The Big Bang Theory* may well have a salutary effect on physics.

If *The Big Bang Theory* were simply standard sitcom fare, intended as a laugh-fest, there would be little need to dig deeper and look behind the curtain to examine its fictional universe, the characters that populate it, and the situations they find themselves in. But the show itself is a rich vein waiting to be tapped: like us, the characters are part of the human comedy, and we see ourselves—to a greater or lesser degree—in them.

Using the metaphor of the Big Bang, this book begins with the show's creation by Chuck Lorre and Bill Brady, examining its origin: the unsuccessful 2006 pilot, untitled and unaired. We then look at the successful 2007 pilot, which properly sets the stage for the discussions to follow.

We meet the actors who play the key roles, and turn a critical eye to those roles: like elemental particles, the characters interlock to bind into a whole.

We take a detailed, guided tour of Pasadena, ground zero for the boys.

We also bone up on the science that informs the show. Even if science wasn't your favorite subject in school, we'll explain it to you in a realistic manner, and you'll see how it forms the backdrop to the show.

After class, it's time to cut loose, have fun, and explore the world of fandom. Especially for first-timers who want to get their geek on, I'll point out the fans' hot spots, known as conventions (or cons), where one goes to hobnob with hobbits, discourse with dragons, soar through the galaxy on metal-finned spaceships, and go up, up, and away with superheroes.

In addition, to give you plenty of context, I've provided a detailed explication of each episode's title and plot.

Finally, to help guide you, a reader-friendly, annotated glossary explains who's who, what's what, and gives you everything else you need to unravel the mysteries of the show's many pop culture references.

In short, this book is your definitive guide to *The Big Bang Theory*'s universe and everything in it.

Ready to beam into the world of *The Big Bang Theory*?

Please stand still as we energize . . .

Part 1

A BRIEF HISTORY
OF TIME

In which we learn about the show's creators,
the unaired 2006 pilot, and the aired 2007
pilot that successfully launched the show

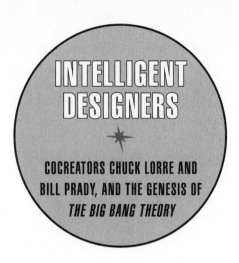

INTELLIGENT DESIGNERS

COCREATORS CHUCK LORRE AND
BILL PRADY, AND THE GENESIS OF
THE BIG BANG THEORY

1. *In the beginning, Lorre and Prady brainstormed and came up with two ideas for sitcoms.*
2. *In the first, the show would revolve around a young single woman making her way in the world.*
3. *In the second, the show would revolve around geeky, high-IQ scientists who live in their own closed universe and can't relate to women.*
4. *And lo!, Lorre and Prady combined the two ideas to come up with a premise: they would be neighbors—the beauty and the geeks—and help one another to get through life.*
5. *And Lorre and Prady labored mightily and, alas, produced a sucky pilot, and so went back to the drawing board.*
6. *Katie, the female lead, was dumped, and the perky, likable Penny was added, and they saw that it was good.*
7. *They saw that the test audience liked Sheldon and Leonard, the two geeky physicists with good hearts, and lo!, they decided that two more geeks would be added.*
8. *So they said, let there be Howard and Rajesh to add to the humor! And they saw that was good.*
9. *And because this was a show about science, they brought forth a UCLA physicist to check the facts. And verily I say unto you, that was a good thing indeed.*

10. *And they looked back on their labors and said, Behold, I give you a sitcom that won't insult its audience's intelligence, and may it go forth and multiply unto many seasons.*

11. *And CBS' Leslie Moonves looked down on their creation, and yea, he committed to buying the sitcom, because the second pilot, unlike the first one, was not sucky.*

12. *And Lorre and Prady saw everything they had made, and, behold!, they saw that it was good, and they smiled, and so righteously they celebrated.*

13. *Then the popularity of the show multiplied its audience manyfold, and that was very good, and verily, the show was renewed unto its seventh season, and there was joy in Mudville—er, Tinseltown.*

14. *And then Chuck Lorre and Bill Prady rested.*

When Chuck Lorre and Bill Prady went to CBS' president and CEO Leslie Moonves to sell him on the idea of *The Big Bang Theory*, they eschewed the normal procedure of "pitching," which involves coming up with a one-line summary (a "logline") and using it to open an enthusiastic verbal presentation backed up by a printed "bible" that fleshes out details about characters and settings. Of course, since it takes a lot of ideas to come up with one that a network might be interested in, the "pitchers" go in and throw a lot of balls, hoping the network will "catch" one.

Rather than pitch *The Big Bang Theory*, Lorre and Prady went whole hog and filmed an actual pilot, so CBS could see *exactly* what they were offering. Fortunately, though CBS passed on the initial go-round, *Big Bang*'s creators were encouraged to go back to the drawing board, reboot the concept, and come back, which they did a year later. This time, CBS liked what they saw and committed to buy four seasons.

In retrospect, it's not too surprising that Lorre and Prady were able to come up with such a winning concept. Between the two of them, they have a wealth of experience in the film and television industries. At the time he pitched the show in 2006, Chuck Lorre's credits included *Grace Under Fire*, *Cybill*, *Dharma & Greg*, and the hugely successful *Two and a Half Men*. Bill Prady, who began his writing career with Jim Henson (*The Muppets*), worked with Lorre on *Dharma & Greg*; he'd also worked on *Married with Children*, *Dream On*, *Star Trek: Voyager*, and *The Gilmore Girls*. Prady, a former computer programmer who worked at the Small Computer Company, knew a coworker who, like Raj, couldn't talk to women unless he was drunk. Prady also had a friend in Brooklyn named Lenny who fixed RadioShack computers.

Fortunately, the original title for the show (*Lenny, Penny, and Kenny*) was discarded in favor of a catchier one, which had more of a *bang* to it: *The Big Bang Theory*, with its intentional double entendre.

Grounded in real science and supplemented by pop culture references, the show is a tacit acknowledgment that geeks *rule*.

As Bill Prady pointed out in an online interview posted on Bob Andleman's website: "Our show is about the feeling of being an outsider, which is a feeling we all share."

Chuck Lorre agrees. In an interview with Michael Idato of the *Brisbane Times*, Lorre elaborated: "Regardless of the fact that they're dealing with quantum mechanics, they're still dealing with feeling and emotions, and those are the things that are commonly shared. The heart of the show is a feeling that you don't quite get it, or you think you've got it but you haven't. That's the universal way in for these characters—wanting to participate in the world but not feeling like you know how."

Though some reviewers have pointed out that the character of Sheldon Cooper is the undisputed star of the show and, therefore, indispensable, the reality is that, as Prady pointed out at a press conference at Comic-Con 2009:

> The characters all work in balance. I think they work best as a group. I think Jim does magnificent work, but I also think they all do. If you look at those amazing scenes with Kaley that Jim does, where you're watching him do crazy stuff, remember the comic

genius of the person who's holding on to the reins of the horse—
that's the *other* person in the scene. You'll see that the comic success
of that big character is based on the timing of the person working
with him. Sometimes it's not as flashy.

If you watch what Kaley or Johnny does with him, you know the
thing is Jim's character, not Jim himself. Sheldon is insufferable,
except that Leonard suffers him. So we accept him as sufferable.
And so it takes an amazing piece of performance from Johnny
Galecki to be the person that could put up with that.

The show is no one-trick pony. In order for it to remain funny
and fresh, its characters must evolve, just as they would in real life.
As Bill Prady pointed out to Luaine Lee of thestar.com,

> We have an amazing ensemble on *The Big Bang Theory*. And we get
> to do twenty-three or twenty-four shows a year. It is an opportunity
> to learn more about them and get more depth to them. I think
> that's something we try to do in learning about where Sheldon and
> Leonard come from by meeting their mothers. You know, they
> come from very, very different backgrounds. And that's our attempt
> at also getting deeper into the characters.

Now that four seasons have aired and the main characters are
firmly established, the show has the luxury of adding new characters, delving more deeply into the secondary characters to flesh
them out, and taking calculated chances with the established
story line.

Currently, the show averages over 13 million viewers in the
United States alone. Watched in almost seventy countries worldwide, the four geeks and a girl have proven to be a winning combination from Albania to Venezuela.

But in the *very* beginning, it *didn't* start with a big bang, but a
whimper.

TO BADLY GO WHERE NO ONE HAS GONE BEFORE

THE 2006 PILOT

*U*ntitled and unaired, the first pilot of *The Big Bang Theory* ("Final Sales Version, Project #27601") was presented to CBS executives on May 1, 2006. It didn't sell, but because it showed promise, CBS encouraged Chuck Lorre and Bill Prady to go back to the drawing board and rework it for a subsequent presentation.

Traditionally, a pilot is added as a bonus feature in a DVD set, but neither the principals nor CBS saw fit to do that with this one. Given its lackluster qualities, it's unlikely that it will ever be made generally available.

There are no authorized copies available from any source, but bootleg copies appear—and then immediately disappear—from websites like YouTube. CBS' lawyers must play a constant game of Whack-A-Mole to keep it from the public's view.

Because it's officially not available, there has been a great deal of discussion online about its specifics: its plot, its emphasis on sex, and, most significantly, its miscasting of major characters. Given that some of its key elements were repurposed for the 2007 pilot, this elusive episode bears an extensive look under a 2-micron microscope.

If the 2007 reboot was a refreshing glass of lemonade—tart, sweet, and with a unique zing—the 2006 pilot was a lemon.

Principal Cast

Dr. Sheldon Cooper (Jim Parsons)
Dr. Leonard Hofstadter (Johnny Galecki)
Katie (Amanda Walsh)
Gilda (Iris Bahr)

Episode Summary

The episode opens with Thomas Dolby's "She Blinded Me With Science," a song about a man in love with a Japanese girl named Miss Sakamoto. Tangentially connected to the episode itself, the music strikes a discordant note, foreshadowing the many problems in the pilot.

After making deposits at a sperm bank to raise quick cash for dinner that night at the Bombay Palace, Dr. Leonard Hofstadter and Dr. Sheldon Cooper walk past an obviously distraught young woman, cell phone in hand, arguing with her mother about coming home temporarily because she has no other place to go.

Though Sheldon doesn't want to get involved, Leonard does, and he prevails on Sheldon to stop and help. The woman agrees to let them buy her dinner, because she's broke and has few options, and we get the distinct impression that this is how she gets through life, by appearing to be gracious and taking men up on their offers to help in every way possible. Katie's true colors are seen over dinner, when she verbally attacks and belittles Sheldon, then takes advantage of Leonard's offer to temporarily stay in the boys' shared apartment.

Sparks fly when the three go home. One of the doctors' colleagues, a woman named Gilda, comes over to visit and sees Katie, whom she perceives as a threat to her budding relationship with Leonard. But when Katie makes it clear that she's disinterested in both Leonard and Sheldon, everyone is happy—except Sheldon, who views the shrewish Katie as having already overstayed her welcome. Katie, who knows a good thing when she sees it, wins Leonard over with her initial insistence that she'd stay "three days, a week tops," but of course it proves to be much longer.

The episode ends in a local bar, where Katie has taken Sheldon, Leonard, and Gilda out dancing. On the dance floor, Katie, dressed in tight, revealing clothing, is "poetry in motion" (from the show's theme song), but the others jerk spasmodically, like frogs galvanized with electric shocks. Looking on, Katie apologizes for her convulsing acquaintances by explaining to a curious onlooker, "They don't get out much."

Guess Who's Coming to Dinner

In a group cast and crew interview at an annual William S. Paley Festival, Bill Prady said, "The 2006 pilot, while including the basic Leonard/Sheldon dynamic, had huge conceptual mistakes that we steered away from when we made the second pilot."

When pressed by the audience for clarification, Prady explained:

> The key difference in the original pilot was the conception of the female lead. The original character [called Katie in that version] was envisioned as a street-hardened, tough-as-nails woman with a vulnerable interior. The idea was for the guys, who would approach her with honesty, to draw the real, sensitive Kate out.

Katie the Shrew

The woman in question, played by Canadian actress Amanda Walsh, appeared only in the unaired 2006 pilot, though her official website erroneously credits her for being a "series regular" on the show in 2007.

In creating Katie's character, Lorre and Prady violated the prime directive of casting a sitcom: make the lead characters likable. In Katie, unfortunately, there's far too little to like.

Though Lorre and Prady's intentions were good—having a character who was damaged goods, who through the kindness of strangers like Leonard and Sheldon becomes whole—the end result required them to permanently jettison her in favor of a more relatable and sympathetic female lead.

Katie, the proverbial bad penny, soon begins to create unintended havoc in Sheldon and Leonard's otherwise routine lifestyle. We get the sense that no matter where she goes, chaos will result. Katie lives in a universe essentially populated only by herself: *her* needs, *her* concerns, and *her* unending, often insoluble, problems.

Early on, when she's offered a free dinner by Leonard and Sheldon, she's characteristically wary and tells them, "You guys can buy me dinner, but that's the end of it"—as if *she's* doing *them* a favor by allowing them to pay for her meal. Her expectation is that they will want sex with her for payment afterward; their expectation is that they're doing a good deed to help someone who's down on her luck, with no financial or sexual strings attached.

Though Leonard and Sheldon buy her dinner, that's not the end of it; in fact, it's just the beginning, as she begins her endless, running commentary on how life sucks in general and how her life in particular sucks big-time.

When Sheldon, for instance, complains about his table's location at the restaurant (a scene recalling his sofa seat in his apartment), she asks, "What's his problem?" And apropos of nothing, she asks, "Have you ever seen a lady naked?" She follows that up by nonsensically insisting that he call himself "Skippy."

All attack and no tact, Katie doesn't see, or care, that she's biting the hand that feeds her. Sheldon reluctantly agrees, because of Leonard, to help her out, without any demands for repayment. In return, she lets loose a barrage of blasts belittling Sheldon, whom she's sized up as a loser.

Leonard fares no better. After a late night of dancing at a bar, Katie returns to the apartment, where she breaks a lamp, partially disrobes in front of him, wipes his whiteboard clean—erasing equations that were months in the making—and throws a tantrum after he suggests she accept responsibility for her self-destructive behavior. She bolts from the apartment, after drawing a penis with testicles on his whiteboard. She thinks *he's* acting like a real dick.

The Bitch Is Back

Is that the end of contentious Katie? Unfortunately, not by a long shot. She returns to the apartment because she has no other option. Explaining her actions to Leonard, she rhetorically asks, "Where else can I live rent-free without banging some loser?"

Where indeed?

The prospect of Katie moving in for an indefinite stay strikes fear in Sheldon, who realizes she's a wicked witch. When she nonchalantly asks him about his testicles ("Hey, how they hanging?"), he can only reply, stone-faced, "At the moment, they are making a fear-based journey up the inguinal canal."

Both Sheldon and Leonard are nice guys, always accommodating, whereas Katie's a loser-user who takes advantage of their kindness and generosity, and then repays them with insults. To her, Leonard's just another chump, the kind of guy she can easily manipulate without having to give anything in return—not even a word of thanks.

Well aware that she is attractive, Katie makes it clear that she considers herself sexually off limits to her new, albeit temporary, roommates. Feeling threatened, Gilda notices and confronts Katie, who unwraps her towel to expose her naked body. She says, "You mean by giving them a shot at this? Never going to happen."

Those are the key words. She can undress in front of them, show off her cleavage and as much skin as possible, and talk endlessly about sex, but it's hands-off, boys; you can look but not touch; I'm saving the goods for *real* men. But what you chumps can do is feed me, listen sympathetically to my problems, and then give me free food and lodging. In exchange, I'll give you a hard time.

Don't Kiss Me, Kate!

Though glimmers of goodness from Katie occasionally shine through, it's clear that in this incarnation she's a poor fit for the show, which test audiences made abundantly clear. At a Paley Festival, Bill Prady remarked, "What we didn't anticipate, though, is how protective the audience would feel about our guys. Early screenings of that version of the pilot led audiences to beg that the 'mean lady' would stay away from the 'sweet guys.'" In other words, it's time for someone to drop a house on this wicked witch.

Sex, Sex, Sex!

Nothing exceeds like excess.

Chuck Lorre, who created the sex-saturated sitcom *Two and a Half Men*, injected a strong component of sex into this pilot: repeated references to male masturbation, recreational sex, semi-nudity, sexual exposure, sexual innuendo, a sexual drawing, and endless erotic bantering, all of which distracted from the inherent appeal of the show.

What works in terms of sex for *Two and a Half Men* doesn't work for *The Big Bang Theory*. Why? Because the former is *all* about sexual relationships, whereas the latter is about human relationships, of which sex is but one component (albeit a prominent one). By giving the 2006 pilot more emphasis on the sexual "bang" and less on the scientific "theory," the focus strayed too far afield from the premise's essential core: the culture clash between the geek world and the real world, as perceived by Leonard and Sheldon.

When Leonard asks Sheldon, "Don't you ever wonder if we're missing out on things?" Sheldon laments, "I don't even know who you are anymore." The road less traveled is Sheldon's route, but it is not for Leonard, who wants to take a walk on the wild side. To him,

Katie represents that adventurous road and all that it promises. The so-called "perfect life" Sheldon alludes to is not what Leonard wants. Their clash is the expressive heart of the show.

Grating Gilda

Like Katie, Gilda is another character miscalculation. Played by Iris Bahr, Gilda is a geeky brunette who works with Leonard and has a frenetic speech pattern that is difficult to follow. Her short bursts of rapidly spoken words are like bullets sprayed from a machine gun.

Gilda is torn between Leonard and Sheldon. Though she professes to have a romantic interest in Leonard, a relationship she plans to build slowly over a period of time, she's already had sex with Sheldon at a *Star Trek* convention—which she admits to Leonard, to Sheldon's mortification. "He was doing such an effective job portraying a Vulcan caught up in the *pon farr* mating fever that I couldn't say no," she explains as Sheldon looks guiltily on.

Initially suspicious of Katie, whom she deprecatingly calls "Princess Aureola," Gilda's presence adds little to the 2006 pilot. For the subsequent pilot, Gilda was dumped and her character retooled as Dr. Leslie Winkle, who refuses to be intimidated by Sheldon and who delights in calling him "dumb ass," which so thoroughly fries his integrated circuits that he can offer only feeble protests and inadequate ripostes when his characteristic rapier-like wit fails him.

Sex and Sheldon

Those two words should not go together. The Sheldon we know and love is asexual, but in the 2006 pilot he's quite the cheeky little monkey. He's not only sexually active, but he admits to Leonard that he has a fetish for "hindquarters."

Sheldon's characterization as a super-bright but essentially horny physicist was a major miscalculation. Painting Sheldon this way puts him on the same plane of existence as Leonard, when in fact our Sheldon is aloof from the human race in general; he is totally disinterested in sex, which sets him apart from his immediate circle of friends, all of whom are anxious to experience the joy of sex. Sheldon is happiest when he can cite obscure facts, trivia, and commentary to befuddle, amaze, and amuse.

In the show we know and love, Sheldon is so asexual that Penny has to ask his friends what his deal is: "women, men, sock puppets?" But in the 2006 pilot, he's not only sexually aware, but even sexually experienced. Though he maintains that his interest in female buttocks is merely a biological imperative, "a classic evolutionary response," we know differently. He's just plain horny. (Over dinner, when Katie asks him if he's ever seen a woman naked, he replies that he's seen six, and "not all of them were relatives.") And who can blame him? It's normal.

But we don't *want* a normal Sheldon. We also don't want an abnormal or subnormal Sheldon; we want a *supra*-normal Sheldon, one who is worlds apart from the rest of the human race.

A sexually aware Sheldon would fundamentally change the tone of the show and provide less comic fodder; an asexual Sheldon sets up innumerable points of conflict between his world, in which sexual imperatives are conspicuous by their absence, and the normal world of everyone around him, where sex and sexuality are omnipresent.

Sheldon: The Show's Nucleus

Clearly, what the fledgling show needed was more emphasis on the relationship between Leonard and Sheldon, and their interactivity with the outside world. Just as clearly, Sheldon's character, with his unique worldview, stands apart from, and above, his fellow geeks. His character would principally be the one around whom the story lines would revolve.

Rebooting

Open to suggestions from CBS, the show's creators recognized the essential heart of the show lay in main characters' relationships. By fine-tuning Sheldon's character, while leaving Leonard's alone, and dropping the combative female characters, the show was ready for its reboot: an opportunity to let Sheldon shine.

Once the viewer embraces Sheldon's wonky worldview, the stage is properly set for divine comedy.

Perspectives

Chuck Lorre: We did the "Big Bang Pilot" about two and a half years ago, and it sucked . . . but there were two remarkable things that worked perfectly, and that was Johnny and Jim. We rewrote the thing entirely, and then we were blessed with Kaley and Simon and Kunal. (A panel at San Diego Comic-Con in 2008)

THE SUCCESSFUL REBOOT

THE 2007 PILOT

Principal Cast

Dr. Sheldon Cooper (Jim Parsons)
Dr. Leonard Hofstadter (Johnny Galecki)
Dr. Rajesh Koothrappali (Kunal Nayyar)
Mr. Howard Wolowitz (Simon Helberg)
Penny [no last name on record] (Kaley Cuoco)

Episode Summary

In this seminal episode, Sheldon and Leonard intend to make deposits at a high-IQ sperm bank to raise money to buy fractional T-1 bandwidth for their computers at the apartment, but Sheldon gets cold feet and convinces Leonard they should leave.

When they return to their apartment with takeout from the Tandoori Palace, they spy Penny, the new neighbor across the hall, unpacking. A perky blonde wearing cutoff shorts and a revealing top, Penny gets Leonard's attention, and he immediately falls in love with her.

At Leonard's request, he and Sheldon invite her over for lunch and get to know her. She's from Nebraska, believes in astrology, and is a waitress at the Cheesecake Factory. Then she unexpectedly shares with them the story of her recent breakup with a boyfriend of four years, which sets her off on a crying jag.

Unsure as how to console her, Sheldon and Leonard are relieved when she stops crying and thanks them for their kindness. She also asks to use their shower because hers isn't working.

Exit Penny and enter Howard and Raj, who are unaware that there is a lady on the premises. When Penny emerges, with a towel wrapped around her bodacious bod, Raj is characteristically rendered mute, and Howard's personality changes: he's suddenly the lady's man—or so he thinks, as he begins complimenting her. It doesn't take long for Penny to peg Howard: he fancies himself a player, but he's far from it.

Penny, realizing that Leonard is smitten with her, asks him for a favor, to which he agrees even without hearing her out. She wants him to retrieve her television from her ex-boyfriend's apartment, and so, on a knight's errand, Leonard and Sheldon sally forth to slay a dragon for the damsel in distress ... and come back empty-handed and without pants.

Penny, who is grateful they made a good-faith effort, takes them all out for dinner. On the way to the restaurant, Sheldon sizes up the male occupants of the car and reassures a dubious Leonard that "I don't know what your odds are in the world as a whole, but as far as the population of this car goes, you're a veritable Mack Daddy."

Ch-ch-ch-ch-changes

The difference between the 2006 and 2007 pilots is night versus day. Whereas the former was permeated by darkness—in tone and appearance—the latter was suffused with optimism and light.

The principal difference is the transformation of the female lead, from bad girl to good: the bitchy Katie replaced by Kaley Cuoco's Penny, who is easy on the eyes and, even more important, likable. Literally the girl next door, Penny is optimistic, good-hearted, and achingly vulnerable—a stark contrast to the street-smart and cynical Katie, who had a veneer of toughness to mask her vulnerabilities.

Penny, who is anxious to turn over a new leaf, is on her own, living in her own apartment, working a full-time job, and able to get by with a little help from her new friends. She is winsome and approachable, and it's easy to see how Leonard is so easily smitten.

But the transformation of the female lead was not sufficient to substantially change the pilot from unsuccessful to successful; that required the transformation of another main character: Sheldon.

Sheldon undergoes two dramatic changes. First, though it's not stated, it's clear that he is not attracted to Penny, though we don't yet know why; as the series unfolds, we learn that Sheldon is asexual and, thus, simply disinterested in women. Second, Sheldon's speech patterns subtly change. His diction is more controlled, finessed, replete with dramatic pauses and emphases. This suggests that, as with every other aspect of his life, Sheldon's speech puts him apart from and above his peers. By thus distancing himself, Sheldon's alien nature dramatizes his "stranger in a strange land" posture: he is of us, but he's clearly not *one* of us.

The final significant change between the two pilots is discarding Gilda and adding two more male geeks, Howard Wolowitz and Rajesh Koothrappali. Howard is Jewish, lives with his mother, and has a master's from MIT; Rajesh is an Asian Indian, lives alone, and has a doctorate.

These welcome changes—reinventing the female lead, fine-tuning Sheldon, and adding two more boys to the geek squad—struck all the right notes with the audience. *The Big Bang Theory* was ready for prime time. But although the reactions from critics and fans were positive, not everyone agreed.

Perspectives

NPR's Linda Holmes, on March 9, 2009: CBS's *The Big Bang Theory* is an odd little show. The Fall 2007 pilot was so atrocious that I couldn't wait for it to be over, but since then, I've gradually seen friends give in to it, to the point where it has many followers in common with *How I Met Your Mother*. There are two good comedic performances at its center from Johnny Galecki and Jim Parsons as roommates and nerds Leonard and Sheldon—I am not a fan of Kaley Cuoco, who plays their obligatory hot neighbor, but two out of three really isn't bad for a show that airs on the same night as *Two and a Half Men*.

On January 6, 2010: As I've mentioned, I truly despised the pilot of CBS's *The Big Bang Theory*, which aired in the fall of 2007. I found it unfunny, obnoxious, stilted, and tired. But now, having been persuaded to try it again this fall—and intrigued by the fact that its audience was steadily growing, which very rarely happened—I've really come to love it . . . Making Penny real has opened up all kinds of comedic possibilities that haven't transformed it into life-changing art, but have made it into a very good half-hour sitcom, which is an enormous change from the pilot—which is still just as excruciating as it was the first time I saw it.

IGN.TV: The writing in this episode was some of the best we've seen in a standard sitcom in some time—it's very smart. We'll be the first to admit, however, that not everyone will love the show. Let's face it, not everyone wants to see a sitcom about nerds playing *World of Warcraft* and Klingon Boggle. That being said, the pilot was a great start for the series. If the writing remains at the level seen in the pilot, we're certain the show will continue to be worth watching. (Sept. 28, 2007)

ELEVEN REASONS WE'RE MAD FOR
THE BIG BANG THEORY
· · · · · · · · · · · ·

1. Jim Parsons' body language and exquisitely delivered dialogue.
2. Simon Helberg's comic delivery. Ka-*pow!*
3. Science advisor Dr. David Saltzberg getting the science right.
4. Sheldon's colorful pop culture T-shirts. Go, Flash!
5. Howard's idiosyncratic wardrobe and the alien pin he wears on the collar of his turtlenecks.
6. An inebriated Sheldon, who lets it all hang out. Literally.
7. The galaxy of guest stars: Summer Glau, Katee Sackhoff, George Smoot, Neil deGrasse Tyson, Stan Lee . . .
8. The *e-v-i-l* Wil Wheaton! *Mwa ha ha!*
9. *Star Trek* over *Star Wars*. Intelligent science fiction over space fantasy. It's a no-brainer.
10. Costumes. They're never a drag.
11. Episode titles: Baffling brainteasers, conundrums for cogitation.

Part 2

THE STARS' TREKS

In which we meet the actors and the characters they portray

A NIGHT TO REMEMBER

✦

"AND THE GOLDEN GLOBE
GOES TO . . ."

*I*n the category of "Best Performance by an Actor in a Television Series—Comedy or Musical," the competition for 2010 is fierce, and it's anyone's guess as to who will win because they all richly deserve the honor.

Each nominee will tell you that it's an honor just to be nominated, but in their heart of hearts, they're there to win. This year's nominees:

Alec Baldwin in *30 Rock* (NBC)
Steve Carell in *The Office* (NBC)
Thomas Jane in *Hung* (HBO)
Matthew Morrison in *Glee* (Fox)
Jim Parsons in *The Big Bang Theory* (CBS)

The joint presenters for the award are Matt Bomer (*White Collar*, USA Network) and Kaley Cuoco (*The Big Bang Theory*). When Kaley opens the envelope, her expression gives away the winner's name before she officially reads it. We *know* it's Jim Parsons . . . and it is.

"Oh my God, Jim Parsons!" she says breathlessly, with a hand on her chest. As she jumps up and down in excitement, Parsons works his way through the usual crowd of well-wishers, gets onstage, and hugs Kaley. She is beside herself with joy for him.

James Joseph "Jim" Parsons takes the microphone and says, "Kaley, if you can't tell, is on the show with me."

We can tell.

Kaley is off to his left, with a hand over her chest, and she's still in a happy state of semi-shock. She wanted this *so* much for Jim, and now it's his time to bask in the limelight. He's now summited the twin peaks of television recognition: the Emmy in 2010 for "Outstanding Lead Actor in a Comedy Series" and now the Golden Globe.

The applause dies down, and an emotional Jim Parsons speaks:

> One day, you're waiting to see if CBS is going to put this show on the air . . . waiting to see if anyone's going to come back after a prolonged writer's strike . . . waiting as the days go by . . . and suddenly you're at the Golden Globes with your whole cast and crew. It's such an honor to be with all of you. The writers, my writers (how crass), thank you for providing a character that I get to enjoy playing, and there's so much interest in playing, week after week. Hollywood Foreign Press, thank you. It's such an honor.

To the catchy theme music of *The Big Bang Theory*, he leaves the stage as Kaley gives him another hug; hand in hand they walk offstage, with Matt Bomer.

Team Effort

Though Jim Parsons as Dr. Sheldon Cooper is clearly the Copernican star of the show, it takes an ensemble cast to bring out the best in his performance: Penny, a likable character with whom we can identify; Leonard, his roommate, colleague, and friend of seven years; and Howard and Raj, who started as friends of Leonard's and became Sheldon's, too.

The lead actors and supporting cast are buttressed by the talented writing team, and an estimated three hundred staffers who help to serve up a half hour of laugh-out-loud comedy recorded before a live audience.

Unlike *Star Trek*, which advances the idea that outer space is the final frontier, *The Big Bang Theory* reminds us that inner space—to know oneself—remains the undiscovered country for Penny and the boys.

Sheldon might ask, "In what universe would people want to watch a television show about geeks such as us?"

To which millions of viewers shout in unison: "*This* one!"

THE SEARCH FOR SPOCK

THE EVOLUTION OF DR. SHELDON COOPER

Biography of Sheldon Cooper

Sheldon Lee Cooper is a senior theoretical physicist at Caltech. He has a bachelor's degree (BA), two master's degrees (MS, MA), and two doctorates (PhD, ScD). His aspiration is to win the Nobel Prize in Physics. He lives with his roommate and colleague Dr. Leonard Hofstadter at 2311 N. Los Robles, Apt #4A, in Pasadena, California. His computer of choice is an Alienware M17x laptop. (He has likely upgraded to the M18x.) In addition to the PC, he also uses a MacBookPro.

Biography of Jim Parsons

Name: James Joseph "Jim" Parsons
Birth date and place: March 24, 1973, in Houston, Texas
Height: 6'2"
Vocation: Actor
Residence: Los Angeles, California
Education: University of Houston, Texas (BA in theater, 1996);
    University of San Diego, California (MFA in Dramatic Arts, 2001)
Awards for the role of Sheldon Cooper: Television Critics Association award for "Individual Achievement in Comedy";

the National Association of Broadcasters Chairman's Award; the Emmy Award for "Outstanding Lead Actor in a Comedy Series"; the Golden Globe Award for "Best Actor in a Television Series Musical or Comedy"

Trivia: He was voted "Friendliest" in his high school graduating class. The only class he failed in college was meteorology. He has never seen any of the *Star Trek* movies. He played a would-be Klingon in *Garden State* (2004). He auditioned for fifteen failed TV pilots before landing the title role in *The Big Bang Theory.*

An Elemental Explication

Meteorology is the study of weather—not meteors.

Jim Parsons: The Stars My Destination

Like the character he plays, Jim was born in Texas—Houston, not Galveston. But unlike his character, Jim's academic background is in theater, not the hard sciences. He obtained his undergraduate degree from the University of Houston, where he acted in numerous plays.

Even in his two-year classical theater program at the University of San Diego, Jim stood out. As Rick Seer, the program director, told Olivia Martinez in an interview for *The Vista*, "Jim is a very specific personality. He's thoroughly original, which is one reason he's been so successful. But we worried, 'Does that adapt itself to classical theater . . . to the kind of training that we're doing?' But we decided that he was so talented that we would give him a try and see how it worked out."

After graduation, Jim moved to New York, where he worked in commercials, had minor roles in several movies, and appeared in recurring roles on *Judging Amy* and *Ed.* He also auditioned extensively for televisions pilots, since winning one would guarantee regular work—the equivalent of a full-time job in the industry.

The first time he auditioned for Sheldon, after Johnny Galecki declined to audition for the role, Jim Parsons' gift for physical comedy made an indelible impression on the show's cocreator Chuck Lorre. Thinking the first audition had been a fluke, Chuck asked him to return for a second, in which Jim proved that his previous performance was no accident: Jim had *nailed* it.

The character of Sheldon requires that Jim "rattle off line after line of tightly composed, rhythmic dialogue, and then do something with his face or body during the silence that follows," wrote Andrew Dansby, who interviewed Jim Parsons on set for the *Houston Chronicle*. Sheldon's distinctive prosody holds a great appeal for Jim as an actor. Sheldon's speech patterns are unlike those of any of the other characters on the show, all of whom tend to be very conversational and normal-sounding. Sheldon, though, speaks in a carefully modulated speech pattern that fits his personality: very controlled, with specific emphases and a rhythmic pattern ideally suited for long, complex sentences. As Jim told Lewis Beale of *Newsday*, the writers "brilliantly use those words that most of us don't recognize to create that rhythm. And the rhythm got me. It was the chance to dance through that dialogue, and in a lot of ways still is."

An Elemental Explication

Prosody is not *what* is said but *how* it is said. According to Wikipedia, "In linguistics, prosody is the rhythm, stress, and intonation of speech. Prosody may reflect various features of the speaker or utterance: the emotional state of the speaker; the form of the utterance (statement, question, or command); the presence of irony or sarcasm; emphasis, contrast, and focus; or other elements of language that may not be encoded by grammar or choice of vocabulary."

For instance, in "The Lizard-Spock Expansion" (2-8), Sheldon explains to Raj the specifics of how to play an ancient Oriental hand game that has been updated for our time: "Scissors cuts paper, paper covers rock, rock crushes lizard, lizard poisons Spock, Spock smashes scissors, scissors decapitates lizard, lizard eats paper, paper disproves Spock, Spock vaporizes rock, and, as it always has, rock crushes scissors."

Reading the words gives a *sense* of what Sheldon said, but not *how* he said it, which underscores Jim's comedic genius. He's got the Right Stuff.

Jim credits the writers more than himself. As he told Frazier Moore of the Associated Press, "It's all right there in the script. I'm not trying to eschew credit or be falsely modest, but there's a part of me that feels like I didn't come up with anything. For me, for the most part, it's very clear: It's the words."

But acting is an interpretive art, and it's Jim's ability to take those words, no matter how prolix, and reel them off with precision and authority. It is because Jim does so with such assurance that we can see Sheldon as a person rather than just a character—a person whose life has been shaped by the very uniqueness we see in his speech.

Early Sheldon

Growing up in East Texas, Sheldon was in many ways a stranger in a strange land. Living deep in the Bible Belt with no interests in sports, tall for his age, and with an IQ that set him apart from, and put him at odds with, others, Sheldon found solace in science, which relies on testable theories and the precise beauty of mathematics, where there is only *one* right answer. We can surmise that he had few, if any, friends as a child, because he wouldn't have considered any of his peers bright enough to talk to, much less bond with.

With a fervent Christian for a mother, a combative older brother, a "very contentious" twin sister, and a redneck father whose chief interests were football and hunting, Sheldon had to look elsewhere for a role model with whom he could identify and whom he could emulate. He found that role model on a television show called *Star*

Trek, set in the future, where diverse races get along, intelligence is held in high regard, and, above all, logic reigns supreme.

Spock

When Spock first appeared on *Star Trek: The Original Series* (1966–1969), it soon became clear that he, not Captain James Kirk, would become the enduring character of the franchise. The stereotypical commander—resolute, handsome, and a lady's man—is hardly a unique character. But Spock, who is half Vulcan and half human, and must come to grips with his riven heritage, intrigued fans (especially young women, many of whom saw him romantically as the ultimate male challenge, the man who could not be seduced—except, of course, by them). As Leonard Nimoy explained in *Star Trek: Where No Man Has Gone Before (A History in Pictures)*, Spock is "struggling to maintain a Vulcan attitude, a Vulcan philosophical posture and a Vulcan logic, opposing what was fighting him internally, which was human emotion." Spock is torn between his cultural roots on the planet Vulcan and the new world of Starfleet in which he must perform his duties as science officer, a key position on the bridge.

Logic is Spock's compass, pointing to true north. Surrounded by flawed humans whose emotions often prove baffling, Spock is, in that sense, above and beyond, and also apart from them. He sees the world differently, unsullied by the distraction of human emotions. As he explained in *Star Trek: The Original Series*, "Nowhere am I desperately needed as among a shipload of illogical humans" ("I, Mudd," 2-37).

But logic, as Spock realizes, is not enough on its own. Rather than the handicap he once thought it to be, his human side ultimately gives him an advantage, a new perspective, and an insight into humans, whom he must understand.

Though it takes time, Spock does eventually embrace his human side, which he comes to accept as an integral part of who he is. Spock is the unique biological product of a logical race and an illogical race, and as such he stands alone.

Like Dr. Sheldon Cooper.

Sheldon and the Science of Reasoning: Logic

It's easy to see the appeal Spock would have held for an impressionable young Sheldon. Like Spock, Sheldon wanted to purge himself of his human emotions; he didn't want to be a part of the real world in which he was trapped, or one of those by whom he was surrounded—the rednecks with deep-rooted prejudices, the Christians who closed their eyes to all things rational and put all their faith in Creationism.

Realizing that science, not religion, would be his salvation, he aggressively pursued advance degrees: At eleven, he began college; at fourteen, he became a graduate student; and at sixteen, he earned the first of two doctorates. (At fourteen, he had also won the [fictional] Stephenson Award.) We can logically assume that Sheldon focused entirely on his studies, to the exclusion of everything else.

Because of his academic accomplishments, Sheldon drew a lot of attention in his chosen field of physics. We know that at twenty-three he began full-time work as a theoretical physicist at Caltech, but we don't know what accounted for the time between when he obtained his second doctorate and left for California. (I'm guessing he stayed in Texas, so he could be close to his mother, and pursued his postdoctoral studies. But we don't know for sure.)

Cathedra mea, regulate meae

An Elemental Explication

"*Cathedra mea, regulate meae*" is Latin for "My chair, my rules." In the flashback in "The Staircase Implementation" (3-22), Sheldon says the phrase to Leonard to indicate that, insofar as his apartment is concerned, he's selected a specific lawn chair as exclusively his, and he also makes the rules (as outlined in the extensive roommate agreement).

In a telling flashback episode ("The Staircase Implementation," 3-22), set three and a half years before the first aired episode ("Pilot," 1-1), we see Sheldon interrogating Leonard, who answered his ad for a room-mate. The dynamic between the two tells us what we've suspected all along: Sheldon sets the rules, and others must simply abide.

The combustible chemistry between Sheldon and his previous roommate prompted the latter to caution Leonard: "Run away, dude. Run fast, run far," but Leonard disregards it. He also disregards an even stronger warning sign: in large red letters, dripping down a bedroom wall, Sheldon's former roommate painted "Die, Sheldon, Die."

By the time of the pilot, Leonard has become Sheldon's best friend. For Sheldon, it was a turning point. Before Leonard, Sheldon deliberately kept everyone at arm's length. But living with Leonard, with whom he has common interests, Sheldon's hard veneer finally began to crack. He eventually allowed his inner circle to include Raj, Howard, and, most significantly, Penny, with whom he would not otherwise have socialized, because if she hadn't happened to be his neighbor, they never would have met.

To Sheldon, the petty concerns of humanity—especially the emotional churn of interpersonal relationships, dating, and sex— are merely distractions from what is truly important: the attainment of knowledge and making his mark on the world. (Unlike most people, to whom knowledge is a means to an end, for Sheldon, the pursuit and attainment of knowledge is its own justification and reward.) To Leonard and Howard, the dating and mating game is paramount: they want women in their lives, both emotionally and sexually. Sheldon does not; he's completely disinterested.

Sheldon's problem is that he must, like all of us, live within immutable biological limits. Born in 1980, he worries about living long enough to bear witness to the promising breakthroughs that consume the attention of today's scientists and thinkers: cold fusion and the unified field theory, to name two. His greatest desire is to live long enough to witness the Singularity, with its promise of immortality by merging human consciousness and a mechanical body, which has been predicted to occur in 2045. By reaching the Singularity and becoming a cyborg, he could explore the universe as a perpetual thinking machine—Sheldon 2.0, as it were.

An Elemental Explication

"So if computers are getting so much faster, so incredibly fast, there might conceivably come a moment when they are capable of something comparable to human intelligence. Artificial intelligence . . . Maybe we'll scan our consciousnesses into computers and live inside them as software, forever, virtually . . . the transformation of our species into something that is no longer recognizable as such to humanity circa 2011. This transformation has a name: the Singularity."

—Lev Grossman on the Singularity
("2045: The Year Man Becomes Immortal," Time, Feb. 10, 2011)

In the meantime, Sheldon must suffer the handicaps of being human, a biological life form whose limited lifespan, physical fragility, and possibilities of mental disabilities threaten to derail his dream of taking the next step in human evolution: to become the New Man, *homo novus*, and boldly go where no Sheldon has gone before.

Asexual Sheldon

Most people are hardwired for sex, but not Sheldon. He would acknowledge its biological necessity for procreation, but little else. To him sex is a needless distraction and, based on the empirical evidence he sees in the complex interrelationships between Leonard and Penny, Penny and her boyfriends (past and present), and Howard and any female, Sheldon has come to the inescapable conclusion that sex usually creates more problems than it solves.

Research psychologist Jesse Bering sheds some light on asexuality in *Scientific American*:

> If it exists as a fourth orientation, true asexuality would be due neither to genetic anomaly or environmental assault; although little is known about its etiology (psychologist Anthony Bogaert believes it may be traced to prenatal alterations of the hypothalamus), by all appearances most asexual people are normal, healthy, hormonally balanced and sexually mature adults who, for still uncertain reasons, have always found sex to be one big, bland yawn. Asexuality would therefore be like other sexual orientations in the sense that it is not "acquired" or "situational," but rather an essential part of one's biological makeup.

During the seven-plus years that Leonard has known him, Sheldon has never made the beast with two backs. He has had ample opportunity with women who found him attractive but who soon realized that he had no interest in, as Leonard says in "The Dumpling Paradox" (1-7), "nudity, orgasms, and human contact."

Even Spock was biologically compelled to have sex once every seven years, due to a condition called *pon farr*, in which, like other Vulcans, he went into heat, suffered a blood fever, became violent, and would die if not mated with someone with whom he shared an empathic bond. If it were not for *pon farr*, there would probably be no Vulcan race at all.

In the aired pilot, when Sheldon tells Leonard he's not sure he can "do this"—produce sperm for donation—Leonard reassures him that he's a "semipro." In that conversation, it's clear that Sheldon occasionally masturbates. And as Jesse Bering asserts in *Scientific American*, it's virtually impossible to masturbate to orgasm without thinking of an erotic image (go ahead, try it yourself)—which is "why [he finds] it so hard to believe that self-proclaimed asexuals who admit to masturbating to orgasm are really and truly asexual. They must be picturing something, and whatever that something is gives away their sexuality."

Which raises an interesting question: what might Sheldon think of? For now, we can only speculate.

Does Sheldon Have Asperger's Syndrome?

In any discussion of Sheldon, the suggestion that he has Asperger's syndrome will inevitably come up, and with good reason: he exhibits many of its traits.

In an interview with Noel Murray for *A.V. Club*, Jim Parsons states:

I'd heard of the disorder but I didn't know what it was *at all*. And when I asked the writers if Sheldon had Asperger's, they said, "No, he does not. That's not what we're doing." Okay. But it made me curious. And I don't know why, but Johnny [Galecki] read that book *Look Me in the Eye* by Augustan Burroughs' brother [John Elder Robison], who wrote about his life with Asperger's. I think Johnny purchased it and took it with him on a trip, and when he came back he said, "You've *got* to read this. You're going to die. The Sheldon comparisons." And I immediately went and I got it. And that was as much "research" as I've done on it. Which was very fun research, because it was very applicable human stories about living with Asperger's. And the comparisons *were* undeniable.

In fact, Sheldon has so many common traits of Asperger's that he would likely be diagnosed as having it if he went to a psychologist for testing. However, were the show's cocreators to acknowledge that, it would significantly change the tenor of the show. In "The Luminous Fish Effect" (1-4), for instance, Sheldon's new boss fires him for comments his boss take to be an insult. Someone with Asperger's would not have intended an insult, and neither did Sheldon; he was just being honest, and he expressed confusion afterward at what he considered an irrational response on his boss' part. If Sheldon had Asperger's, and Dr. Gablehauser knew that, he'd have taken that into account and perhaps not fired him. It would put everything in a different light.

Because *The Big Bang Theory* is a television sitcom and not a documentary about Asperger's, it doesn't pay for it to become too serious or clinically accurate in regards to a known medical condition. If we perceive Sheldon's cognitive dissonance with the world around him as a personal quirk, it's funny. But if we have to see him struggle with Asperger's, and everyone he knows realizes he's so afflicted, it would fundamentally and irrevocably change our perception of Sheldon, the expressive heart of the show. So the show's cocreators are quick to downplay the obvious connection, agreeing that, sure, he's got some of the traits, but he doesn't have the condition.

Be that as it may, the fact that Sheldon *does* have some of the traits is key to his character. If he were just another supersmart geek like the other boys, the show would lose its center. Sheldon's Asperger's traits—as long as they aren't named as such—are what make him both hilarious and extraordinary. It's a delicate line that the writers must carefully tread. After all, it's best not to tinker with a winning formula.

MORE ON ASPERGER'S SYNDROME
· · · · · · · · · · · ·

We get the name from Dr. Hans Asperger, an Austrian pediatrician who termed it "autistic psychopathy": *autism* (self) and *psychopathy* (personality disease). Clinical psychologist Tony Attwood, in *The Complete Guide to Asperger's Syndrome*, wrote that, "He observed that the children's social maturity and social reasoning were delayed and some aspects of their social abilities were quite unusual at any stage of development."

In his book, Atwood cites the Gillberg diagnostic criteria for Asperger's syndrome. Five of the six defining criteria include: social impairment (extreme egocentricity), narrow interest, compulsive need for introducing routines and interests, speech and language peculiarities, and nonverbal communication problems.

From the very first episode, we see these in full force:

Social impairment: Sheldon's reluctance to meet Penny, his new neighbor; his acknowledgment to Leonard regarding his deliberately small social circle; his pointing out that his whiteboard containing mathematical formulas is noteworthy but Leonard's is merely "a derivative restatement"; his factual comments about Penny's interest in astronomy

Narrow interest: his desire to view *Battlestar Galactica*'s third season, only *this* time with commentary

Compulsive need for introducing routines and interests: his adherence to playing Klingon Boggle; his insistence on sitting in *his* seat on the couch

(continued on next page)

(continued from previous page)

Speech and language peculiarities: his prolix explanations

Nonverbal communication problems: his inability to comfort Penny when she bursts out in tears

The sixth criterion, motor clumsiness, clearly does not apply, given Sheldon's dexterity with video games. But one need not meet all criteria to receive a diagnosis; social impairment along with four of the other five is sufficient.

The World through Sheldon's Eyes

Watching Sheldon at work and at play is to witness a markedly different set of behaviors from the norm. He sees and interprets the world in absolutes, in binary: 1/0 or off/on. In Sheldon's world, there is no gray scale. He also expects the world to change to accommodate him.

Q: How does Sheldon change a lightbulb?

A: He inserts it in the fixture and waits for the room to revolve around him.

Of course, Sheldon's *wanting* the world to be ordered specifically to his needs and desires is unrealistic and impossible, but therein lies the humor: he simply doesn't *understand* why things are the way that they are, because shouldn't we live in a logical, not an emotional, world? Because he sees himself as logical and virtually everyone else as illogical or stupid, he becomes frustrated with them. In "The Gorilla Experiment" (3-10), he fails in teaching Penny the rudiments of physics. She's visibly distraught and he can't figure out why she's crying. When he asks her, she replies, "Because I'm stupid!" He insensitively responds: "That's no reason to cry. One cries because one is sad. For example, I cry because others are stupid and it makes me sad."

A few more cases in point: when Sheldon feels he needs a bigger budget to conduct his research, the obvious solution is for the school to simply fire other people to free up funding. To him, the human dimension of the equation is a nonissue. People's livelihoods are expendable when it comes to his research, which always takes precedence. For Sheldon, nothing comes between him and his goal of winning a Nobel Prize in Physics, which he sees as a foregone conclusion. In instances where he's had serious rifts with others, it's inevitably been over his work. When he refuses to join Leonard in presenting a jointly written paper in "The Cooper-Hofstadter Polarization" (1-9), and Leonard goes at it alone, things quickly deteriorate when the two duke it out in public. In another instance, when Sheldon refuses to share credit with a graduate student in "The Cooper-Nowitski Theorem" (2-6), he summarily dismisses her; she runs out of his apartment as Penny looks on. Most significantly, when the boys tamper with Sheldon's experiment in the North Pole in "The Monopolar Expedition" (2-23), he deliberately isolates himself and declares that he has no friends—he stands alone.

The Cheese Doesn't Stand Alone

It's been a long road for Sheldon, who for most of his life has traveled solo. In "The Monopolar Expedition," the betrayal by his buddies, whom he implicitly trusted, stuns him. Blinded by his pursuit of science, he puts himself and his needs first, and fails to see his own dictatorial behavior as group leader. He has come far, but must take to heart Spock's immortal words to Kirk in *Star Trek: The Wrath of Khan*: "The needs of the many outweigh the needs of the few, or the one."

Spock finally acknowledged that no man is an island; so, too, must Sheldon. Ultimately, he needs his friends more than he will admit. Socially, he still has some evolving to do.

SHELDON:
A FICTIONAL FACE OF REAL HOPE
· · · · · · · · · · · ·

Sitcoms are intended to be a laugh riot, an entertaining thirty minutes carefully crafted to take your mind off the real world. They're escapism, pure and simple. But occasionally, there's a sitcom with something more to offer.

Because Sheldon has many characteristics associated with Asperger's syndrome, he has put a human, albeit fictional, face on the condition. That face is also empathic; we care about Sheldon and want him to succeed. The proof is in the numbers: in one poll of 34,516 fans on the-big-bang-theory.com, two-thirds voted for Sheldon as their favorite character.

Though the cocreators never intended Sheldon to be the poster boy for those with Asperger's, he has had a measurable impact, according to Dr. Tony Attwood, a practicing clinician and the author of *The Complete Guide to Asperger's Syndrome*, who in an e-mail to me wrote about the salutary effect Sheldon's character has had within the community:

The character does portray many of the clinical signs of Asperger's syndrome, and parents say the character is representative of someone with Asperger's syndrome. Interestingly, teenagers and young adults with Asperger's syndrome identify positively with the character. He is a hero, and the scenes and script are perceived as very funny. Scenes could be used to train clinicians in the diagnostic characteristics and also used to teach those with Asperger's syndrome about social and especially interpersonal situations. The show has had a very positive influence in the Asperger community.

For those who have the syndrome, and for their family and friends who support them every step of the way, *The Big Bang Theory* offers more than laughter. Sheldon Cooper speaks to and touches them in a way that no other role model has ever done. Brilliantly portrayed by Jim Parsons, Sheldon Cooper gives them a voice—and hope.

Long after the show airs its final episode, that will be its enduring legacy.

The Quotable Jim Parsons

Affinity for Sheldon: I would say that, yes, I am fond of him. It's not anything necessarily that I've done. It's as much the writing. He's such a non-malicious character. He comes by his faux pas so honestly. He doesn't have time for it, and frankly, it doesn't occur to him. There's some version of arrested development in his brain socially, dealing with people. He's just really busy doing a lot of other things, and nobody ever asked that of him. One wonders how capable he is of actually ever getting there. Perhaps that's season seven, God willing. ("The Geek Shall Inherit the Earth," Jan. 1, 2010, *American Way*)

Asexuality: You'd never be able to have the Penny-and-Sheldon relationship if he was more sexually threatening to her. It opened us to this brother-sister combativeness and helpfulness, but the bottom line is that there is a sort of a yin and yang to them, and I think if sex was in the way, it would be a very different relationship, more like the relationship between her and Leonard. (Allie Townsend, "Big Bang Theory: The Jim Parsons Interview," *Time* magazine, Sept. 23, 2010)

Asperger's syndrome: We had already shot and aired several episodes before I was ever asked the Asperger's-or-autism question. I asked the writers, and they were like, No, he doesn't have it. It's been useful to us to utilize some of those "Aspergian" traits, but we need to be able to move away from it if we want to. ("10 Questions: Jim Parsons," *Time* magazine, Feb. 21, 2011)

Geek cred: I feel like my geek cred in this realm ran out around *Star Wars*' time. I was completely into that, but I didn't know any of the other stuff, really. I knew of *Star Trek*, but that's the only thing that's come up that people do ask about. (IGN TV, April 10, 2010)

Joy of solitude: I'm not more into science, and I haven't really gotten more into comic books or games. But if I have to be sincere about it, though, I think I've grown a greater appreciation for letting myself enjoy time alone. Because he enjoys it so much, you know? He not only enjoys it, but I think he prefers it. It's easier for him to get things done when he's alone. Other people get in the way. And it's one of the things that I do admire about him. Some people think he's somewhat cut off from society, and I guess that's not always great, but that ability to be content alone like that—I think that's really nice. He's really comfortable with himself in many ways, which is admirable. (Will Harris, "A Chat with Parsons of *The Big Bang Theory*," Bullz-Eye.com, Dec. 4, 2009)

Memorizing lines: A lot of the time, I'll go online. I'm very good friends with Dictionary.com and Wikipedia. And then as far as literally memorizing the words, I'll have note cards. I do note cards all week. And in longhand, I write out all my lines again and again and again. And on weekends, I drill them. I walk around with my note cards for each scene and do one scene at a time. And I'll go to my computer, and I'll type the whole scene out on my [Microsoft] Word document and then I'll go back and I'll do the second scene . . . It's maddening. I will not lie to you, I literally want to kill myself sometimes. (Julie Miller, "*Big Bang Theory*'s Jim Parsons on Learning

Lines, Emmy Nods and Cast Ping-Pong Deathmatches," Sept. 4, 2009, Movieline)

Penny and Sheldon: What makes it enjoyable is that, in this case, they're so different. I've said from the beginning, of the five characters in this piece, [Penny and Sheldon] are polar opposites of each other, her being the most earthbound and tactile, and him being the most, literally, in his head. And that's fun! And just sticking them on stage at the same time, sparks begin to fly immediately because they're so different. (Angel Cohn, "More *Bang* for Your Buck," TWOP.com, May 3, 2010)

Physics: I bought *Physics 101* that the Smithsonian put out. I thought, "Well, that sounds smart to get, why not?" . . . I didn't get very far in the *Physics 101* book. We talk about Newton and I'm just gone. (Comic-Con 2009)

Science: The science part is extremely easy as far as being able to tell you why it's authentic. We employ David Saltzberg, who is a physicist who teaches at UCLA. He not only fact-checks, but he supplies a great deal of [the material]. We need Sheldon to talk about something or teaching Penny whatever, and [Saltzberg will] come up with something. He sends over this diagram on this whiteboard and he'll throw in little inside jokes that I don't find funny because I don't know what the heck he's talking about. ("Jim Parsons on the Science of Sheldon," NPR, Sept. 28, 2010)

Scripts: I always laugh. I literally laugh as I'm reading it through every time. We are very lucky. I've heard that there's a lot of shows that have to go through tons of major changes all week. We rarely get that. These scripts are in such fine condition when they get to us, which is why they're funny immediately, because they're already worked over. I don't know when the writers are sleeping or seeing their families. (Rebecca Murray, About.com, at the 2009 British Academy of Film and Television Arts/Los Angeles TV Tea Party)

Sheldon's lovability: The somewhat unspoken collaboration between us—me, Chuck, and the rest of the writers—is simply that we have to walk up to the line. We cannot cross it. And we've had to go through scenes where we've had to correct on the spot, going, "We've gone too far. We must bring this back. The audience is not pleased with the way you are talking to Penny." We can be biting, and he can observe something in a situation, maybe get snarky about it, but he can't—it can't be malicious. And it's a fine line, but it isn't just—it is also the words, carefully chosen, especially to someone like Penny that you don't want to be put in a position where people are groaning. Well, not always, at least. (H.B. Foreman, "Jim Parsons and Johnny Galecki are making big sparks," *Delaware County Magazine*, undated)

Sheldon reaching out: That Sheldon engages other humans is the salient point for me. He tries. I mean, he means well. He just doesn't have the tools for it. And I think what's endearing is that he really is a stranger in a strange land. And he knows his limitations many times and tries to deal with them. The fact that he deals with them very badly is where the comedy comes from. (Luaine Lee, thestar. com, May 7, 2010)

Venue remuneration: As an actor on a TV series, I get a wonderful paycheck, and it's a consistent paycheck, which doesn't always happen when you're doing theater or movies. Both are hard in their own ways . . . I don't miss cashing unemployment checks and am not stupid enough to say that, but yes, to a degree, I enjoy the rat-race aspect of it. (Michelle Kung, "*The Big Bang Theory*'s Jim Parsons on Twitter, Parakeets, and *Star Trek*," May 6, 2010, *Wall Street Journal*: Speakeasy)

Verbal salience: As strange as this may sound, I really feel like I let the words bring it out of me. Literally, especially with preparing for the audition and for the first show, the struggle to learn the words—I did this on TV once, showing people—I put a pencil between my teeth to help with articulation, because sometimes the constructs of the sentences are such that it's a full-muscle workout to get it out.

But I have found that it really informs who [Sheldon] is. There is so much going on, he's so busy inside his brain . . . (Abbie Bernstein, "Jim Parsons on *The Big Bang Theory*, Buzzy Media)

Wil Wheaton: He seems to be completely okay with the fact that his entire name became a mantra of vengeful hate. That didn't seem to bother him. He was so fun to have on the set, and he was such a good guy, just in general, but what a wonderful foil for Sheldon. And it makes such sense, because as a person and an actor—he was playing himself, though slightly different, obviously—of course Sheldon's the angriest at this human who is so *un*hurtful. There's nothing wrong with Wil Wheaton! (Will Harris, "A Chat with Parsons of *The Big Bang Theory*," Bullz-Eye.com, Dec. 4, 2009)

GREAT EXPECTATIONS

DR. LEONARD HOFSTADTER

Biography of Leonard Hofstadter

Dr. Leonard Leaky Hofstadter is an experimental physicist at Caltech. His IQ is 173. He is a longtime friend and roommate of Dr. Sheldon Cooper.

Biography of Johnny Galecki

Name: John Mark Galecki
Birth date and place: April 30, 1975, in Bree, Belgium
Height: 5'5"
Vocation: Actor
Residence: Los Angeles, California, but spends time in Chicago, where his immediate family lives
World Wide Web: No official online presence
Factoids: Good friends with actress Sara Gilbert; dated colleague Kaley Cuoco for two years. He was originally considered to play the role of Sheldon but opted for the more "normal" role of Leonard. He believes in maintaining his privacy and does not participate on any social networking sites.

John Galecki: A Star Is Born

At age eleven, John Mark "Johnny" Galecki had already established himself as a rising star in Chicago's thriving theater scene. His big acting break came when he appeared as Rusty Griswold in *Christmas Vacation*, starring Chevy Chase. Two years later, he was handpicked by Roseanne to be her son in a television movie, *Backfield in Motion*. That, in turn, led to a major role on *Roseanne*, as David Healy, Darlene's boyfriend.

Johnny can play the cello and can also draw, a talent he showed at an early age. He lives in Los Angeles, though he frequently travels to Chicago, where his siblings live.

Unlike other actors who feel a compulsive urge to discuss their private affairs in public, especially on the internet, Johnny does not have a Twitter account, nor is he personally involved on MySpace or Facebook. "I don't understand the current frame of mind in our society that seems to say that any action is not of value until it's broadcast somehow," he said in an interview with Brent Furdyk for "Inside the Box" on tvweekonline.ca.

Not surprisingly, when news broke that he and costar Kaley Cuoco had dated, it was Kaley who broke the silence.

It's a Small World After All

In the acting profession, it's not so much who *you* know but who knows you. Chuck Lorre, a cocreator of *The Big Bang Theory*, was also the co-executive producer of *Roseanne* from 1990 to 1992, during which time Johnny played Darlene's boyfriend. Darlene was played by Sara Gilbert.

When casting began for *The Big Bang Theory*, Johnny got the nod. Sara came on later as Dr. Leslie Winkle, a regular character, but her status was changed to "recurring" when the writers decided they couldn't come up with enough story lines with her to warrant "regular" cast status.

Mommy Dearest

Like his roommate Sheldon, Leonard Hofstadter comes from a dysfunctional family.

Leonard's parents—his father, an anthropologist, and his mother, a psychologist and neuroscientist—eschewed any semblance of normalcy to raise their children in a rigorous world in which family activities were merely opportunities to conduct hands-on research.

As Leonard points out in "The Peanut Reaction" (1-16), "My parents focused on celebrating achievements, and being expelled from a birth canal was not considered one of them." In other words, birthdays were nonevents, and, as a result, he never had one until his friends took pity on him and threw him a surprise party.

Christmas, too, was not a time for religion, family, or the season itself, but simply another opportunity to conduct research. As Leonard explains in "The Maternal Congruence" (3-11), "In my family, holidays weren't so much celebrated as studied for their anthropological and psychological implications on human society . . . We presented papers and then broke off into focus groups and critiqued each other."

Not surprisingly, just as Leonard's parents distanced themselves from personal and cultural celebrations, they physically distanced themselves from their children. In "The Maternal Capacitance" (2-15), we learn that the hug-deprived Leonard, at ten, "built a hugging machine . . . I got a dressmaker's mannequin, I stuffed it with an electric blanket so it would be warm, and built two radio-controlled arms that would hug me and pat my back."

The surrogate mother was so emotionally and physically comforting that Leonard's father borrowed it, though he eventually found solace in a real woman's arms—his secretary's—which was the catalyst for Leonard's parents' inevitable separation and acrimonious divorce.

Despite his nontraditional upbringing, his parents' ill-fated union did produce three remarkable children, though Leonard is considered the black sheep: he's outclassed by his older siblings, including a brother who teaches law at Harvard and a sister who is a medical researcher on the verge of an important breakthrough in the field of diabetes.

The net result of Leonard's unorthodox family history inevitably took a toll. In "The Cooper-Hofstadter Polarization" (1-9), he tells Sheldon, "I am clearly not the only person who is tormented by insecurity and has an ego in need of constant validation." Leonard seeks validation from his family, his colleagues, his friends, and women he dates. Though he doesn't get positive strokes from his mother, who finds she has much more in common with Sheldon, his colleagues do regard him highly: the Institute for Experimental Physics invited him to present a paper at a conference on Bose-Einstein condensates. When it comes to women, he's learned the hard way that the path to love is strewn with broken hearts, but he perseveres through a string of unfortunate and fortunate relationships, including a Korean spy, a colleague at work (Dr. Leslie Winkle), a fellow scientist whom Penny calls Dr. Slutbunny (Dr. Elizabeth Plimpton, in "The Plimpton Stimulation," 3-21), Penny herself, and Raj's sister Priya.

Despite all the *sturm und drang* in his life, Leonard remains the core of his social group—Sheldon, Howard, and Raj. Both Howard and Raj were initially Leonard's friends, and they follow his lead. Like Leonard, though, they often defer to Sheldon because it makes life easier for everyone.

Sheldon assumes he's the leader of the pack, but we know better—and, eventually, so does Sheldon, after his "friend who's a girl but not his girlfriend," Amy Farrah Fowler, points it out in "The Toast Derivation" (4-17). "I think it's time to face the fact that Leonard is the nucleus of your social group. Where he goes, the group goes . . . What I'm saying, Sheldon, is that your group is Leonard-centric."

It's a bitter pill for Sheldon to swallow, but swallow it he must.

Though all four of the boys are to some degree damaged goods,

Leonard is the most normal and well adjusted, the most diplomatic, the compromiser and the peacemaker. Those qualities give him moral authority, despite Sheldon's oft-voice assertions that everything must be done *his* way, no matter what. While Sheldon is often dictatorial, autocratic, and *assumes* a leadership role by virtue of his intellect, the others don't necessarily share his worldview. They prefer someone who is more a team player, and not a superstar.

In "The Staircase Excitation" (3-22), our brief glimpse of Sheldon's previous roommate and his warnings to Leonard should have made it clear that Sheldon is not your typical roommate, even without the prolix, one-sided roommate's agreement he induced Leonard to sign.

An Elemental Explication

The phrase painted on Leonard's bedroom wall recalls another great moment in pop culture, when we see "Venkman, burn in hell" painted in red on his office door in *Ghostbusters*.

Sheldon is fortunate that Leonard stayed. Not only have they become best friends, but Sheldon is a better person because of Leonard, a wise mediator who knows when to put his foot down, and also when to back off. His salutary effect on Sheldon transformed him from insufferable to sufferable, to the point that he can have social intercourse with Leonard's other friends, who at their first meeting bolted from the apartment to get away from him.

Leonard is not the tallest (that would be Sheldon) or the smartest (again, Sheldon), nor is he the one most likely to attract women (Raj) or the one who dresses in the most distinctive manner (Howard), but he's the calm center of the hurricane's eye. The others all revolve around him.

Though Leonard is a better man for having dated Penny, his relationship with Raj's sister Priya is understandably turbulent. To

Priya's parents, Leonard is an outsider to their culture; moreover, Priya's time in the United States is coming to an end, as she plans to head back to India. What will become of their relationship then?

Though we can't foretell what the future holds for Leonard, we can be sure of one thing: whether it's Priya, Penny, or another woman, he is slowly but surely putting his past, and the feelings of inadequacy, behind him and moving on with life. He's growing up, maturing, accepting his place socially and professionally, and slowly learning that the great expectations his parents placed on him pale in comparison to the very real-world accomplishments he's achieved largely on his own. Leonard is slowly but surely becoming his own man.

The Quotable Johnny Galecki

Acting advice: I think I really lucked out starting [by doing theater], and it was really probably only because I grew up in Chicago and that's such a great community of theater out there . . . Theater audiences don't pull punches. They'll let you know when they're feeling ripped off. (Ann Murray-Yavar, Fancast interview, May 19, 2008)

Visiting Caltech: No, that would be a disaster. I would be terrified that they would ask for advice on some sort of equation. Early on, for the pilot, Jim and I went to UCLA. We got to hang out with those guys and some professors. We learned that there is no way to learn how to think like these people. Basically, the microcosm of it is that, let's read the biography on Einstein instead of what Einstein wrote. We're just not going to understand [physics]. (Julie Miller, "*The Big Bang Theory*'s Johnny Galecki Talks TV Physics, Fans and Cutthroat Ping Pong," Sept. 28, 2009)

Geeks: I think a nerd or geek or dork or dweeb is just someone who's passionate about something. The word *geek* is now a verb. People say, "Oh, I totally geek out on this." Post–fifth grade, it's cool. People wear their geekdom like a badge of courage. Everyone claims they're a geek—especially hot women. (Novid Parsi, "Geek Love," Time Out Chicago: Movies on Demand, May 4, 2009)

Jim Parsons: Jim's story, to me, is so incredible. Having met him four years ago when he was living in Brooklyn and pounding the pavement for Dimetapp commercials, he is talented, but he works so, so hard. Every struggling actor should read and pay attention to his story, because it's hopeful, and not just because he didn't win the Lotto. He worked hard and paid his dues for a long, long time. And still, with the attention he gets, he is such a great guy, and it is still all about the work for him, for all of us—except for the rock-star component. (Bill Harris, torontosun.com, April 4, 2010)

Penny: I think in many ways, unconsciously, Penny's character is slowly trying to mold Leonard into the man of her dreams. And she ends up dating the guy that owns his favorite comic book store, which just throws him into a tizzy . . . But when she dates someone who is very similar to him, it gets under his skin quite a bit. But I think she is sending him a not-so-subtle message at the same time. These subtleties are really, really fun to play. (Will Harris, bullz-eye. com, Apr. 13, 2009)

Actors' creative interpretation of characters: That's never come up. We're very much on the same page. In a series, you really need to stay open-minded. It's not like a play or a film, where you can create and fully commit to your character's backstory. These characters are apparently going to be here for a few years. We still have a whole lot to learn about them. You might all of a sudden learn that your character's father was an alcoholic. We just did a flashback episode in which you see how Sheldon and Leonard met. There were a lot of surprises there. You can't really claim too much ownership of your character. They really do belong to the writers, and in many ways, you're just their puppet. (Noel Murray, *A.V. Club*, May 24, 2010)

Smarts: I thought it might be a show that made fun of smart people. Now I think it's a show that much more often defends smart people. (Maureen Ryan, "Having 'Big' fun on a hit comedy," *Chicago Tribune*: The Watcher, Jan. 10, 2010)

LUST IN SPACE

MR. HOWARD WOLOWITZ

Biography of Howard Wolowitz

Howard Joel Wolowitz, who holds a master's degree from MIT, is an engineer at Caltech, and his accomplishments include codesigning a waste disposal system for the International Space Station (ISS), performing long-distance maintenance on Mars Rovers, and designing components for a fly-by spacecraft that took pictures of Saturn.

Biography of Simon Helberg

Name: Simon Maxwell Helberg
Birth date and place: December 9, 1980, in Los Angeles, California
Height: 5'7"
Vocation: Actor
Residence: Los Angeles, California
Marital status: Married to actress Jocelyn Towne
Education: Attended New York University's Tisch School of the Arts but is not a graduate
Twitter verified account: @simonhelberg (97,022 followers as of May 1, 2011)

Simon Helberg: A Star Will Rise

A lifelong resident of Los Angeles, Simon has acting in his blood. His father is Sandy Helberg, who has appeared principally in TV shows. Raised Jewish, Simon Helberg is no geek, though he's played one on television as Seth in *Joey*, and also in the movie *National Lampoon's Van Wilder*. He's a professional pianist and also holds a black belt in karate, which he earned at age ten. Of the principal cast of *The Big Bang Theory*, Simon has the most television and movie credits, dating back to 1999 when he appeared as a minor character in the movie *Mumford*.

Simon also appeared in a web-based series that debuted in 2007 and ran for twelve episodes, a comedy show that foreshadows his role as Howard Wolowitz in *The Big Bang Theory*: "The series . . . follows real-life bumblers Derek Waters and Simon Helberg trying in vain to pick up girls in Los Angeles," said *USA Today* (April 2007).

Simon Helberg is currently raising funds through Kickstarter for an independent film titled *I Am I*. His wife, Jocelyn Towne, wrote the film and will be directing and starring in it; Simon will be in the film, as will Jason Ritter. Simon told smashinginterviews.com, "It's about a girl who never knew her dad growing up. She meets him at her mother's funeral. He has a form of retrograde amnesia which is a disorder called Korsakov's Syndrome . . . It's sort of a twist on a love story. It's dark, funny, and heartbreaking."

When Did You Last See Your Father?

In "The Precious Fragmentation" (3-17), we learn that Howard was abandoned by his father, leaving him to grow up with his mother. We aren't told why, but Howard's reaction to a touchstone from his past—the discovery of a sitcom toy in a box of auctioned goods at a garage sale—brings up a wellspring of emotion. "Oh, my God. An Alf doll. When I was eleven, my mother got me one to help me sleep after my dad left. I used to pretend that my dad had moved to the planet Melmac, and Alf was going to bring him back to me. But he never did. Where's my daddy, puppet? Where is he?"

We never find out, nor does Howard.

Lacking a father figure, Howard, an only child, grew up with only his mother for guidance, and presumably, except for the time he attended MIT, he's always lived with her—even though he's now twenty-seven and working full-time as a faculty member at Caltech's Department of Applied Physics, where he was hired right out of college, after earning his bachelor's and master's degrees.

Among his close friends, he's the only one who lacks a doctorate degree, but he's unapologetic about it. As he told a wealthy benefactor named Mrs. Latham ("The Benefactor Factor," 4-15), "I'm an engineer. Most engineers don't bother with a PhD."

But even Mrs. Latham puts him down, minimizing his accomplishments by calling him a "space plumber."

The lack of a doctorate on his résumé is an omission he cannot forget, because his peers won't let him. In any formal gathering, where his closest friends are all addressed with the honorific of "doctor," Howard is always called, simply, "Mister." It's a sore point with him, especially since Sheldon, who has two doctorates, enjoys pointing it out on every possible occasion. To make matters worse: even Howard's fiancée has a doctorate, and draws a bigger salary than he does.

His lack of a father figure, his overactive imagination, and his inability to see himself as others see him are at the root of why Howard had largely been unsuccessful with women.

To everyone else, Howard rides an underpowered Vespa scooter, but to him it's a powerful motorcycle, a "hog" he rides just like bad-boy biker Marlon Brando. To women, he initially comes across as creepy, peppering them with hoary pickup lines and excessive compliments. The first time he meets Penny ("Pilot," 1-1), without knowing anything about her, he begins trying to ingratiate himself. As Sheldon points out, explaining why he preferred to join Leonard on his knight errand, "Oh, right, yes, I could have stayed behind and watched Wolowitz try to hit on Penny in Russian, Arabic, and Farsi."

Though grounded in reality in his work, which includes engineering marvels such as a zero-gravity space toilet for the International Space Station, it's his life away from the office that really fuels his fantasies, not only in fandom, where he can play computerized game quests using avatars, but especially his sexual fantasies, which, in his twenties, dominate his life.

Though Jewish, Howard is not strict and enjoys non-kosher meals. Moreover, he's shown little interest in pursuing girlfriends of his own faith; instead he has been on a relentless pursuit of *shiksas* like Penny.

An Elemental Explication

Shiksa is a Yiddish word, often used in a derogatory context, to denote a WASP-like woman whose attributes, especially physical, are such that even a good Jewish boy cannot resist.

In the four years we've seen Howard at play, we get the distinct impression that his failure to connect, as it were, with women is due largely to his inability to relate to them as people: he principally judges, and perceives, women as sex objects. It explains why, for instance, he's immediately attracted to Penny but has no interest in Amy Farrah Fowler, a brainy plain Jane.

Howard's obsession with being with the perfect woman extends into his fantasy life as well. Resorting to self-manipulation during bubble baths, he dreams of a blonde *shiksa*, an actress named Katee Sackhoff (Captain Kara "Starbuck" Thrace) from the sci-fi television series *Battlestar Galactica*, in "The Vengeance Formulation" (3-9).

He actually meets one of his dream girls in real life ("The Terminator Decoupling," 2-17), a petite, brown-haired actress named Summer Glau who plays a Terminator in the television show

Terminator: The Sarah Conner Chronicles. During this brief encounter, Howard blows it big-time. He refuses to follow Leonard's common-sense advice of introducing himself with a simple hello, which Howard asserts "always creeps girls out. I need to come up with something that's funny, smart, and delicately suggests that my sexual endowment is disproportionate to my physical stature."

As always, Howard relies on his familiar crutch: a pickup line. This time, he comes up with "It's hot in here. It must be Summer." But Raj steals the line and uses it, to her amusement. Still, Howard manages to dismiss Raj and takes his place—and then he bores Summer with endless trivia and, finally, exasperates her to the point of no return after he unwisely asks if it's okay if he takes a photo with his phone to post on his Facebook page, "one where it looks like we're making out?" He returns, crestfallen, though his buddies want to pump him for information.

"Terminator broke my phone," he shamefacedly admits.

It's a scenario with which he's quite familiar, for it's the story of his life—his *real* life, not his fantasy world. He constantly encounters disappointment at the hands of young women everywhere. He just can't catch a break because he's his own worst enemy.

Another example: in "The Cooper-Nowitzki Theorem" (2-6), when a cute female grad student named Ramona Nowitzki approaches the boys at a lunch table in a Caltech cafeteria, she only has eyes for Sheldon. But, of course, Howard is oblivious to the fact that she's totally disinterested in him. He introduces himself: "Howard Wolowitz, department of engineering, codesigner of the International Space Station's Liquid Waste Disposal System," to which she responds, simply, "Eww." As he presses his case, she responds: "Again, eww." But Howard persists.

Howard is simply obtuse. He can't, and won't, take no for an answer. He can't really help himself, because he simply cannot relate to women in any meaningful and adult way. To him, all it takes to win the fair lady is to introduce himself, show his sly grin, and spring a line that will grab her attention and, ultimately, get her into bed with him.

The Man Who Fell to Earth

For Howard, the journey from lust to love can only begin when he hits rock bottom, which he does at Penny's hands. After two years of being on the receiving end of his unsolicited compliments, Penny delivers a verbal atomic bomb that devastates him. In "The Killer Robot Instability" (2-12), Howard, in the company of his friends at Sheldon's apartment, puts his foot firmly in his mouth. He begins what he considers his slow dance, "our little tango . . . the carnal repartee, the erotic to and fro. But as delicious as the appetizer might be," he tells Penny, "at some point we will have to succumb and eat the entrée while it's still . . . hot."

Penny lowers the boom. "You think I'm flirting with you? I am not flirting with you. No woman is ever gonna flirt with you. You're just gonna grow old and die alone."

Humiliated in front of his best friends, his morale and ego crushed, Howard immediately leaves, going "home to live my creepy, pathetic life."

At Leonard's urging, Penny goes to Howard's house to make amends, during which time he finally speaks from his heart and not his penis. Penny sees his human side when he confesses his greatest fear: "Look at me. What chance do I have if I don't try too hard?"

Penny responds, "Well, you'd have a terrific chance. I mean, you're smart, you're funny, you have a cool job. You build stuff that goes into outer space . . . Look, I'm telling you, I've known you for, like, a year and a half, and this is the first time I feel like I'm talking to a real person. And you know what? I like him. He's a nice guy."

True to form, Howard misconstrues her comments and goes for a kiss. She plants one on him—with her fist.

It is Penny, though, who indirectly proves to be the salvation to Howard's dating woes. As she observes, Howard does have good qualities, if only he'd let them come to the surface, breaking through what she once called his "creepy candy coating" ("The Creepy Candy Coating Corollary," 3-5). In that episode, though Howard doesn't know it, Penny will change his life forever by agreeing to fix him up with a friend—a graduate student working in microbiology who, part-time, works as a waitress at the Cheesecake Factory. It turns out that Bernadette Rostenkowski will be able to see in him what other women have not, principally because they've never seen him for who he is, only for who he pretends to be.

"Three Dates Mean Sex? Who Knew?"

"In love," the French proverb goes, "there is always one who kisses and one who offers the cheek." In the budding relationship between Howard and Bernadette, it is Howard who is cheeky and Bernadette who offers the cheek. Having gorged himself with unsurpassable sexual fantasies—couplings with Hollywood stars like Katee Sackhoff and Summer Glau—it's unlikely that any ordinary woman will be able to measure up, and initially Bernadette cannot. Howard, wedded to the idea of dating and mating with the perfect girl, is in love with a fantasy construct that can exist only in his imagination.

As Howard might say, you only live once, so why not go for it? In his case, as he tells Penny in "The Vengeance Formulation" (3-9), that means he wants, "Well, you know, more like Megan Fox from *Transformers*, or Katee Sackhoff from *Battlestar Galactica*."

Penny brings him back to reality. "Howard, you're going to throw away a great girl like Bernadette because you're holding out for some ridiculous fantasy?"

Howard, of course, doesn't see that as absurd—until his own conscience, in the form of Katee Sackhoff sharing an imaginary bubble bath with him during one of his masturbatory sessions in the tub, pricks him. "I want to know why you're playing make-believe with me when you could be out with a real woman tonight . . . You've got a wonderful girl in your life, and you're ignoring her in order to spend your nights in the bathtub with a mental image and a washcloth."

The point is clearly made, and Howard realizes that Penny and Katee are both right. So naturally he proposes to Bernadette—and she turns him down. After all, they hardly know each other. They've been on only three dates, and haven't even had sex yet.

Howard begs for forgiveness and a second chance, which she grants. A relationship takes time to build, she knows, and Howard needs to realize that, too. She's experienced and mature, but he still has a lot of growing up to do.

Once Howard embraces the idea that, after all these years, he has a viable chance with a smart, attractive woman who likes him as he is, he realizes his good fortune, and begins to woo her.

Mommy Dearest

In addition to letting go of his erotic fantasies, Howard must also disengage himself from his mother, who sees him not as an adult man but still her little baby boy.

Though Howard is not a strict Jew, we get the impression his mother is, and one of her big concerns is whom he'll eventually marry. In "The Dumpling Paradox" (1-7), when Howard, in the house he shares with his mother, shacks up with Penny's hometown friend Christy, his mother threatens to cut him out of her will if he continues the relationship. Wisely (for a multitude of reasons), Howard decides he has no future with Christy, and they go their separate ways.

But as Howard's relationship with Bernadette evolves, it's clear that he'll have to make a choice between his mother and her. It's not realistic, Bernadette tells him, to expect her to live in the same house with his mother. It's time for him to stop being a mama's boy—something he's loathe to do, because his mother has always been his safe haven, and he associates their home with security.

In the end, Howard finally sees the light. He can no longer live at home and masturbate in the bathtub, dream of marrying a Hollywood film star, and in the process push away his best hope for building a real life with a real woman. In "The Herb Garden

Germination" (4-20), Howard finally pops the question again; and this time, Bernadette is ready. She doesn't even allow him to finish his proposal; she preempts him and accepts. And thus begins the next phase of Howard's life.

In the last four years, we've seen Howard change and grow. In the pilot, he's a classic horndog, excited by the mere prospect of a woman in Sheldon's apartment. Howard, who considered himself a lady's man and a smooth operator, has come to realize that it's not just about sex but an ongoing, long-term relationship. With his impending marriage to Bernadette, which will require him to finally move out of his mother's house, he's no longer a boy but a man, though he still has a lot to learn about women.

The Quotable Simon Helberg

Girls: He's just delusional. In his head, he's got this all figured out. He's done his work and he thinks he knows what to do to pick up girls. He's got it down—how to dress, those sweaters, and tight, tight pants, knowing multiple languages, pickup lines—so he just goes with it. And some people just have that confidence and swagger, and he's got it. I liken him to James Bond. He knows—or he thinks he knows—how to get the girls." (tvguide.com)

Auditioning: I auditioned for the second version of the pilot. They had already shot a pilot . . . My character wasn't in it. Then they rewrote it and restructured it and added my character . . . When we shot the actual pilot, I could tell something really special was happening beyond the status and brilliance of Chuck [Lorre] and Jim [Parsons]. At that point I sort of had a feeling we might at least get a shot of getting it on the air, and we did." (Melissa Parker, *Smashing Interviews Magazine*)

Bernadette: Things are never smooth, but then again, Howard is not smooth. He's learning the ways. I couldn't have seen it in *any* way. If I did, I wouldn't even think it would be a down-to-earth girl. It's nice, and you can see he's never really had girlfriends before. You get to see this human side of him you've never seen. I think it's time. He's worked; he's earned it. It'll be interesting to see how he copes with how this whole thing will affect his relationship with his mother. His heart certainly belongs to his mother. (tvguide.com)

Cast: The characters are completely inept in the world. I think everyone can relate to feeling sort of like an outcast or an underdog in some way. You watch these guys, and you'd assume they have the whole world figured out, or the universe figured out in an equation, but they literally can't figure out how to function with girls, with other human beings. It's really fun to watch people fall on their faces, trying to crack that human condition . . . In some ways, they are the biggest morons in the world, but their IQs are higher than most people. It's a great combination of the overconfident nerds, inept almost like aliens. ("Interview with Simon Helberg," seat42f.com, March 17, 2008)

Fans: We are just very lucky to have this enormous group of loyal die-hard fans. Nerds are really scary when they get into large groups—you don't want to mess with them. So it is good to have them on your side like we do. It is the greatest thing to have such loyal passionate people watching our show; it really fuels us. (Mike Gencarelli, moviemikes.com, January 4, 2011)

Marriage: He's growing up! The most amazing part is he found a great person as opposed to a prostitute or a mail-order bride . . . He ended up being in the healthiest relationship of all these people and moving the farthest along . . . Having not had a father figure and having a mother in this unhealthy, symbiotic, bizarre relationship— as much as he talks about sleeping with girls, I think he probably is looking for a real companion, a future wife and mother. He puts on this front of being a ladies' man, but it's really because he's trying whatever possibility there is. Most of them are strikeouts. Until now.

(Joyce Eng, "*The Big Bang Theory*: Howard Makes a 'Simple and Sweet' Marriage Proposal," tvguide.com, April 6, 2011)

Mother: This woman named Carol Anne Susi. I think she's worked a bunch as a character actress. She's from Brooklyn. And she's a small woman. And she's the nicest lady, but she just yells at me all night long . . . I don't think we'll ever show Howard's mother. I mean, I don't know if you'd want to see a face put to the voice of that character. I think they like that dynamic of having her just existing in this ominous, overbearing way. (Will Harris, bullz-eye.com, December 28, 2010)

Biography of Rajesh Koothrappali

To see but not necessarily be seen, to hear but not necessarily be heard, and to speak but not to young women because of his selective mutism—those are the crosses that Dr. Rajesh Koothrappali must bear.

An Asian Indian, Raj is an alien who holds a H-1B nonimmigrant visa and works as an astrophysicist at Caltech.

Biography of Kunal Nayyar

Name: Kunal Nayyar
Birth date and place: April 30, 1981, in London
Height: 5'8"
Vocation: Actor
Residence: Los Angeles, California
Education: University of Portland in Portland, Oregon (BS in business); Temple University in Philadelphia, Pennsylvania, (MFA in acting)
Twitter verified account: @kunalnayyar (103,975 followers as of May 1, 2011)

Kunal Nayyar: A Rising Star

Born in London, Kunal attended high school in New Delhi, India (St. Columba's School), obtained a BS in business from the University of Portland in Oregon, and a master's in fine arts in acting at Temple University in Philadelphia.

Unlike the other principal cast members, who have extensive television experience, Kunal had previously appeared only on NCIS (*Naval Criminal Investigative Service*) in one episode as a terrorist, and had a small part as a pizza delivery man in *S.C.I.E.N.C.E.* (though of course there are no small parts—only small actors).

No Slumdog

Rajesh grew up as one of six children in New Delhi, India, but he lacked for nothing because he comes from a wealthy family. His father, a gynecologist, has all the creature comforts money can buy: a large house, servants, and a leased Bentley. The beneficiary of an excellent education, Raj's affliction—an inability to talk to females to whom he's attracted—gave rise to the erroneous belief within his family that he might have homosexual tendencies, especially after they learned of his bromance with Howard. (His otherwise traditional parents, though, are enlightened: they talk warmly of a homosexual couple they know in town and their adoption of a baby boy.)

H-1B Nonimmigrant Visa

Raj is in this country legally, but he's not an American citizen. He's here on a work visa, which allows him to stay in the United States for up to six years, contingent on continued employment by his sponsor, Caltech, because he's in a "specialty occupation" considered desirable by immigration officials. As he explains to his friends in "The Pirate Solution" (3-4), "My visa's only good as long as I'm employed at the university . . . I don't want to go back to India. It's hot and loud, and there's so many people. You have no idea—they're everywhere."

What the others take for granted—their U.S. citizenship, and all the privileges it entails—Raj cannot. He must remain gainfully employed or risk deportation. It's a concern that's uppermost in his mind. A year later, as recounted in "The Apology Insufficiency" (4-7), when he panics during an FBI interview investigating Howard, Raj volunteers far too much information about himself. "Please don't send me back to India," he begs. "It's so crowded! It's like the whole country is one endless Comic-Con, except everybody's wearing the same costume: Indian Guy . . . I love this country! Baseball, the freedom, the rampant morbid obesity! From California to the New York island, I'm a real Yankee Doodle boy!"

Resident Alien

A cultural outsider, Raj straddles two worlds. His past, represented by India, is what he escaped from. Though he cites Hinduism when it suits him, like when he needs ammunition to support his views in discussions with Priya, he otherwise wants little to do with the world he left behind. He eschews Indian cuisine, preferring American fast food and ethnic foods from other cultures; he hasn't gone back home since moving to California; he doesn't date Indian women; and he has no intention of ever going back to India to live.

Though he has had a few one-night stands with American women, he's been unable to make any of them work because that would require verbal communication, which is his roadblock to successful relationships. Once he resolves that little issue, he won't have any problem meeting women: Penny, Bernadette, Sheldon's sister Missy, and actress Summer Glau have all made it clear that they consider him an interesting, attractive man—but not when he clams up and stands mute.

SIGNS OF SELECTIVE MUTISM
· · · · · · · · · · · ·

Raj clearly exhibits symptoms of selective mutism. On its website, the American Speech-Language-Hearing Association explains some of the signs of this condition:

- Consistent failure to speak in specific social situations (in which there is an expectation for speaking, such as at school) despite speaking in other situations.
- Not speaking interferes with school or work, or with social communication.
- Lasts at least one month (not limited to the first month of school).
- Failure to speak is not due to a lack of knowledge of, or comfort with, the spoken language required in the social situation.
- Not due to a communication disorder (e.g., stuttering).
- It does not occur exclusively during the course of a pervasive developmental disorder (PPD), schizo-phrenia, or other psychotic disorder.

From the beginning, Raj shows these symptoms. When Penny asks him if he works with Leonard and Sheldon at the university, his silence is misinterpreted by her. "Uh, I'm sorry, do you speak English?"

Howard explains, "Oh, he speaks English; he just can't speak to women."

In the episode's closing scene, as Penny and the boys head out to dinner and they decide where to go, she tries to get his input. "Any ideas, Raj?" Again, he appears flustered and, again, it's Howard who speaks for him. "Turn left on Lake Street and head up to Colorado. I know a wonderful little sushi bar that has karaoke."

> With those two scenes, Raj's essential character is firmly established: he can, but doesn't, talk to young women to whom he's attracted. It is his Achilles' heel.

Unlike other guys who can talk to pretty ladies without clamming up, Raj is not merely tongue-tied—he's really mute. His selective mutism renders him, for all practical purposes, socially invisible, unless he drinks and assumes his alternative persona—an obnoxious, loud braggart. Most of the time, Raj is the invisible man in a world where it pays to be seen and heard. At work, his career opportunities are limited: in "The Pirate Solution" (3-4), he seeks an alternative subject of study, stellar evolution research, which is headed by Professor Laughlin. Though well qualified for the position, when a comely brunette from MIT named Dr. Millstone appears, Raj blows the interview by getting drunk on sherry and propositioning her: "Would you like to hear more about it in my hot tub?" Then, to Professor Laughlin, "So, when do I start?"

To no one's surprise but his own, he doesn't get the job.

Outside of work, especially in his small circle of friends, Raj fares no better, because his posse includes Penny, with whom he can't talk unless he's drunk. Any other woman he chances to meet presents the same dilemma. His only hope is to keep silent and have it misinterpreted in his favor, which happens in "The Middle Earth Paradigm" (1-6), when Cheryl, attending Penny's Halloween party, tells him, "Wow, I have to say you are an amazing man. You're gentle and passionate and, oh my God, you're such a good listener!"

Though Raj occasionally gets lucky and lands a one-night stand, his selective mutism makes it impossible to have an ongoing relationship. Indeed, in "The Herb Garden Germination" (4-20), there seems to be someone for everyone, except Raj. Though Penny is temporarily without a boyfriend, Sheldon has a girl who's a friend in Amy Farrah Fowler, Leonard has Raj's sister Priya, and even horny Howard has Bernadette Rostenkowski, the girl of Raj's dreams.

In "The Griffin Equivalency" (2-4), Raj finally has his day in the sun, but it's not a pretty sight. Having discovered a new planetary body beyond the Kuiper belt, Raj is lauded as a visionary—one of thirty under thirty years of age—by the redoubtable *People* magazine. For the first time in his life, he's the center of attention, and it goes to his head, so much, in fact, that his geek buddies refuse to attend the awards ceremony. Penny chastises them and joins Raj— an engagement she soon regrets. Drunk on heady fame and an unending supply of booze, Raj's boorish alter ego emerges from the shadows.

The next morning, Raj goes to Penny's apartment, hoping to slip an apology note under her door. She refuses to accept the note, and demands he apologize to her directly. He squeaks, "Sorry!" and she hugs him and says, "Oh, sweetie, it's okay."

Penny understands the demon Raj struggles with, and recognizes that when he's not drunk, he's a nice guy who has a lot going for him.

Raj's Exotic Looks

It's not that Raj is physically unattractive. In fact, in "The Thespian Catalyst" (4-14), Bernadette reassures him, "You're such a cutie . . . You're a hottie." But he can't overcome his selective mutism. Even in instances when a woman is interested in him, as was Sheldon's sister Missy ("The Porkchop Indeterminacy," 1-15)—who greets him with, "Hi, cutie pie. I was hoping you'd show up," after she shoots down Howard and Leonard—Raj is tongue-tied and stumbles over his words when the experimental medication he was taking begins to wear off.

What a cruel irony! Unlike Leonard, Howard, and Sheldon, all of whom look like geeks, Raj is photogenic. In fact, when he takes the opportunity to dress up, as he did when escorting Penny to a *People* magazine reception, he's tall, dark, and handsome. But

those advantages are nullified when he is verbally noncommuni-
cative. To women, he's seen but seldom heard, unless he's drunk as
a skunk.

Bernadette

Just as Howard yearned for the likes of Summer Glau and Katee
Sackhoff, Raj also has feelings for a woman he cannot have—
Bernadette, who, from the beginning, only has eyes for Howard.
She's friendly to Raj, but Bernadette's feelings for him are clearly
platonic, though he holds out hope that somehow her ongoing
relationship with Howard will implode.

In "The Herb Garden Germination" (4-20), buoyed by the rumor
that Bernadette is thinking of breaking up with Howard, Raj bears
witness, along with the rest of the inner circle, as Howard drops to
one knee to propose to her. Placing full faith in the rumor, Raj is
hopeful. Soon he will have his long-awaited chance to make his
move, after Bernadette dumps Howard. But as it turns out, Howard
never completes his proposal because of Bernadette's preemptive
acceptance. The resultant response reduces Raj to tears, though not
tears of joy. Now he will have to find a woman on his own, instead of
poaching his best friend's fiancée.

Ironically, it's another member in the inner circle who winds up
being the turning point for him. Commiserating about their lack of
relationships in "The Roommate Transmogrification" (4-24), Raj
and Penny's defenses are down, and after being friends for four
years, the unexpected—and, after the fact, unthinkable—happens:
they both wake up the next morning in Penny's bed.

Penny realizes what's happened and wakes up Raj to tell him,
"This never happened," and he nods in agreement. After what might
have been a sexual encounter, Penny's understandably perplexed and
angry. "Still can't talk to me?"

Raj, who is no longer under the influence, reverts to his classic
mode: he is speechless.

Bromance

Though Raj's own parents and siblings, as well as other people, like Leonard's mother (a psychologist), think that Raj may have homosexual tendencies, that's not true. Raj is clearly hetero, even though he is in a bromance with Howard. They are the very best of friends, just like Sheldon and Leonard; moreover, Raj indisputably has an eye for the ladies.

But in the four years after Penny moved in across the hall, life has moved on for Howard. Now engaged to a smart, lovely young lady, he will soon be spending more time with Bernadette and thus less time with Raj. So Raj is going to have to find a life for himself, one outside of the construct principally built around Howard and also Leonard and Sheldon. The boys-only club has already expanded to include Penny, Priya, Bernadette, and Amy; clearly, the boys are slowly becoming men.

Howard has grown up and is moving on, and it's time for Raj to do the same. He will have to seek treatment for his selective mutism if he wants to enjoy what everyone else in his social circle already has: the joy of connecting with another human being of the opposite sex. Only then will he be complete, and not forever on the outside looking in.

The Quotable Kunal Nayyar

Auditioning: I auditioned for the part during pilot season in 2007. They were looking for a first-generation American of Indian descent. But they were also looking at other ethnicities as well, Chinese or Japanese. It didn't have to be Indian, even though the guy's name was Koothrappali. So when I went in there, because I am from New Delhi, I wanted to bring that side of me. ("Kunal Nayyar Interview," moviemikes.com, January 16, 2011)

Bromance: There's definitely a bromance there. That's what is so lovely about this season—you're seeing that they can't live without each other. In the next few episodes, you really see how dependent Leonard is on Sheldon and Penny. But I think Raj and Howard are endearing. I also love that Raj is becoming more needy and effeminate, like the wife in their relationship. (*The New York Post*)

Character evolution: I think we will see Koothrappali evolve and become a little more social with women. Hopefully, his inability to speak will evolve soon. He will always be socially awkward but hopefully he will figure it out a little bit. Or maybe we will learn that he has a secret at home, like a talking robot or something. ("Kunal Nayyar from *The Big Bang Theory* Talks with Chit Chat Gal," Oct. 12, 2007)

Geekdom: I love *Star Wars* and *The Lord of the Rings* and video games and stuff. The comic book world is a separate world altogether, one that I don't know. I read Archie comics growing up in India, but in terms of superhero comics, I have no idea.

In the comic book store episode, they built an entire comic book store on set. Fascinating. We just got an Emmy nomination in art direction because of how amazing the sets are. I was like a child. Before you know it, you're touching all the magazines and playing with the toys. *What's wrong with me? I'm germing everything.* And you know a lot of stuff is rented, and you've got to give it back in one piece, but I'm touching. (2009 Comic-Con press conference)

Raj: Not only does he have trouble mingling with the outside world, he also has trouble mingling because he's a foreigner. It's a double-edged sword he's fighting. He feels very comfortable with these guys because they're everything to him—you know what I mean? He's so dependent, especially on Howard, but these guys are his family and his life, because he feels completely at ease with them. Inside Raj lives a beast, like a rapper or like a player or like a mogul, because every time he drinks he becomes this smooth, suave, picking-up-girls kind of guy. So I think there's a beast that lives inside him. (CNN, SciTechBlog, April 12, 2010).

Science: The stuff they talk about here is the stuff that geniuses talk about, people who are so advanced in that field. I only studied physics when I was a kid growing up. I don't know any more about physics than the layman does ... They talk about a lot of theories ... A lot of the equations come up on the board; I have no idea what they are. (Julie Zied, The Ziedgeist, "Interview: Kunal Nayyar of *The Big Bang Theory*, May 16, 2008)

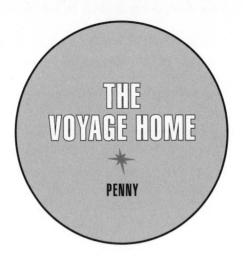

THE
VOYAGE HOME

PENNY

Biography of Penny

Penny, a native Nebraskan, works as a waitress and bartender at the Cheesecake Factory. She has a high school diploma. She lives across the hall from Sheldon and Leonard. She aspires to be an actress.

Biography of Kaley Cuoco

Name: Kaley Christine Cuoco
Birth date and place: November 30, 1985, in Camarillo, California
Height: 5'6"
Vocation: Actress
Residence: San Fernando Valley, California
Education: High school diploma
Factoids: She was a nationally ranked tennis player, which explains her prowess at ping-pong, the recreational pastime of the cast members of *The Big Bang Theory* between takes. She rides horses and once broke her leg in a riding accident, missing two episodes. She began modeling and acting at age seven. She loves to bowl. She's a vegetarian.

Awards: Teen Choice Award for Breakthrough Actress (2003)
Twitter verified account: @KaleyCuoco (167,468 followers as of
  May 1, 2011)

Kaley's Story: Wish Upon a Star

Kaley Cuoco began acting professionally at age seven, when she appeared in *Quicksand: No Escape*, a television movie in which she played the role of Connie Reinhardt. She's had other acting jobs (mostly TV, though she had a role in the film *Virtuosity*), but her breakout role, for which she was ideally cast, was a teenage girl named Bridget Hennessy in the TV show *8 Simple Rules*, based on the bestselling book *8 Simple Rules for Dating My Teenage Daughter* by W. Bruce Cameron.

This popular show would likely have had a longer run, if one of its principals—actor John Ritter in the role of Paul Hennessy, the father—had not unexpectedly died. (The subsequent episodes showed the family mourning and then moving on, just as they would in real life.)

The three seasons Kaley spent in her role of a typical American teen girl paved the way for the opportunity to audition for *The Big Bang Theory*, since the two roles dovetailed perfectly. For *The Big Bang Theory*, she'd play the female lead, a high school graduate living on her own and working a low-paying job, though she aspires to be an actress.

When the cocreators began work on the initial pilot (the unaired version), they had wanted Kaley to audition, but she wasn't right for the role as originally written. It's a good thing that she didn't, because had she taken the role of cruel, unlikable Katie, it may have prejudiced CBS against her for the reboot. (Canadian actress Amanda Walsh, who portrayed Katie in the unaired pilot, did not reprise the female lead role in the aired pilot.)

8 Simple Rules put Kaley on the map, and *The Big Bang Theory* propelled her into stardom.

Penny

At first glance, Penny evokes a classic stereotype: the blonde bimbo, a woman notable only for her looks and certainly not her intellect. She's no Suzanne Somers, who as Chrissy Snow in *Three's Company* (1976–1984) undeniably reinforced the "jiggle and giggle" stereotype. It would be a mistake to characterize Penny as such, since she has more depth.

Penny was born in Omaha, Nebraska, and grew up on a farm, where she learned the importance of self-reliance at an early age. She's not the type of woman who wants, or seeks, a sugar daddy. She'll make her own way in the world.

Though Penny dropped out of community college, she's obviously brighter than most people—especially men—give her credit for. She was able to rebuild a tractor on her own at age twelve, and actively participated in rodeos where she rode horses, lassoed animals, and hog-tied them in record time. Penny's emotional quotient is high: naturally outgoing and obviously cute, she started attracting male attention early on, and began dating when she was fifteen. At sixteen, she was a member of the Queen's Court in her high school's annual homecoming celebration.

From what we know of her early dating experience—relayed by her father, Wyatt ("The Boyfriend Complexity," 4-9)—Penny's choices of what he termed "the skateboard idiots, the white rappers, and all those sweaty dumb asses with their backward hats" tells us that she deliberately overlooked the quiet nice guys who would have wanted to date her if they only had a chance—the geeks who would later become the Leonards of the world, the guys who would go on to make a substantial contribution to society.

Wyatt's greatest fear is that his daughter will marry poorly, which explains why he beseeched Leonard not to give up on her. "Then stack the deck," he urges him. "Cheat. Lie. I don't care. I want grandkids before I die, and I want them to grow up in a house without wheels."

In addition to being sexually active in high school, Penny also enjoyed an occasional toke. Both were signs to her father that his little girl was growing up, though perhaps not in the way he had intended. Was she simply rebelling because she knew her father had hoped for a boy? His nickname for her, after all, was "Slugger."

The farming life was not for Penny. Once she graduated from high school, and after an abortive attempt at securing her associate's degree at a community college, she decided to make a clean break from her past. Like Dorothy Gale, who grew up on a farm in the plain wasteland of Kansas, Penny wanted to be transported to a magical place where she could be transformed from a corn-fed Husker to a movie star. Hollywood beckoned, and she came.

A pragmatist, Penny soon realized that she wasn't going to be discovered while waiting tables at a restaurant, even one called Cheesecake Factory. She realized that she'd have to pay her dues and appear in small theater productions and hope to catch the eye of a talent scout. She recognized that success wasn't going to come cheap, and so she came up with the money for acting lessons, which were expensive but necessary.

With stardust in her eyes, she's blind to the fact that making a career as an actress is statistically not in her favor: 1 in 1.5 million, according to Zachary Turpin's website bookofodds.com. But, as is always the case, the odds are irrelevant when blinded by the light. Penny's lot in life is to realize her dream as a film star, and not settle for being a farmer's wife. It's a big risk, knowing that with each passing year, her good looks are slowly fading, in an industry that feeds on the young and beautiful.

Just as she invested time and money into her fledgling acting career, she made a similar investment in her boyfriend Kurt, a tall, muscular man with whom she lived for four years. Whether or not he could be lumped in with the young men Penny dated when she lived in Nebraska is speculative. But, clearly, Kurt was hardly husband material: he cheated on her, which ended that relationship. Distraught, Penny moved out of their apartment and into her own place. She is, finally, on her own.

An Elemental Explication

In September 2007, Penny moved into apartment 4B at 2311 Los Robles in Pasadena, but without the benefit of a roommate to share expenses. From what we can infer, based on a sublet posting in the lobby of the apartment building, rent is approximately $1,200 a month. Given that she earns minimum wage at the Cheesecake Factory plus tips, the rent alone must be a major financial stretch for her.

The Girl Next Door

Unlike the apartment's previous occupant, Penny will have a dramatic effect on the men across the hall. Sheldon and Leonard, who lead cocooned lives, will be drawn out by her in different ways: Sheldon will find a true friend, and Leonard an on-again, off-again girlfriend. In the larger context of their restrictive social world, which largely consists of fandom in its various guises, both real and imaginary, Leonard and Sheldon are the proverbial Lost Boys of Peter Pan's Neverland: they live in a magical world of their own where they never have to grow up, until Penny (in the guise of Wendy) draws them into the real world.

Wendy and the Lost Boys

Neverland is a place of fantasy where Peter Pan and the Lost Boys live, and the real world is where a young girl named Wendy lives with her parents. Wendy accepts the Lost Boys into her life and into her home, as she prevails upon her parents to adopt all of them. They ultimately leave Neverland behind, but Peter Pan refuses to come along. His place is in Neverland and he knows it, just as he knows it's a place for children, not grown-ups.

In chapter 17 of James Barrie's novel *Peter and Wendy* ("When Wendy Grows Up"), we see Wendy, now a mother, whose daughter

Jane takes her place. And in time, Jane's daughter Margaret will do the same—a cycle that will never end. As each young girl makes a Blakeian journey from innocence to experience, they become adult women and can no longer visit Neverland. They must leave it behind forever, and keep only their fading memories.

That novel, adapted from Barrie's play *Peter Pan; or, the Boy Who Wouldn't Grow Up*, is a prism through which we see refracted Penny's relationship with not only Sheldon and Leonard, but also Howard and Raj. By being accepted as part of their formerly cloistered world, she opens up their lives to infinite and different possibilities. The Lost Boys have been found, and, in a larger sense, they are finally coming home.

Leonard: Sexual Maturity

Penny's presence makes Leonard grow up romantically. Before Penny, his only female relationship was a brief liaison with a North Korean spy whom Sheldon providentially exasperated to the point of her abrupt departure. Unlike Sheldon, Leonard yearns for a normal relationship with a woman. In Penny, he finds a neighbor who becomes a friend, a lover, and then a friend again.

Their complicated relationship is compounded by the presence of Raj's sister Priya, a beautiful young lawyer, whom Penny resents because, as she tells her gal pals Bernadette and Amy, Penny is the one who was principally responsible for "turning Leonard into quality boyfriend material" ("The Zarnecki Incursion," 4-19). So, quite naturally, she resents the time and money she invested in a boyfriend that didn't pay off, which recalls her four years with Kurt, whom she now knows to be little more than a muscle-bound jerk.

Leonard has moved on, and Penny is now relegated to friend status. But had he not met Penny, would Priya find him attractive? Less tolerant than Penny, Priya sarcastically observes that Leonard is "a boy trapped in a man's body." She may not want to wait for him to grow up, as Penny did after she pulled him out of Sheldon's closed world.

Howard: Emotional Maturity

From the first time she meets him, Penny recognized Howard's type: more an adolescent boy than a man, trying way too hard to impress. Howard has much in common with the Warner Bros. cartoon character Pepé Le Pew, a French skunk who is constantly on the make. As noted on Wikipedia, Pepé "cannot take 'no' for an answer, blissfully convinced that the girl is flirting with him, even when she physically assaults him."

Doesn't that sound just like Howard?

Penny's met his kind before—all words and no action—and, from the beginning, she patiently tolerates his verbal assaults disguised as endless compliments about her appearance, until she finally puts her foot down and unintentionally humiliates him in front of the others ("The Killer Robot Instability," 2-12).

Though some would consider her treatment of him harsh, and needlessly so, others feel he had it coming. Now, finally, he knows where he stands with her and the rest of the female population who have been needlessly accosted because of Howard's emotional immaturity.

It is Penny, though, who finally draws him, albeit indirectly, out of his role as a devoted mama's boy whose false bravado masks his insecurities. Howard has never had an authentic, mature relationship with a woman who accepted him on his own terms until Penny reluctantly serves up her coworker and friend Bernadette on a blind date, which has its ups and downs but eventually results in a marriage proposal ("The Herb Garden Germination," 4-20). Had Penny not introduced the two, Howard would probably still be spinning his wheels romantically and looking for a one-night stand or a quick score, even if it meant paying for it. Howard, finally, has left his fantasy world, his Neverland, and embraced reality and a real woman, not a fantasy construct.

Raj: Social Maturity

Just as Penny's presence in Howard's life irrevocably changed him, she's had a salutary effect on Raj. She considers him such a close friend that, in "The Roommate Transmogrification" (4-24), as she and Raj share bottles of wine, she opens up to him and admits that she "screwed up" in letting Leonard go. In turn, Raj asks her, "What's wrong with me, Penny?" She comforts him, saying that if he and Leonard weren't friends, she'd be on him "like the speed of light squared on matter to make energy." The next morning, when they wake up in bed, they discover it's with each other.

Sheldon: Interpersonal Maturity

Of the four boys-turned-men, Sheldon is the most lost. He is, in fact, basically Peter Pan. "All children, except one, grow up," wrote James Barrie in *Peter and Wendy*, referring to Peter. Now we can add Sheldon, the man-child.

Penny's relationship with Sheldon is unique: because of his asexuality, she knows she never has to worry about a misguided pass. She has a maternal attitude toward him, which he embraces; distanced geographically from his biological mother, who lives in East Texas, Sheldon views Penny as a surrogate mother/big sister on the scene. When Sheldon is sick, she tucks him into bed and sings "Soft Kitty," and, when the time comes, he reciprocates.

As seen in a flashback episode ("The Staircase Excitation," 3-22), Sheldon has come a long way: at one point completely unable to relate to people, his interactions with Penny over the years have sensitized him to a world in which women are an integral part. First Penny and then Amy Farrah Fowler—women are now on his radar, though never in a sexual way. To him and Amy, sex is just an undesirable part of the human comedy. In "The Herb Garden Germination" (4-20) they pretend to have had sex to test their theory on meme propagation. Afterward, Sheldon tells her,

"Pretending to have intercourse with you has given me great satisfaction."

Penny refuses to be intimidated by Sheldon or take the supercilious crap he dishes out to his other friends, which sets her apart from them. She cares for him deeply and looks after him on an ongoing basis, but she's nobody's fool, and to underestimate her is a big mistake. Penny's one smart cookie.

Though she hasn't yet climbed up the ladder of success at work, nor has she made any inroads as an aspiring actress, Penny has caused great change among the two young men who introduced themselves to her, the girl next door, some years ago. She's certainly had a salutary effect on all the boys, which we can see by simply imagining the effect of her omission on their lives: they would have been lost without her. But with her, they've moved from Neverland to the real world. Sheldon recalls Peter Pan as he explains his relationship with Wendy to her daughter: "She is my mother." Wendy's daughter replies, "He does so need a mother," to which Wendy agrees, "Yes, I know. No one knows it so well as I."

Penny is not only Sheldon's Wendy, but Leonard's, Howard's, and also Raj's.

She is the ship's rudder that finally steers them in the right direction.

The Quotable Kaley Cuoco

Auditioning for the show: I auditioned two years ago and didn't get it. I auditioned again and didn't get it. Chuck [Lorre] told me I was not the girl for the show. And then a year later, he rewrote the whole thing, called me, and said, "I'm sorry. Will you come back?" And I said, "No, I'm busy now." He sent me the script, and he rewrote the whole thing. I came in two days later and got the job. It was all an incredible timing thing for me. (Brian Ford Sullivan, "Live at the San Diego Comic-Con: *The Big Bang Theory,*" *The Futon Critic*, July 25, 2009)

Being one of the boys: I think now going into our fourth season, Penny has definitely become one of them. I don't see her any longer as that hot girl next door whom Leonard pines after. I see that she's one of their friends. She understands them and has patience with them. She understands them on a level that most women—I would say most human beings—don't understand them. (Karen Heyman, "*The Big Bang Theory* Q&A: Kaley Cuoco," for "Inside the Box" by Brent Furdy)

Breaking up with Leonard: I think it was super realistic, actually. Relationships are up and down, and people get together, and they break up, and they're not friends, and they're friends. I mean, this stuff happens all the time. So I think it actually was perfect timing, and you never know what's going to happen with them. (teentelevision.com, Sept. 21, 2010)

Breaking up with Johnny Galecki: This is the first time I've ever talked about it, ever. It was a wonderful relationship, but we never spoke a word about it and never went anywhere together. We were so protective of ourselves and the show, and didn't want anything to ruin that. But that also made it sad, too. That's not the kind of relationship I want—I don't want to be hiding. We couldn't do anything. It wasn't as fun as we wanted it to be. Everyone was always asking, and we deny-deny-denied. (Hudson Morgan, "Justify Her Love," CBS Watch! Magazine)

Casting: Originally, I was a little nervous that it was going to be the blonde next door to two goofballs, which we've seen before. But if you've seen the show, it's so not like that at all. Penny, like myself, likes these guys very much and actually wants to be friends with them more than they want to be friends with her. I think they were the mean ones at first. They wanted nothing to do with her. She just annoyed them. So I just love these guys in life and it shows on the show. We love each other. (2009 Comic-Con)

Character: She's definitely not perfect. She has a lot of stuff going on, too, which is cool. Penny started out as "the girl next door," but they've been writing some really great, fun stuff for me. She's a real girl. She's smart in her own way, and I think I represent the audience, like I'm looking at [the boys] through their eyes, because they are so different than we all are used to. I didn't know where the character was going to go; I still don't. But she has totally grown. Penny wants to do things. She doesn't want to waitress for the rest of her life, and she has struggles every day. And, yeah, she has a lot of depth. (H.B. Foreman, "Kaley Cuoco's career is making a big bang in Hollywood")

Cheesecake Factory: I went into the Cheesecake Factory a couple of times recently, and I'm always, like, "Why is everyone looking at me?" And fans are saying, "Do you know anything about the Cheesecake Factory? We love you." I always forget that my character works there. They always give me funny looks, but it's very cute. (H.B. Foreman, "Kaley Cuoco's career is making a big bang in Hollywood")

Geeky fans: They love the show. They're just genuine about the show. I really feel like people love the show. So the fans that come up know everything about it, want to know more about Penny, and kind of think Penny is real: "So what would Penny do tomorrow?" and I'm like, "I don't know. I don't have a script in front of me!" They really believe, and I don't want to take that away from them, but at the same time it's sweet. (2009 Comic-Con)

Her own geekiness: I refuse to pick up on any of those things. I still want to live my life, okay? I don't live in *The Big Bang Theory*, I don't know anything about physics, and I'm never going to learn anything about physics. (2009 Comic-Con)

Johnny Galecki: [One] time I was driving a Vespa in the Dominican Republic with my cast-mate Johnny Galecki on the back like a little bitch. I ran us right into the wall, and he went flying. I almost killed Johnny Galecki. I'm dead serious . . . I've had so many [accidents], I can't even count. (Mike Moody, digitalspy.com, Feb. 15, 2010)

Howard Wolowitz: I think it's nice to cut through the sleaze of the character and see some humanity there, and that is unbelievably fun to play. Every season, the writers give more and more layers to these characters, and make them more and more real, and to see that there's kind of a bleeding heart under his ridiculous character . . . (teentelevision.com, Sept. 21, 2010)

The show: It has a lot of heart. People like Jim Parsons and Johnny Galecki, and I think the writing that was in season two was the best season. The love between Penny and the guys was really heartfelt. I think in the first season, no one believed the cute girl was going to like them and all this silly stuff. I think the characters have really grown, and they love each other. It's really nice to see. (Fred Topel, craveonline.com, Sept. 8, 2009)

Work environment: Oh my gosh, we barely even work here. We just mess around, we're laughing. We all have lunch together every day. It's very cute. Everyone is very close. We already know these characters so well. It's very easy. (Ann Murray-Yavar, Fancast Interview, May 14, 2008)

SHOOTING STARS

THE SUPPORTING CAST

*7*he principal cast of a show appear in virtually every episode. In *The Big Bang Theory*, that would be the Fantastic Five: Penny, Sheldon, Leonard, Howard, and Rajesh. Or, if you prefer, Sheldon and his "C-Men." Backing them up is a growing list of engaging supporting characters. (I have omitted actors who have appeared only briefly.)

Note: The boldfaced names are arranged alphabetically by the character's last name; in cases where no last name is known, he or she is alphabetized by first name.

ALICIA
played by Valerie Azlynn

In "The Dead Hooker Juxtaposition" (2-19), Alicia, like Penny, is an aspiring actress; however, Alicia decides the traditional route of appearing in local productions and hoping to be discovered isn't her plan. She instead tries sleeping her way to the top, which works: she's cast as a dead hooker in *CSI* after sleeping with one of the producers.

A tall, shapely, attractive blonde, she's not only competition to Penny, but she's a classic manipulator. A few cheap words of flattery to any male is sufficient to enlist him as her willing lackey. Though the boys can't see Alicia's deception, Penny can, and she goes to work to protect her "peeps" from Alicia's depredations.

STEPHANIE BARNETT

played by Sara Rue

Though Howard had hoped she'd be his main squeeze, Stephanie abandoned him for Leonard. But she was kind enough to fix him up with her roommate. Her medical expertise came in handy, time and again, especially when temporarily depriving Sheldon of speech with the aptly named "Sheldondectomy."

Sheldon's hope was that Stephanie would be a permanent addition to their *Star Trek* outings, in which she could serve as Dr. McCoy, a medical officer on an Away Team. Unfortunately, her relationship with Leonard didn't work out, and we haven't seen her on the show since.

BETHANY

played by Molly Morgan

In "The Gothowitz Deviation" (3-3), Bethany is an employee at the Gap by day and a goth princess at night. She almost gets it on with a delighted Howard, until their visit to a tattoo parlor pricks him the wrong way, and he's exposed as a fraud: he's obviously no goth. Bethany immediately splits, along with her friend Sarah, leaving Howard and Raj to fabricate a cover story for their failure.

MR. CHEN

played by James Hong

An employee at Szechuan Palace, Mr. Chen is not sweet but sour when an overbearing Sheldon comes to complain in mangled Mandarin about the preparation of his food: Sheldon asserts he's been served orange, not tangerine, chicken.

MARY COOPER

played by Laurie Metcalf

Sheldon's mother, Mary, a fundamentalist Christian who warred incessantly with her late husband, knows her son "Shelly" like no other. When all else fails in dealing with Sheldon, it's time to call Mary, who can always set things straight.

MISSY COOPER
played by Courtney Henggeler

Sheldon's fraternal twin sister Missy is one of the few people who can call him "Shelly" and also twist a private part of his anatomy like a pretzel to reinforce her point—particularly when he interferes with her dating life, which she makes clear is off limits.

A social opposite of Sheldon—she's charming, friendly, and draws other people to her naturally, especially men—Missy is delightfully normal in every way, which provides a sharp contrast to her more intellectually gifted brother, who chafes when she tells him that she refers to him as a rocket scientist, which he considers insulting.

Unfortunately, her only appearance to date was in "The Porkchop Indeterminacy" (1-15), but one hopes she drops in on Shelly more often, if only to *twist* things up a bit.

DR. CRAWLEY
played by Lewis Black

Nicknamed "Creepy Crawley" early in his life, this noted entomologist appears in "The Jiminy Conjecture" (3-2) as the tiebreaker for a bet between Sheldon and Howard. Visibly distraught over recent life changes—he has lost his wife to a rival, paid through the nose for the divorce settlement, lost his job at the university, and will soon be forced to live with his daughter—Dr. Crawley, aptly played by comedian Lewis Black, is the picture of a frustrated man who, toward the end of his career, vents his frustration against an indifferent world.

DR. AMY FARRAH FOWLER
played by Dr. Mayim Bialik

Amy, a girl who's a friend to Sheldon but not his girlfriend, is a neuroscientist. (Art imitates life: Mayim has a PhD in neuroscience, making her the only principal cast member with a bona fide degree in a hard science. As Barry Kripke would say: Vewy impwessive.)

Amy's presence suggests that there really is someone for everyone, because she is in many ways as peculiar as Sheldon. Howard and Raj find her online and fix her up on a blind date with Sheldon, prevailing upon him to meet her, though he is highly skeptical ("The Lunar Excitation," 3-23). Over time, Amy wins him over, though as a good friend, not a romantic interest.

DR. ERIC GABLEHAUSER
played by Mark Harelik

The head of the physics department at Caltech, Dr. Gablehauser hits all the right notes in his dealings with Sheldon, whom he reluctantly agrees is a genius, but possibly a crazy one (though Sheldon asserts he's clearly not, because his mother had him tested). Dr. Gablehauser is not as smart as Sheldon, but he's the boss, and Sheldon would do well to remember that.

PROFESSOR GLENN
played by Rick Fox

In "The Love Car Displacement" (4-13), Professor Glenn is revealed as an old boyfriend of "Bernie" (Bernadette), to Howard's mortification. A study in contrasts, Glenn is tall and Howard is short; Glenn is handsome and Howard is geeky; Glenn is outgoing and personable and Howard is defensive and annoying; Glenn is confident and Howard is not.

Played by former NBA Lakers star Rick Fox, Professor Glenn shows that a measure of a man is not his height but his heart, whereas Howard reveals himself to be needlessly suspicious and insecure.

LALITA GUPTA
played by Sarayu Rao

In "The Grasshopper Experiment" (1-8), Lalita is a blast from Raj's past. A childhood acquaintance, Lalita was, as Raj recalls, fat, obnoxious, and prone to kicking him in the testicles. So when his parents fix him up with a date with her—she's now a dental student at USC— he abhors the idea, until he meets her and sees that she's become a lovely young lady. But it's not Raj who enchants her; it's Sheldon. Raj, who constantly points out how fat she used to be, represents her past, whereas a deferent and charming Sheldon strikes all the right notes, lyrically comparing her to an Indian princess.

DR. BEVERLY HOFSTADTER
played by Christine Baranski
Christine Baranski, a comic legend, brings an authority to the role of Dr. Hofstadter that comes from years of acting experience. Dr. Hofstadter, a psychologist and neuroscientist, has a closer relationship with Sheldon than with her own son, Leonard, who as an adult still seeks her long-delayed approval, which she's bestowed on her other children but not on him. She especially enjoys probing Penny, Howard, and Raj's psyches to lay them bare for close examination.

Over drinks, she gives her seal of approval to Penny, her new drinking-pal gal. She urges her son, who was then dating Penny, "to take very good care of this young woman" ("The Maternal Congruence," 3-11).

ZACK JOHNSON
played by Brian Thomas Smith
The kind of guy Penny used to date before meeting Leonard, Zack is big on brawn and small on brains. After breaking up with Leonard, Penny dates him and realizes there's a considerable intellectual gap between the two men. Leonard, Penny complains, has ruined stupid guys for her. Even so, Zack's a presence in her life, though more as a friend than a lover, just as he's a presence in the boys' lives, notably participating in a costume contest in which he dresses as Superman.

An amiable and likable guy, Zack is without pretensions. He was once the butt of the boys' jokes, but they now accept him for who and what he is.

JOY
played by Charlotte Newhouse
In "The Desperation Emanation" (4-5), Joy is Leonard's blind date who, unfortunately, is no joy at all. Loudmouthed, brassy, and adept

at self-defense against men (she takes pride in knowing "a hundred different ways to rip a guy's nuts off"), she is the date from hell— until she volunteers that she'll be "giving it away" at her cousin's wedding after she hits the open bar. (No fool, Leonard changes his tune and decides to be her date to that event.)

DENNIS KIM

played by Austin Lee

In "The Jerusalem Duality" (1-12), Dennis is a Korean child prodigy whom Dr. Gablehauser is wooing with the help of Sheldon and his friends. Dennis is a younger, even more obnoxious version of Sheldon—and, as Sheldon discovers, he is intellectually more gifted. No longer the wunderkind, Sheldon plots to dethrone Dennis, and succeeds by distracting him with a girl his own age.

The model for Dennis Kim may be Kim Ung-yong, a Korean child prodigy whose IQ is estimated at 210. Kim was multilingual by age two (Japanese, Korean, German, English), at age five he could solve high-level math problems (differential and integral calculus), and at age eight was invited by NASA to study in the United States. Four years later he finished his university studies and began working for NASA. Eventually he returned to his homeland, got his doctorate in civil engineering, and took a teaching position at Chungbuk National University.

PRIYA KOOTHRAPPALI

played by Aarti Mann

Priya is Raj's baby sister and is currently in a relationship with Leonard, to his great surprise, given that she's firmly put him off in the past. Though Raj feels protective toward her, even he must admit that she's no longer a little girl but a grown woman, thus capable of making her own decisions as to whom she'll snog.

Priya's ongoing relationship with Leonard, however, is not without its critics—namely Penny, who belatedly realizes that she had a pretty good thing going with Leonard and laments her loss. His and Priya's relationship, though, is built on a shaky foundation. In "The

Roommate Transmogrification" (4-24), we learn that Priya is soon headed back to India. That is news to Leonard, who assumed she was in Los Angeles for the foreseeable future. Also in that episode, her parents learn that she's dating Leonard. The result: nobody—Priya, her parents, or Leonard—is happy.

DR. V.M. KOOTHRAPPALI

played by Brian George

Sitcom fans will likely remember Brian George from *Seinfeld* (1990–1998), on which he played Babu Bhatt, an Indian restaurateur who was deported after he failed to file immigration paperwork.

We've only seen Dr. Koothrappali on Raj's laptop, and even then too infrequently, because in those few scenes he is hilarious. He represents the past, the old world that Raj has left behind. As a gynecologist, Raj's father can certainly afford to travel, so perhaps one day we'll see him show up stateside to check up on his son, whom he and his wife fear may have become too Americanized. Seen with his wife in video chats with Priya and Raj, Dr. Koothrappali is dismayed to learn that Priya is dating Leonard—a fact Leonard deliberately reveals, as Priya bolts.

MRS. KOOTHRAPPALI

played by Alice Amter

More traditional than her husband, Mrs. Koothrappali is obviously concerned about their daughter Priya, now dating a "white" boy, and their son Raj, who still suffers from selective mutism and whose closest relationship is with another man (not that there's anything wrong with that). Romantically unattached at thirty with no prospects in sight, the clock is ticking for Raj, whose mother fervently wants him to marry an Indian woman and begin raising a family.

BARRY KRIPKE

played by John Ross Bowie

Barry is a Caltech scientist who delights in bedeviling Sheldon, and has a real knack for needling him with practical jokes that are

ROTFLMAO-worthy. In "The Vengeance Formulation" (3-9), Barry releases helium in Sheldon's closed office while Sheldon is on the phone doing an interview with NPR, and as Sheldon's voice becomes increasingly high-pitched, he finally squeaks in outrage, "I found the nozzle, Kripke. I'm going to kill you!" Also humorous, although not intentional, Barry has rhotacism and cannot pronounce the letter "r." So when he tells Sheldon in "The Friendship Algorithm" (2-13) that "I have no interest in becoming your friend," it comes out as: "I have no intewest in becoming your fwiend."

KURT

played by Brian Wade

Penny's ex-boyfriend of four years, and a muscle-bound caveman, Kurt is one of the few people on the show who causes Sheldon's testicles to rapidly ascend to his inguinal canal. Though brains may eventually triumph over brawn between Kurt and the others, in the short term, Kurt's curt ways and imposing physique are enough to make the boys quake in fear, lest they relive their youthful days and find their pants around their ankles, which was Sheldon and Leonard's fate in "Pilot" (1-1).

MRS. LATHAM

played by Jessica Walter

In "The Benefactor Factor" (4-15), the benefactor in question is Mrs. Latham, who is wooed by Caltech president Dr. Siebert for a sizeable donation. Mrs. Latham, in turn, is wooing Leonard, who reminds her of a boy she once dated. Recalling Benjamin Braddock and Mrs. Robinson in *The Graduate* (1967), Leonard's sexual involvement with a woman his mother's age is, he insists, not mercenary. Though Dr. Siebert congratulates him in the cafeteria for taking "one for the team," Leonard doesn't see it that way at all. He maintains that he has feelings for her, though no one believes him.

TOBY LOOBENFELD

played by D.J. Qualls

In "The Loobenfeld Decay" (1-10), Toby is a research assistant at Caltech recruited by Sheldon to perpetuate a ruse—he's "Leopold Houston," a recovering drug addict, and Sheldon's first cousin. By enlisting Toby, Sheldon, who believes a lie will have more credibility if buttressed with history, hopes this will provide an excuse to justify Leonard's absence at one of Penny's performances. She's going to sing, though she obviously can't carry a tune in a bucket.

Sheldon's plan backfires, though, when Toby makes himself at home on his couch, sitting next to Penny, as a rueful Howard looks enviously on.

MIKAYLA

played by Jodi Lyn O'Keefe

In "The Vegas Normalization" (2-21), Mikayla is a hooker with heart who is hired by Raj and Leonard to provide the "Jewish girlfriend experience" to Howard, who is down in the dumps because he couldn't score in Sin City.

RAMONA NOWITZKI

played by Riki Lindhome

In "The Cooper-Nowitski Theorem" (2-6), Sheldon finally meets his match. Ramona, a tall redhead, is a graduate student at Caltech who is smitten by Sheldon's intellect and becomes his Girl Tuesday. In short order, she insinuates herself into his life, at work and at home, assuming multiple roles, including research assistant, food handler, and, most significantly, draconian overlord keeping him focused on his work. Realizing that he will have to sacrifice everything on the altar of scientific knowledge—all work and no play makes Jack a dull boy—Sheldon decides that Ramona's stifling presence is more than he can take. He has unwittingly created a Frankenstein monster who threatens to consume his life.

Ramona's withering looks at Sheldon as he lamely attempts to restore order to his life make her a standout, and her gift for physical comedy, juxtaposed against Sheldon, is icing on the cake. Let's hope we see her in a future episode.

SPECIAL AGENT ANGELA PAIGE
played by Eliza Dushku

In "The Apology Insufficiency" (4-7), Paige is an FBI agent doing a background investigation on Howard, who's up for a promotion if he can get his security clearance upgraded to, presumably, top secret. But, honest to a fault, Sheldon unwittingly sabotages Howard's plan when he reveals the Mars Rover incident ("The Lizard-Spock Expansion," 2-8) to the agent.

Each of the boys interact differently with Angela: Sheldon is initially suspicious; Raj, worried about his immigration status, is nervous to a fault; and Leonard unwisely hits on her, not realizing she's married to a Navy SEAL, to his chagrin and embarrassment.

DR. ELIZABETH PLIMPTON
played by Judy Greer

In "The Plimpton Stimulation" (3-21), Dr. Plimpton is a cosmological physicist from Princeton University who visits Caltech with Sheldon as her host. What Sheldon doesn't know is that she has an alter ego, nicknamed "Dr. Slutbunny" by Penny. The good doctor is quick to hop in the sack with any male in sight—including Leonard, Raj, and Howard.

The visit, fortunately, proves vocationally unfruitful for Dr. Slutbunny, who decides to stay at Princeton after all.

BERNADETTE ROSTENKOWSKI
played by Melissa Rauch

Upgraded from supporting cast member to a regular, though she doesn't appear in every episode, Bernadette is a breath of fresh air. Penny may be the obvious blonde hottie next door, but Bernadette's looks are deceptive. In glasses and conservative clothes, she's deliberately desexed, which belies her lusty nature. With her glasses off and nearly naked in bed with Howard, she's obviously a beauty, more than capable of firing up his pocket rocket ("The Cohabitation Formulation," 4-16).

Nicknamed "Bernie" by a former boyfriend, she's now Howard's fiancée ("The Herb Garden Germination," 4-20), to his endless delight and Raj's endless despair. Her secret admirer, Raj can't help imagining exotic and erotic fantasies about her.

Bernadette has livened up the show and injected a much-needed sexual dynamic, especially since Penny and Leonard's on-again, off-again relationship has provided too few sparks since their breakup. (And, of course, Sheldon and Amy's relationship provides no sexual spark at all.)

SARAH

played by Sarah Buehler

In "The Gothowitz Deviation" (3-3), Sarah is Bethany's wingwoman. Approached by Howard and Raj dressed as goths, Sarah is almost convinced the boys *are* goths, until Howard's yelp of pain when pricked by a tattoo needle reveals their ruse: they only *pretended* to be goths because they wanted to score with goth girls. Not that anyone cares . . .

DR. SIEBERT

played by Joshua Malina

The president of Caltech, Dr. Siebert, solicits Sheldon, Leonard, Howard, and Raj to attend a fund-raising event ("The Benefactor Factor," 4-15), at which Sheldon is conspicuously absent, until Amy Farrah Fowler sheds some light on the matter. Sheldon then shows up, albeit late.

Two years earlier, in "The Monopolar Expedition" (2-23), Dr. Siebert e-mailed Sheldon, telling him to meet him early the next morning in his office. It turned out that he wanted to give Sheldon the good news that his grant proposal to the NSF (National Science Foundation) had been approved.

STUART

played by Kevin Sussman

Stuart is the owner of the Comic Center of Pasadena, a local comic book store that the boys frequent. He's also an artist, with an art degree from the Rhode Island School of Design, and his work has been exhibited locally. A sad sack frequently in the dumps, Stuart manages to go out on two dates with Penny before they decide to remain friends.

The Comic Center of Pasadena is a second home to the boys, especially Sheldon, who retreats, womb-like, to one of its corners when he's profoundly depressed and needs to regress into a comforting childlike state.

CHRISTY VANDERBEL

played by Brooke D'Orsay

In "The Dumpling Paradox" (1-7), Christy is Penny's hometown friend, a buxom blonde with loose morals who comes to visit and wreaks havoc in Howard's life. Madly in lust with her bodacious body, Howard is willing to spend whatever it takes to keep her in his life. But Christy's a user, and Howard's just the latest victim who gets to pay for the privilege of her sexual favors, until his mother puts an end to the shenanigans.

With the exception of Penny's father, Wyatt, and Christy, no one else from Penny's Nebraska days has made an appearance on the show.

WIL WHEATON

played by himself

A child star as Ensign Crusher from the twenty-third century on *Star Trek: The Next Generation* (1987–1994), Wheaton is now in the twenty-first century to put the screws to Sheldon, and takes great delight in doing so. A sharp contrast to his goody-two-shoes image from *Star Trek*, he plays an "evil" Wil Wheaton who stoops to conquer, especially Sheldon, by giving no quarter.

Wil's a great addition to the show, and he needs to make more frequent appearances. Nobody rankles Sheldon like he does.

DR. LESLIE WINKLE
played by Sara Gilbert

Dr. Winkle is not afraid to go toe-to-toe with Sheldon, whom she considers an "East Texas blowhole" ("The Codpiece Topology," 2-2). Calling Sheldon a "dumb ass" is her favorite verbal assault, one that derails him so thoroughly that he is rendered speechless and sputters like a gas engine running on fumes. With some of the others, however, she's the tempting vixen with a sexual itch to scratch, and finds no lack of takers—including both Leonard and Howard.

A female version of Kripke, Dr. Winkle is the other lemon in Sheldon's work life. She was originally a regular, but because the writers couldn't work her into enough story lines, her status was changed to recurring, though "intermittent" is more accurate.

MRS. WOLOWITZ
played by Carol Ann Susi

Unseen but often heard at top volume, Mrs. Wolowitz is most likely to interrupt her son Howard when he's (a) answering the door, (b) on the phone with one of the other boys, (c) playing by (and with) himself, or (d) having coitus in his bedroom with a girl. Mrs. Wolowitz, a traditional Jewish mother, raised Howard on her own after her husband abandoned the family when Howard was only eleven.

In "The Engagement Reaction" (4-23), news of her son's impending marriage to a *shiksa* puts Mrs. Wolowitz in the hospital— or so Howard thinks. It was a simple misunderstanding; in fact, his mother is charmed that there's going to be a doctor in the family— Dr. Bernadette Rostenkowski.

WYATT

played by Keith Carradine

Wyatt is Penny's father, who makes his first (and, to date, only) appearance in "The Boyfriend Complexity" (4-9). Given that Penny makes a reference to her father "Bob" in "The Maternal Capacitance" (2-15), it seems logical that "Bob" would be a nickname for "Robert," a first name, and Wyatt is his surname. Penny's last name has never been given, but I propose that it's Wyatt.

During a revealing episode ("The Boyfriend Complexity"), we see Penny through a new lens: that of her father, who explains a lot about her dating background, to Leonard's amusement. As with Raj's parents, Wyatt is deeply concerned about his daughter's poor choices in the past and, therefore, sees Leonard as his best hope. Well educated, earning a good living, and with excellent career prospects, Leonard is a stark contrast to the morons Penny dated back home.

Part 3

BEAMING DOWN TO PASADENA

In which we transport ourselves to sunny Pasadena, California, to explore terra firma

THE SHELDONIAN UNIVERSE

✦

FROM THE COUCH TO THE COSMOS

*T*he lord of the manor, the master of his domain, Sheldon is permanently fixed in time and place. From his favorite spot on the couch to deep space, we can see how Sheldon's universe, like the Big Bang itself, is naturally expanding, to include not only himself, but Leonard, then Howard and Raj, and then Penny . . . and eventually, the rest of the world.

And it all started with a leather couch.

1. HOME SWEET HOME

The Couch

In "The Staircase Implementation" (3-22), a flashback episode in which we see how Leonard came to be Sheldon's roommate, we learn that the couch is Leonard's contribution to the apartment, not Sheldon's. Sheldon's deliberately designed, sparsely furnished living room only included two lawn chairs, one of which is his "by eternal dibs" because of its ideal location.

When tenants from a first-floor apartment were moving out, they sold the leather sofa to Leonard for $100, and, with Raj's help, he moved it into Sheldon's apartment. It didn't take long for Sheldon to realize that the sofa was a quantum leap in comfort over the plastic web-covered lawn chairs. Then of course he had to try sitting on each of the three cushions to determine which one was optimum: the end one on the left side, facing the TV. That spot is now at the dead center of Sheldon's universe, as revealed in "The Cushion Saturation" (2-16). As only Sheldon could put it: "That is my spot. In an ever-changing world, it is a single point of consistency. If my life were expressed as a function on a four dimensional Cartesian coordinate system, that spot, from the moment I first sat on it, would be 0,0,0,0."

From that vantage point, Sheldon ponders his place in the universe.

Sheldon's Bedroom

The couch is the center of the Sheldonian universe, and all geographical points expand from there. The next node is Sheldon's bedroom, his sanctum sanctorium, his Fortress of Solitude where no one else is allowed to enter. The first time he meets Leonard, as he's showing him around, Leonard asks whether the room they're standing in was his. "No, this is my room," Sheldon replies. "People don't go in my room."

Over the years, though, Sheldon has mellowed somewhat. In "The Psychic Vortex" (3-12), he graciously gives up his bedroom to a tall, lovely brunette named Martha. Later, in "The Plimpton Stimulation" (3-21), he goes to great lengths to prepare his bedroom for a visiting guest, Dr. Elizabeth Plimpton from Princeton University.

The Elevator, or Up the Down Staircase

Permanently out of order, with yellow tape across its exterior, the fourth-floor elevator is a reminder of the folly of man—or, more specifically, of Leonard, whose foolish experiment in Sheldon's apartment created a combustible situation, chronicled in "The Staircase Implementation" (3-22). Leonard's hubris prevents him from admitting that Sheldon, an insufferable know-it-all, is dead right on this count, a fact he realizes when the rocket fuel he's been fooling around with explodes in the elevator—without him in it, thanks to Sheldon, who not only saved the day but also his life.

The elevator remains in a state of stasis. From the time Leonard first met Sheldon to the current day, its lack of functionality means that everyone in the apartment complex must hoof it up and down the stairs, which is obviously a major pain for those who live on the fourth floor, like Sheldon, Leonard, and Penny.

Penny's Place

If Sheldon's apartment is the calm center of the hurricane, with everything else in the world swirling around him, Penny's apartment is where the tornado touched down to wreak havoc. Penny's and Sheldon's apartments are worlds apart: his is one of order, and hers is one of disorder. It's the close proximity of Penny's chaos to Sheldon's ordered world that causes flux in his time-space continuum, leaving him with no choice but to make an incursion to set things straight. In "The Big Bran Hypothesis" (1-2), Sheldon uses Penny's apartment key to trespass and clean up what he calls "a swirling vortex of entropy." Penny wakes up the next morning, and from across the hall Sheldon and Leonard hear her yell, "Son of a bitch!" When she realizes that the boys took it upon themselves to tidy up her place without her knowledge or consent, she storms over to verbally attack an oblivious Sheldon with a barrage of sarcasm.

Sheldon's orderly world is epitomized by his apartment, but even the demigods have to occasionally climb down from the heights of Mount Parnassus. In Sheldon's case, he had to descend into chaos by staying in Penny's apartment when he accidentally locked himself out; his spare room key, which Penny had, turned out to be in his apartment as well, where it obviously shouldn't have been, and where it could do him no good.

In "The Vegas Renormalization" (2-21), the mere thought of having dinner with Penny in her apartment strikes him as absurd. He sarcastically responds, "Sure, why not? And after the Sun's down, we can all pile in my pickup and go skinny-dipping down at the creek. 'Cause today's the day to stop making sense."

But Sheldon is left with few options. With his friends in Las

Vegas, he can either accept Penny's offer of temporary lodging or check in at a local hotel, so he takes her up on the offer. Besides, what's the advantage of having friends unless they can offer you a few benefits?

The Apartment Complex

Sheldon and Leonard's shared apartment, #4A, is located at 2311 North Los Robles in Pasadena (zip code 91104). Across the hall is Penny's apartment, #4B; we finally learned the number in February 2009 ("The Financial Permeability," 2-14), when Sheldon was discussing money matters with Penny. (We also learned that, based on Dr. Beverley Hofstadter's count of the mailboxes in the lobby, there are approximately thirty-six apartments in the building.)

Later, in October 2010, their address becomes a concern when Sheldon goes to great but futile lengths to hide from Amy Farrah Fowler, whom he feels has impure designs: she wants to raise the level of their involvement from friends to the next step. (She actually prefers stasis, but Sheldon misinterprets a comment she makes.)

In any case, if you were to try to go visit them at 2311 North Los Robles, you'd discover that the avenue runs north–south and, on its northern terminus, intersects Woodbury Road. The last street address on N. Los Robles Avenue is 2099.

So where would the apartment actually be?

For the inspirational source of the set designs, an online sleuth named The Flash, posting on "The Big Bang Theory Forums" in April 2010, says:

I'm sure it's Brookmore Apartments at 189 N. Marengo Avenue (brookmoreapts.com). It's a 1920s apartment building a block and a half from City Hall. It's near Caltech and the Cheesecake Factory, and Euclid is one of the streets you can take to get [from] there to Caltech. I lived in the building for two years, and the inside looks like the exact replica of the *Big Bang Theory* apartments. Exposed brick, stairwell looping around the elevator, very similar front doors as the

RIGHT:
Brookmore Apartments, possible inspiration for the apartment building where Penny, Leonard, and Sheldon live

LEFT:
Exterior shot of the Brookmore Apartments

RIGHT:
Pasadena City Hall

show. And the Brookmore Apartments elevator was always broken. Even the laundry room looks the same. A number of Caltech and JPL physicists live there, as well as more than one aspiring actress.

But the view from the four-story Brookmore Apartments doesn't give us what we see from Sheldon's living room, which clearly shows the prominent and unmistakable bell tower at City Hall. On the same forum, another poster said that based on what he determined, that background shot was made from "a commercial building owned by Western Asset . . . 385 E Colorado Blvd."

2. DINING

None of the boys has ever shown any culinary interests, except for Sheldon, who once tried to improve the taste of scrambled eggs ("The Luminous Fish Effect," 1-4), but they clearly enjoy dining out and bringing home takeout, especially ethnic food: Indian, Japanese, Thai, Italian, Chinese, and Korean. They also enjoy American fast food.

Ironically, the alien, an Americanized Raj, prefers chicken nuggets to fare from his native India, though Sheldon is particularly smitten with its cuisine, notably "the intoxicating aroma of kadhai paneer" ("The Vegas Renormalization," 2-21).

Sniffing my way around the alphabet soup of dining locations mentioned on the show, I discovered that most, but not all, of the locations are fictional.

Fictional Locations

Chinese food: Szechuan Palace ("The Tangerine Factor," 1-17), where Sheldon thinks he's getting orange chicken, not the advertised tangerine chicken. (This may, in part, explain why the restaurant later closed down.) In "The Cushion Saturation" (2-16), Leonard breaks the bad news to Sheldon that he's been getting their Chinese takeout from **The Golden Dragon** instead. Chows is mentioned by Dr. Leslie Winkle in "The Codpiece Topology" (2-2).

Indian food: House of Tandori ("Pilot," 1-1); **Mumbai Palace** ("The Jiminy Conjecture," 3-2).

Italian food: Giacomo's ("The Cooper-Nowitski Theorem," 2-6).

Thai food: Siam Palace ("The Adhesive Duck Deficiency," 3-18).

Real-World Locations

Bob's Big Boy Restaurant (bobspasadena.com), located at 899 E. Del Mar Blvd: They serve up their famous "original double-decker cheese-burger," which predates McDonald's Big Mac. In "The Irish Pub Formulation" (4-6), Priya Koothrappali gets her first taste of American fast food when she enjoys a Bob's Super Big Boy hamburger.

The Cheesecake Factory (thecheesecakefactory.com), located at 2 W. Colorado Blvd: In "Pilot" (1-1), we learn that Penny works there as a waitress. In subsequent episodes, we learn that she earns minimum wage (currently $7.25 an hour plus tips), has never gotten a raise, receives tips as a waitress and a bartender, and may or may not have a predilection for adding her own special sauce (i.e., saliva) to Sheldon's hamburger when he unwisely pisses her off.

With more than two hundred items on the menu, the Cheesecake Factory offers far more than just cheesecake. The restaurant serves salads, pizzas, pastas, fish, seafood, steak, and their trademarked Glamburgers. Because Penny and Bernadette work there, it's a spot frequented by the boys. Gastronomically fussy, Sheldon finally eschews the Big Boy hamburger to chew on the Cheesecake Factory's Barbecue Burger. His standard order is a "barbecue bacon cheeseburger, barbecue sauce, bacon and cheese on the side" ("The Panty Pinata Polarization," 2-7).

DelTaco (deltaco.com), located at 844 Union Street: A fast-food chain that serves Mexican food. In "The Maternal Congruence" (3-11), Dr. Beverly Hofstadter talks about her recent visit with Penny, where they got drunk at this bar. It's actually not a bar; it's a fast food place that doesn't even serve alcohol, so they obviously

The Cheesecake Factory on Colorado Blvd

didn't come here. But because the name is identical, it may be confusing to the unwary.

Hot Dog on a Stick (glendalegalleria.com), located in the food court (California Terrace Eateries) at the Glendale Galleria: This place serves all-turkey hot dogs and, in some locations, veggie dogs. The dog is dipped into a special batter, cooked in soy oil, and then skewered. The sixty-five-year-old restaurant chain also offers French fries, cheese on a stick, hot dogs in buns, funnel cake sticks, and freshly squeezed lemonade. In "The Cornhusker Vortex" (3-6), Howard mentions it to Raj. Howard, though, wasn't interested in a skewered hot dog; he was interested in the counter girl—who verbally skewered him.

Lucky Baldwins, located at 1770 East Colorado Blvd, and 17 South Raymond Ave: The full name is Lucky Baldwins Trappiste Pub and Cafe. It's a British pub with breakfast, lunch, and dinner, and a great place to go if you are a beeraholic: they have sixty-three beers on tap. In "The Irish Pub Formulation" (4-6), Sheldon gives Leonard a napkin from this restaurant, purportedly written on by a waitress named Maggie McGeary, which says, "Leonard, call me if you're interested in coitus. Sincerely, Maggie McGeary."

Luigi's Pizza (luigiortegas.com), located at 1655 E. Colorado Blvd (with another branch in Oxnard at Fremont Square, 606 N. Ventura Rd): This combination Italian/Mexican chain offers pizzas and hoagies as well as tostadas, tacos, and burritos. In "The Toast Derivation" (4-17), Sheldon orders pizza for takeout but thinks the owner doesn't sound Italian enough, and thus questions the restaurant's ethnic authenticity. On that count, he may have a point ...

Marie Callender's Restaurant & Bakery (mcpies.com), located at 2300 E. Foothill Blvd: In "The Cornhusker Vortex" (3-6), Howard's trying to make amends with Raj and suggests that after they hit the La Brea Tar Pit and have lunch, they go to Marie Callender's for pie. Raj responds, "I'd like that." But, of course, Howard is sidetracked by another dish—a beautiful girl who walks by—and they have to forgo the pie. Which is too bad, because Marie Callender's has a mouth-watering selection of pies, cakes, and other desserts.

P.F. Chang's (pfchangs.com), located in Paseo Colorado, 260 E. Colorado Blvd, Suite 201: In "The Large Hadron Collision" (3-15), this is where Howard is planning on taking Bernadette for Valentine's Day, for the "P.F. Chang's for Two."

Quiznos (quiznos.com), located at 766 East Colorado Blvd, Ste 100: Of the two locations in Pasadena, the one the boys most likely frequent. Famed for its toasted submarine sandwiches, Toasty Torpedoes, and Toasty Bullets, this is what Amy alludes to in "[The Alien Parasite Hypothesis (4-10)]" during her conversation with Sheldon, who knows nothing about her field but insists she's slicing the brain specimen in her lab too thin. She tells him that under a two-photon microscope, she's sliced it just right, but it'd be "too thin if I were making a foot-long brain sandwich at Quiznos." Brain food, eh?

Fun fact: Jim Parsons has done ads for Quiznos. (You can find his 2003 "Raised by Wolves" ads on YouTube.)

Souplantation (souplantation.com), located at 201 S. Lake Ave: Beau-ootiful Soo-oop! Beautiful, beautiful soup! But wait, there's more: tossed or prepared salads, bakery goods, hot pastas, and desserts! In "The Hamburger Postulate" (1-5), Sheldon ponders dropping Souplantation from his scheduled weekly list of dine-in options because "the name always confused me anyway ... You can't grow soup." But in "The Euclid Alternative" (2-5), he has a change of heart and wants to stop there because "it's creamy tomato soup day."

3. SHOPPING

Penny and the boys do most of their shopping in Pasadena, which has an excellent selection of major retail and specialty stores at the local malls and stand-alone stores.

The greater Los Angeles area offers an extraordinary selection of retail stores, from small one-person shops (like comic book stores) to name-brand stores on Rodeo Drive in Beverly Hills, an international shopping mecca.

These are some of the shops *The Big Bang Theory* cast has patronized.

The Apple Store (apple.com) at 54 West Colorado Blvd is a favorite destination, though the boys aren't big Apple fans, beyond the occasional iPod. Sheldon, of course, praises the late Zune, Microsoft's MP3 player, and talks smack about the iPod to Raj, in "The Staircase Implementation" (3-22).

For Leonard and Howard, the Apple Store is where they go to steal employee T-shirts and try to pick up unsuspecting female customers. And all the boys are happy to go there to mock the unsuspecting employees at the Genius Bar. In "The Terminator Decoupling" (2-17), Leonard tells Sheldon, "We're all going over to the Apple Store to make fun of the guys at the Genius Bar. You want to come?" Sheldon replies, "Oh, I always enjoy that, but I'm a little busy."

Bath & Body Works (bathandbodyworks.com): When Sheldon has to buy a gift basket for Penny, he heads to the Bath & Body Works at 340 E. Colorado Blvd, #119. On another trip there ("The Bath Item Gift Hypothesis," 2-11), he walks away with a bushel of baskets. It's no surprise, then, that the store would come to mind later in "The Large Hadron Collision" (3-15), when he's making comparisons between where he and Penny might each want to go. He even provides a PowerPoint presentation to state his case. He first shows the Large Hadron Collider, then an image of the "Bath & Body Works on Colorado Boulevard. They sell scented soaps and lotions, some of which contain glitter. Now, let's see if we can match the individual to the appropriate destination." Though eminently logical, Sheldon's presentation fails to win Penny over.

Glendale Galleria (glendalegalleria.com) is located at 100 West Broadway. This large shopping mall, due west of Pasadena, is co-located with an Apple Store and a Cheesecake Factory. So after working up an appetite by making fun of the Genius Bar staffers at the Apple Store, the boys can go to the Cheesecake Factory and eat their fill, and after that they can walk off the meal in the shopping complex.

The mall is a favorite destination for Raj, who likes to go there to window-shop and see what catches his fancy. In "The Psychic Vortex" (3-12), he suggests a trip there, which Sheldon declines. But Raj's persistence pays off: Sheldon agrees to go to a university mixer as Raj's wingman.

One Colorado (onecolorado.com), at 24 East Union St, is a city block of twenty-five retail stores, seven restaurants, and a movie theater. Though Sheldon prefers the Pottery Barn, there is a Crate & Barrel at this location, along with the Soap Kitchen (perfect for Penny), and Gold Class Cinemas (for the boys).

Paseo Colorado (paseocoloradopasadena.com), at 280 East Colorado Blvd, is an indoor mall with dozens of stores. Not only is there a Bath & Body Works (store #119), but also a P.F. Chang's China Bistro (#201) and ArcLight Cinemas (#336).

The Pottery Barn (potterybarn.com) is located at 1 E. Colorado Blvd, with a second location specializing in stuff for kids at 511 South Lake Ave. This is where Sheldon buys, among other items, his *Star Wars* bedsheets. We know this because, in "The Euclid Alternative" (2-5), he wants to return a set that "turned out to be much too stimulating to be compatible with a good night's sleep. I don't like the way Darth Vader stares at me."

RadioShack (radioshack.com): Given the boys' love for electronics, we can infer that this is a regular stop for all of them. Sheldon goes there to buy batteries on sale ("The Euclid Alternative, 2-5), likely to the one at 825 N. Lake Ave. (There are 7,200 locations worldwide.)

Had Howard been able to buy off-the-shelf supplies to re-jigger his failed space toilet ("The Classified Materials Turbulence," 2-22), RadioShack would have been the store of choice. It's a virtual electronic cornucopia of wires, switches, remotes, spare parts, and other items—so many that it defies easy description.

Ralph's (ralphs.com) is a grocery store with two locations in Pasadena: 160 North Lake Ave, and 320 W. Colorado Blvd, which is likely the one where Sheldon and Penny shop. It's one of many grocery chains owned by Kroger.

In "The Pants Alternative" (3-18), we learn that it's where Sheldon gets his sliced bologna. We can assume it's where Penny took Sheldon to shop for eggs, since he had time to do experiments because of his recent firing at work ("The Luminous Fish Effect," 1-4).

Victoria's Secret (victoriassecret.com): Penny enjoys buying lingerie. Not your run-of-the-mill stuff from Kmart or Wal-Mart, but the good stuff at Victoria's Secret. In "The Precious Fragmentation" (3-17), she tells Leonard, "FYI, this is a bag from Victoria's Secret." "I'm out," Leonard says, as he releases his hold on the prop replica of the One Ring—also held by the other boys—and follows Penny into her apartment.

She can no longer shop at the Victoria's Secret at 21 W. Colorado Blvd, because that retail store closed in early 2011. Fortunately, the location at 13 W. Colorado Blvd remains open and has man-bait aplenty.

4. COMIC BOOK STORES

A home away from home for the boys, Stuart's comic book store is not only Sheldon's occasional haven ("The Guitarist Amplification," 3-7) when his world becomes too noisy and chaotic, but Shangri-La for himself and the others.

Though comics can be ordered online from specialty stores, it's preferable to get them locally at a retail store, because browsing is part of the excitement. In "The Classified Materials Turbulence" (2-22), Sheldon and the boys are at Stuart's store and, as Stuart is unpacking a new box, Sheldon perks up and says, "Smell that? That's the smell of new comic books. Oh, yes!"

Whether in comic book form or collected in graphic albums, comics are an integral part of the boys' world. In the real world that often disappoints, frustrates, and infuriates them, comics are a safe harbor where they can revel in a four-color fantasy in which evil is punished, the good guys triumph, the guy gets the girl, and what always prevails is truth, justice, and the American way.

Fictional Location

Sheldon and the boys regularly shop at The Comic Center (thecomiccenter.com), located on E. Green St, near Pasadena City College and Caltech. The shop's website advertises its Mystic Warlords of Ka'a Tournament every Thursday. (Patrons will remember the classic Sheldon Cooper vs. Wil Wheaton showdown, when Sheldon was snookered ["The Creepy Candy Corollary," 3-5].) It's also where Stan Lee held a signing ("The Excelsior Acquisition," 3-16), which Sheldon missed.

The Comic Center set design, wrote Wil Wheaton in his blog, is marvelous:

The comic book shop set is incredible, and the attention to detail is unbelievable. Because *BBT* is produced at Warners, and Warners is affiliated with DC, they have tons of DC books (including archival editions that I wanted to, uh, borrow) like you wouldn't believe, tons of sculpted minis and action figures, and posters all over the shop that are actually part of current storylines in comics. Their set-dressing people change those posters and stuff to reflect what's happening in the DCU (DC Universe), which I thought was awesome.

Real-World Location

Comics Factory (comicsfactory.com), located at 1298 East Colorado Blvd. A staffer explained to me in a phone call that although he has never seen any of the actors from *The Big Bang Theory* in his store, he has seen the show's staffers doing research there.

Given that this is the only comic book store in town with an emphasis on print products, it stands to reason that this would be where the boys most often go to get their comic book fix and action figures, which are prominently displayed in Leonard and Sheldon's apartment. A partial listing:

- In the living room, against the large picture window: Robin, Captain Marvel, Green Lantern, and a figure that might be Aquaman
- On top of a bookshelf near the door: Han Solo as a Stormtrooper, the Flash, and Batman
- In the kitchen: Superman
- In Leonard's room: Han Solo as a Stormtrooper with helmet off, standing next to Chewbacca, Viggo Mortensen as Aragorn, and a Superman model
- In Sheldon's room: Green Lantern, whose ass is an emergency cash stash

Comics Factory, where the boys would, in the real world, shop until they drop

Interior shot of the Comics Factory

5. MOVIES

Sheldon takes his film viewing very seriously. When he and the others go out to eat before a movie, he likes to err on the side of caution and factor in enough time to get in line to get tickets, and once inside, his principal objective is to get the best seat in the house. He's even been known to try out various seats and make sounds to find his preferred acoustic sweet spot ("The White Asparagus Triangulation," 2-9). His other priorities include going to the bathroom before show time and leaving enough time to get to the concession stand to buy refreshments.

Fictional Theaters

The boys (especially Sheldon) have been known to stand in line for hours for films of major interest. For instance, in "The 21 Second Excitation" (4-8), Sheldon recalls that he and Leonard stood in line for fourteen hours to see the midnight premiere of *Star Trek: Nemesis* in 2002; in that same episode, all four boys wait to get into **Colonial Theater** to see a midnight showing of the first Indiana Jones movie, with twenty-one seconds restored.

The boys avoid Sheldon like the plague when he gets sick, and in "The Pancake Batter Anomaly" (1-11), they take refuge at the **New Art Theater** to watch a *Planet of the Apes* marathon.

Real-World Theaters

The boys saw *Spiderman 2* (2004) at **AMC Pasadena**, located at 40 W. Union St ("The Creepy Candy Coating Corollary," 3-5), but it has since closed. In addition, in "The Guitarist Amplification" (3-7), a worried Sheldon tells the others that they've got a scant seventeen minutes to show time, "which means we'll need to make all the lights on Colorado Boulevard, plus skip the concession stand and pre-show urination." (They don't make it, and instead kill two hours at Stuart's comic book store while waiting for the next showing of *Time Bandits* [1981].)

The boys' current choices of movie theaters in Pasadena:

- **ArcLight Pasadena** at 336 East Colorado Blvd
- **Laemmle's Playhouse 7** at 673 East Colorado Blvd
- **Regency Academy Cinemas 6** at 1003 East Colorado Blvd
- **Village Roadshow Gold Class Cinema** at 42 Miller Alley

6. MISCELLANEOUS PASADENA LOCATIONS

The boys explore Pasadena when they're not chained to their desks at work. Given the disparity of locations, I'll summarize in alphabetical order.

Fictional Locations

Bowling Alley: Penny and the boys enjoy bowling, especially when pitted against comic book store owner Stuart's team. (To Sheldon's horror, Stuart recruits his archnemesis, Wil Wheaton, in "The Wil Wheaton Recurrence" [3-19].)

We aren't told the name of the bowling alley where Sheldon gets his balls racked, but in Pasadena, the only choice is 300 Pasadena (threehundred.com), which is part of the AMF bowling and recreational centers. It's at 3545 E. Foothill Blvd. The cost to bowl there is $5.25 to $8.25 per person, per game, depending on whether you want to bowl before 5 P.M. or on weekends. (Shoe rental is an additional $5.)

Freemont Memorial Hospital: In "The Peanut Reaction" (1-16), Howard goes to the Freemont Memorial ER on a pretense, but then takes one for the team: he's allergic to peanuts but eats a candy bar to deliberately induce a reaction. In "The Adhesive Duck Deficiency" (3-8), Sheldon drives Penny to Freemont Memorial because she slipped in her tub. And in "The White Asparagus Triangulation" (2-9), Leonard gets stitches after a kitchen accident, and his then-girlfriend, Dr. Stephanie Barnette, takes him to Freemont Memorial, where she works. Freemont Memorial is also where Sheldon shows up, wanting Stephanie to approve a long list of tests he doesn't need. (He's a hypochondriac.)

Kurt's Apartment: In "Pilot" (1-1), Leonard and Sheldon take a drive "halfway across town" (says Sheldon) to retrieve Penny's television. Based on what little we know, we cannot infer Kurt's address.

Marriott (Rose Room): The only Marriott in Pasadena is a Courtyard Marriott (marriott.com) at 180 North Fair Oaks Ave, located in the Old Town area. Though it has nine meeting rooms—the largest being the Huntington Ballroom, which seats two hundred—there is no "Rose Room."

Paintball Outdoors: In "The Dumpling Paradox" (1-6), the boys engage in a real-world, physical team sport (as opposed to a computer game): paintball. There are no paintball parks in Pasadena, though there are plenty of them farther west, especially in Santa Clarita, north of Los Angeles.

Dressed in uniforms and armed with paintball rifles and pistols, in the real world the boys would paint the town red at **Hollywood Sports Park** (hollywoodsports.com) at 9030 Somerset Blvd. According to its website, it's "rated as one of the top five paintball and airsoft fields in the U.S." Spread out over twenty-five acres, "the paintball fields are actual movie sets from such classics as *Starship Troopers, The Haunting, Saving Private Ryan, Godzilla*, and *Supernova*, to name a few."

Real-World Locations

Altadena: North of Pasadena, this is where Howard Wolowitz lives with his mother. In "The Dead Hooker Juxtaposition" (2-19), in an attempt to impress Sheldon's new upstairs neighbor Alicia, Howard lets it slip that, "Oh, actually, I'm, uh, living with a woman in Altadena. Purely platonic. She's also my maid."

Caltech (California Institute of Technology): A private research university with an emphasis on science and engineering, Caltech, where

Sheldon, Leonard, Howard, and Raj are employed, is the vocational backdrop for the show. Its website is at caltech.edu. (See page 122.)

Euclid Avenue: This major thoroughfare runs north–south through Pasadena. On its north end, it terminates at E. 24th St; on its south end, it terminates at highway 71 near San Bernardino county and Riverside county. In "The Euclid Alternative" (2-5), Sheldon is literally taken for a ride on this street, on the back of Howard's underpowered Vespa scooter. Bumping all the way, Sheldon hangs on for dear life while screaming, "Oh, God, not Euclid Avenue!" (A vocal backseat rider, Sheldon's exclamations have an unexpected effect on Howard, who as a result loses control of his bladder, and abandons him on the side of the road.)

Huntington Memorial Hospital is located at 100 West California Blvd. This, not Freemont, is where Howard, Sheldon, Penny, and Leonard would really go in the event of a medical emergency. Huntington has 635 beds and a helipad topside.

Pasadena Municipal Court is located at 200 N. Garfield Ave. After running a red light, Sheldon is summoned to traffic court, where he is summarily fined and spends some time in the pokey for contempt of court ("The Excelsior Acquisition," 3-16).

"Not Euclid Avenue!" yelled Sheldon.

7. CALIFORNIA INSTITUTE OF TECHNOLOGY (CALTECH)

From its website: "The mission of the California Institute of Technology is to expand human knowledge and benefit society through research integrated with education. We investigate the most challenging, fundamental problems in science and technology in a singularly collegial, interdisciplinary atmosphere, while educating outstanding students to become creative members of society."

Caltech, affiliated with NASA's Jet Propulsion Laboratory located north of its campus, has a star-studded list of faculty and alumni that includes thirty-one recipients of the Nobel Prize, six recipients of the Crafoord Prize, four recipients of the Kavli Prize, fifty-five recipients of the National Medal of Science, and ten recipients of the National Medal of Technology, among other honors.

Clearly Sheldon, who is shooting for the stars and hoping to add a Nobel Prize to his already impressive résumé, is in very good company.

The school, which assumed its current name in 1921 after spinning off its preparatory and vocational schools, "owes much of its character to the vision of its troika of founders: astronomer George Ellery Hale, physicist Robert Andrews Millikan, and chemist Arthur Amos Noyes."

Tours

A free guided tour is available for prospective students (check with the admissions office), but for civilians, a self-guided tour is a good way to acquaint yourself with the grounds and the key buildings. It's available for download at marcomm.caltech.edu/pdf/Along_the_Olive_Walk.pdf.

Each numbered stop provides a brief description of the building/ grounds, its history, and its purpose. Your tour starts at the Office of Undergraduate Admissions and the Finance Aid Office (stop #1), at 383 South Hill Ave. The tour is designed to end up back where it started approximately an hour and a half after you begin.

Caltech sign on campus

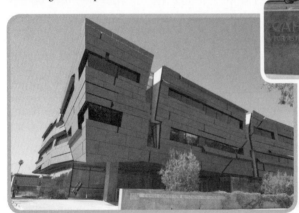

Signage outside the Cahill Center for Astronomy and Astrophysics

The Cahill Center for Astronomy and Astrophysics

The Thomas J. Watson, Sr., Laboratories of Applied Physics

Signage on a locked door to a room containing a laser, at the Thomas J. Watson, Sr., Laboratories of Applied Physics

Fans of *The Big Bang Theory* will especially want to visit the most obvious show-related stops, though the full tour will give you an appreciation of the campus' expansiveness and its extensive range of scientific inquiry. Some don't-miss stops:

Stop #9: Kellogg Radiation Laboratory, Sloan Laboratory of Mathematics and Physics, and Bridge Laboratory of Physics. This is where you would be likely to find Sheldon conducting experiments.

Stop #16: Cahill Center for Astronomy and Astrophysics. This is where you would be likely to find Raj. There are between "200 and 300 researchers" at this location, who:

> work to unravel some of the most profound scientific mysteries of our age, probing such questions as the origin and ultimate fate of the universe; the forces that have shaped the formation and evolution of galaxies, stars, and planetary systems; the nature of the dark matter and dark energy that seem to permeate the cosmos; the behavior of spacetime and matter and energy under extreme conditions, such as those involving black holes; and of course, the perennially fascinating question of whether life exists elsewhere in the universe.

Stop #29: the Thomas J. Watson, Sr., Laboratories of Applied Physics. This is where you'd be likely to see Leonard and Howard working in the lab. "Watson houses research in solid-state electronics and plasma physics. Scientists here are developing lasers and other electronic devices that will be used in light-wave communications systems of the future."

Caltech places in The Big Bang Theory

Though we don't see the campus itself on the show, we have seen the inside of Sheldon's and Raj's offices, and Leonard and Howard in the labs. We've also see a lecture hall, a meeting hall (for socializing), and the cafeteria, where most of the action takes place. It's where the boys hash out topics of the day, egg each other on, chew out each other, and try to fry Sheldon's circuits. All of these locales, of course, are set designs at Warner Bros. studio lot in Burbank. However, if you're visiting the area, you can eat at the university's cafeteria, located at building 42, Chandler Cafe.

Chandler Cafe (626-395-3439) is open from 7:00 A.M. to 3:30 P.M.; the grill and pizza stations are open after 2:00 P.M. The menu includes a wide variety of food (breakfast, lunch, and dinner) for any palate, humorously named (where possible) by station: Bunsen burner (The Grill), Wok Zone (Mongolian BBQ), Bandwidth Bakery (muffins, scones, croissants), Sushi, Deli Epicenter (sandwiches and salads), Pizza Byte (pizza, calzones, and pladines), TechTonics (hot and cold drinks), Cooking 101 (pasta and salad), Salad Fusion (salad bar), Comfort Equation (entrée specials), Soup Station, and Latin Special (burritos and tostadas).

This is, of course, where we most often see Sheldon, Leonard, Howard, and Raj on the show, though we seldom see them actually *eat*. It'd be hard to say their lines with their mouths full, so they mostly play with their food, or look as if they're about to eat the food, which explains why the actors go to the studio commissary to eat before such scenes are filmed.

JPL Tours

You can also tour nearby JPL (jpl.nasa.gov, 818-354-4321), located at 4800 Oak Grove Dr., seven miles northwest of Caltech, where, among other missions, they control the Mars Rover. This is most likely where Howard unsuccessfully tried to woo Penny and Dr. Stephanie Barnett to his boudoir: in an attempt to impress them, he promised to let them drive a Mars Rover by remote control.

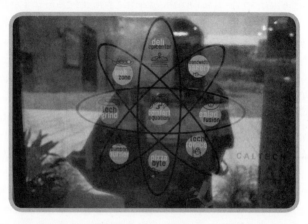

The front door to Chandler Cafe, where the boys would dine during lunch

An interior shot of Chandler Cafe

8. GREATER LOS ANGELES

In terms of what it has to offer—fast food, fine dining, ethnic food, first-class movie theaters, specialty stores, tourist attractions, major theme parks, natural wonders, boutique shops, and all manner of attractions, from pop culture to science and history—the greater Los Angeles area is unquestionably an entertainment, dining, and shopping mecca. Culturally diverse with something for everyone, the city's extensive web of interconnected freeways makes it easy to get around, although traffic during morning and late-afternoon rush hour can be nightmarish.

Though Sheldon's posse tends to stick close to home—Pasadena and nearby Glendale have a lot to offer—they, of course, have the option of going anywhere in the greater Los Angeles area to quench their thirsts, satisfy their appetites, feast their eyes on natural wonders, world-class museums, and state-of-the-art movie theaters, and shop until they drop for anything under the hot California sun.

In *The Big Bang Theory*, there are several prominent LA attractions mentioned or discussed at length. In order of episode appearance, here are the high spots.

Beverly Hills: In "The Dumpling Paradox" (1-7), Christy Vanderbell visits Penny and soon latches on to Howard, who offers to take her shopping, at his expense, at the expensive boutiques in this exclusive shopping district.

Like the proverbial pot of gold at the end of a rainbow, the lure of Beverly Hills beckons shoppers worldwide with its swimming pools, movie stars, and stores catering to the rich and famous. (Where else does the U.S. government offer valet parking at a post office?)

The city of Beverly Hills (beverlyhills.org) justifiably boasts having "more than 100 world-renowned boutiques and hotels ... the famed shopping street is known throughout the world as the epicenter of luxury fashion."

Far from Rodeo Drive, in both geography and ambiance, are the sites where **Renaissance Faires** are held year-round in California, and where the Ren Faires made their first appearance before migrating eastward. Today, California has more Ren Faires than any other state in the country; and although there are no Ren Faires in Pasadena, according to the Renaissance, Medieval & Pirate Faire Directory (renfaire.com), there are several within driving distance, including one only sixteen miles away: **The Original Renaissance Pleasure Faire** (renfair.com/socal). Located at the Santa Fe Dam Recreation Area and held annually in the spring (April to May on weekends only), it's an opportunity to step back in time and sample life circa 1500–1600, the time of England's first Queen Elizabeth.

In "The Codpiece Topology" (2-2), when the boys return to Sheldon's apartment after attending a Ren Faire, all of them are happy except—guess who?—Sheldon, who cites the Faire's historical inaccuracies. The boys are all dressed symbolically: Leonard is a knight in shining armor with a crest emblazoned on his full-length vest, Howard is a colorful court jester in tight shorts with matching hand puppet, Raj is a nobleman wearing ballooned sleeves and pants, and Sheldon is a hooded monk wearing a cross and a rope sash. (He's also wearing period-style underwear that he sewed himself because he prizes authenticity.)

For the boys, the Faire is an opportunity to see performers, hear period music, watch the pageantry of the queen and her court making their way around the fairgrounds, dine on period food (a crowd favorite is the large hunk of turkey leg), quaff beer, buy handcrafted goods, and, for those who share Howard's tastes, ogle the large-breasted women displaying a lot of cleavage in "corsets so tight their bosom jumps out and says howdy."

In "The Panty Piñata Polarization" (2-7), the boys are playing Klingon Boggle, and everyone but Sheldon gets sidetracked when Penny comes over to watch *America's Next Top Model*. An astonished Howard asks, "I'm within driving distance of a house filled with aspiring supermodels?" Actually, he is. From Pasadena to

Hollywood Hills, it is a quick drive. Just take Ventura Freeway (Route 134) west, and Hollywood Freeway (Route 170, turning into Route 101), and you're in the neighborhood of the *very* rich and famous. According to Wikipedia, some of its previous and current residents include Ben Affleck, Sandra Bullock, Cameron Diaz, Zac Efron, Paris Hilton, Angelina Jolie, Madonna, Jerry Seinfeld, and supermodel Gisele Bundchen, who is mentioned by Howard as having been kicked off *America's Next Top Model.*

At the **Robot Fighting League** (botleague.net) members duke it out using—you'll never guess—fighting robots. In "The Killer Robot Instability" (2-12), Barry Kripke warns the boys against entering their robot "M.O.N.T.E." in the Southern California Robot Fighting League Round Robin Invitational, because his own "Kripke Killer" is more powerful, which indeed it proves to be.

The Robot Fighting League holds an annual National Championship at which the competition is intimidatingly formidable. Usually heavily armored with powerful drive trains and weapons galore, including flame weapons, the man-of-war robots are designed for one purpose only: to efficiently and effectively kill the competition.

Goth Clubs: In "The Gothowitz Deviation" (3-3), Howard, aided by his wingman Raj, go goth. Well, faux goth, since their tattoos are merely slip-on sleeves, but in a dark Hollywood goth club, who can tell? Certainly not Bethany and Sarah, the ladies they meet.

There's no lack of goth clubs in Southern California, so Howard and Raj can take their pick of the sepulchral, spooky sanctums where they can hope to seduce sexy sirens. No doubt they consulted the goths' most popular online directory (undergroundmine.com/clubdirectory.htm), which lists clubs by name and also provides website links.

Of course, in order to blend in with the goth crowd, you must look the part. And if you don't want to walk into a retail store to buy your creepers, boots, platform shoes, and chokers, it's easy to shop online. A good source is Rivithead (rivithead.com), which carries a full line of clothing for men and women, complete with accessories. Since Howard and Raj were exposed as goth fakers wearing tattoo sleeves, though, don't look to see them back in those bars anytime soon.

La Brea Tar Pits (tarpits.org): In "The Cornhusker Vortex" (3-6), Raj and Howard visited this popular destination, "home to the world's only active urban Ice Age excavation site." Located at 5801 Wilshire Boulevard in Los Angeles, the onsite museum has "the largest and most diverse assemblage of extinct Ice Age plants and animals in the world. Visitors can learn about Los Angeles as it was between 10,000 and 40,000 years ago, during the last Ice Age when animals such as saber-tooth cats and mammoths roamed the Los Angeles Basin."

Moonlight Roller Rink (fictional): In "The Einstein Approximation" (3-14), Raj tells Howard that it's "Disco Night at the Moonlight Roller Rink in Glendale." Howard and Bernadette, Leonard and Penny, and Raj go there and boogie the night away.

In the real world, they'd go to **Moonlight Rollerway** (moonlightrollerway.com) in Glendale. You can't miss it at night: in blue neon above its front entrance, "Moonlight Rollerway" literally glows. (Underneath in painted letters: Skating Center.) The company website says that it's "the PREMIERE roller-skating rink in all of Los Angeles county . . . Moonlight Rollerway features a regulation-size skating surface and a beautifully maintained maple wood floor . . . It has been featured in more television shows, movies, and music videos than any other skating rink in the world."

Stan Lee's home: One of the advantages of living in Southern California is that it's the entertainment capital of the world and, thus, home to many movie and television stars. The greater Los Angeles area could properly be called Celebrity City.

And who's top of the list for the boys' favorite celebrity? Stan Lee, of course. A frequent guest of honor at comic book conventions worldwide, Lee made a cameo in "The Excelsior Acquisition" (3-16), in which the boys excitedly discuss what Marvel comic each plans on bringing to Lee's signing at the Comics Factory. All the boys get to meet Lee—except Sheldon, who is making a simultaneous appearance at traffic court in town. But never fear! Sheldon does eventually meet his hero, at his personal residence, and even gets his signature—on a restraining order.

STAN "THE MAN" LEE

• • • • • • • • • • • •

Transplanted from New York City to Southern California in 1981, comic book legend smiling Stan Lee (Stanley Martin Lieber) now lives in the Los Angeles area. (Among his many honors, he's got star number 2,428 on the Hollywood Walk of Fame.)

Best known for being the public face of Marvel Comics, Stan Lee was instrumental in cocreating its line of superheroes who, despite their superpowers, weren't invulnerable to the pitfalls and pratfalls of being mortal. They were flawed human beings, just like the rest of us.

For fans wishing to make contact with Stan Lee outside of a convention, the best place is his official website, powentertainment.com. "POW" stands for "Purveyors of Wonder." The site "specializes in new characters and franchises created by Stan Lee, Chief Creative Officer at POW! Entertainment, utilizing Stan's core group of writers."

You can get e-mail updates by submitting yours on his website, and follow him on Twitter, @therealstanlee. And if you don't want to incur his Hulk-like wrath by showing up uninvited at his front doorstep, you can make contact with him by e-mail at fanmail@powentertainment.com.

Note: Lee no longer signs autographs by mail; he will only do so in person at official signings. So if you send an autograph request to his Beverly Hills office, you are doomed to disappointment.

TOUR GUIDES TO PASADENA
AND THE GREATER LOS ANGELES AREA
· · · · · · · · · · · ·

The Pasadena Convention & Visitors' Bureau (visitpasadena. com) will mail you a free packet of information upon request. It includes: a pocket-size color map with high points, a pocket-size color map highlighting the shopping areas, a pamphlet about walking tours of sixteen historic districts, and a fifty-six-page pocket-size Official Visitors Guide with detailed information about the area's community, hotels, restaurants, nightlife, shopping, art & agriculture, fit & fun, Tournament of Roses, signature events, and transportation.

As another option, a free app (at Apple's iTunes store or market. android.com) called Go Pasadena is a handy, up-to-date guide for newcomers about what to do and where to go in the city.

The official Los Angeles guide (online or a hard copy to be mailed to you) can be obtained at discoverlosangeles.com. (The downloadable version, the "Virtual Guide," uses a proprietary format called nxbook.) My recommendation: get the free hard copy.

For information about California as a whole, go to visitcalifornia. com. The Visitor's Guide can be viewed online, downloaded, or ordered in print for free. Numerous guidebooks are available on the Golden State, but the one I recommend is from DK (dk. com), *Eyewitness Travel: California*. At 660 pages, it's portable but obviously not pocket-size. Printed on glossy paper with over a thousand color photos, maps, and diagrams, it's head and shoulders above the competition.

9. GREATER CALIFORNIA

With the wealth of activities in Pasadena and the greater Los Angeles area that command the boys' attention, they have little time to go elsewhere. But when the situation requires it, or the spirit moves them, they go.

In "The Loobenfeld Decay" (1-10), the boys pretend to do an intervention in nearby **Long Beach**. Sheldon tells them, "The *Queen Mary* is docked there. Once the largest ocean-liner in the world, it's now a hotel and restaurant where they host a surprisingly gripping murder mystery dinner." Aboard the *Queen Mary* (queenmary. com), there's certainly plenty to do—dining, tours, sightseeing—but its dinner theater is a tad more sedate than a murder mystery. **Tibbies** (tibbiescarbaret.com) offers a musical production drawing on local talent, among whom are regulars in Disney shows and local theater productions. In addition to singing, the cast performs double duty as waiters.

For an actual murder mystery dinner, you'd have to go dockside to 204 Aquarium Way (Dock #4) to **The Dinner Detective** (thedinnerdetective.com), which offers a four-course dinner "while you solve a gripping murder! Having worked in the professional theater, TV and film industries for over 20 years, our collection of actors and producers have mastered the art of improvisational theatrical roleplaying." The key to its success: "hiding our actors among the customers and leaving everyone to suspect who is part of the show and who is not."

Further north, approximately 382 miles away, reachable by car in six hours via Interstate 5 North, is **San Francisco**, where, in "The Terminator Decoupling" (2-17), Sheldon and his posse travel by train—not car, not plane—to attend a symposium with an address by Nobel Prize–winning scientist Dr. George Smoot. Sheldon's ecstatic to be traveling by train, though it's "seven times as long as flying, and costs almost twice as much," as Howard points out. The decision proves fortuitous because actress Summer Glau is on the train—a rare opportunity for all the boys except Sheldon to make a pass at her.

Sheldon's not interested in the tourist-related activities in San Francisco; he only wants to hear Dr. Smoot's talk and use that opportunity to ride on his coattails by suggesting they collaborate together on a paper. But there's certainly plenty to do in San Francisco. Check sfgov.org and onlyinsanfrancisco.com, to get a sense of the city's restaurants, wineries, museums, performing arts centers, and a long list of sports and recreational activities, especially aquatic, since the city is on the water. (Don't miss Fisherman's Wharf, where the seafood is scrumptious.)

Penny, who likes to ride the famous cable cars, would have three routes from which to choose; alternately, like Sheldon, you could hole up in a hotel and ignore all the attractions the city has to offer. I think Penny's got the right idea: eat, drink, and be merry!

Heading south, **San Diego** is the place you want to be in late July. Prominently mentioned in several episodes on the show, the San Diego Comic-Con International (comic-con.org) is summer's biggest attraction. Celebrating its forty-second year in 2011, the convention draws an international audience of fans and pros alike. For fans of *The Big Bang Theory*, the convention is your only opportunity to see everyone—the principal cast, guest actors, crew, and show creators— at a single event. For the last three years, they've made an appearance at Comic-Con, usually on Friday, announced two weeks before the Con date. (For more information about Comic-Con, as well as tips on how to survive a convention, see pages 171–180.)

In "The Adhesive Duck Deficiency" (3-8), all the boys but Sheldon go up in the mountains to see the Leonid Meteor Shower. There's no mention of their actual location, but plotting the declination (34.48 degrees north, 118.31 degrees west) puts them up in the mountains north/northeast of **Whittier**, about thirty-four minutes away from Pasadena.

Far enough away from the city lights, the stars pop out against a velvet backdrop; a meteor shower looks like white diamonds streaking across the sky. The boys, however, see none of that. They're on a trip, but not a celestial one.

A half hour away from Whittier, Anaheim is where Penny and her friends at work take Sheldon to "the happiest place on Earth," **Disneyland** (disneyland.disney.go.com). Although Howard and Raj assert that Las Vegas is the happiest place on the planet, we know better: like Sheldon, we'd soon become enchanted with Disneyland's many wonders and return with a bag of memorabilia in hand, along with unforgettable memories. "Welcome to the place where imagination is the destination," the Disneyland resort website promises—and it delivers. Divided between the larger Disneyland Park and its more recent sister the Disneyland California Adventure, Disneyland Resort is where kids of all ages can go to experience what Sheldon, in "The Spaghetti Catalyst" (3-20), calls "pure Disney magic." There's also restaurants and gift shops aplenty on both properties, and nearby is the **Shops at Anaheim GardenWalk**, where you can dine at, among other eateries, the Cheesecake Factory and P.F. Chang's China Bistro.

Los Angeles International Airport (lawa.org/welcomelax.aspx), bound by W. Westchester Pkwy on the north, S. Sepulveda Blvd on the east, Century Freeway on the south, and S. Pershing Dr on the west, is the fifth-busiest airport in the world. Encompassing 3,425 acres, it has approximately 100 air carriers (passenger and freight) that come in and out daily. In 2006 alone, LAX handled more than 656,842 takeoffs and landings.

In "The Irish Pub Formulation" (4-6), when Raj meets his sister Priya at LAX, she only has one day to see the sights. It proves to be a layover in an erotic sense, because she only has eyes for Leonard. She declines all of Sheldon's recommendations; she has no interest in going to **Carney's** (carneytrain.com), where she can dine in a converted railroad car, nor is she into going to **Travel Town** (travel-town.org), where she can see a museum devoted entirely to "the rich railroad heritage of Los Angeles," as its website explains.

She obviously has fond memories of her first encounter with Leonard at **Toluca Lake** (tolucalakechamber.com), where Priya, as Sheldon explained, "was enjoying the sweet state of Hindu rebellion in the form of a Bob's Super Big Boy hamburger."

Occasionally, the boys do feel a need for a road trip. In "The Zarnecki Incursion" (4-19), they saddle up like vengeful gods and drive to **Carlsbad** (near San Diego) to hopefully slice-and-dice a thief who stole Sheldon's virtual goods from his *World of Warcraft* online gaming account. Fortunately, Penny, who has no compunctions about fighting dirty, saves the day and convinces the thief to return his ill-gotten gains.

10. THE UNITED STATES

Hawaii (gohawaii.com): In "The Boyfriend Complexity" (4-9), Raj is looking for a star in the Eridanus constellation, Epsilon Eridani, which is 10.5 light-years away. Drunk on wine, Raj calls Hawaii, identifies himself, and says, "I'd like you to reposition the telescope, please, to Scarlett Johansson's house!"

Raj would have called the **Mauna Kea Observatories**, a complex of telescopes operated by astronomers around the world. Sited on top of Mount Manua Kea, which rises fourteen hundred feet, he would have been asking them to reposition one of the two ten-meter tele-scopes, which are shared by several universities, including Caltech and the University of California, and scientific communities.

Actually, since the astronomers do search for heavenly bodies, Scarlett Johansson—a tall, buxom blonde who has appeared in two superhero movies (*The Spirit* [2008] and *The Avengers* [2012])—is, as Mr. Spock would say, a logical choice.

Sheldon cites a secret site of a supercollider as being 12.5 miles southeast from **Travers City, Michigan** ("The Bad Fish Paradigm," 2-1). But don't go there looking for it, because although the DOE accepted seven sites, including Stockbridge, Michigan (211 to 243 miles away from Travers City, depending on the route taken), it finally chose Dallas/Forth Worth, Texas, for the $4.4 billion project. (See *Federal Research: Final Site Selection Process for DOE's Super Collider*, June 1989, issued by the GAO.)

Had Sheldon been able to be a bit more circumspect about the site of the supercollider, he might have gotten the job and, subsequently, been closer to home: Dallas is about five hours away from where Sheldon "Shelly" Cooper was born, **Galveston Island** (galveston.com), which has a population of 57,466 that lives on 208 square miles. A major seaport, Galveston's economy is also based on tourism, health care, shipping, and financial industries.

In "The Electric Can Opener Fluctuation" (3-1), a humiliated Sheldon heads home, dragging his tail, after he prematurely sends an e-mail to everyone "explaining that I have confirmed string theory and forever changed man's understanding of the universe." Home, as they say, is where they *have* to take you in, though "Shelly" is always welcome when he returns to his mother's loving embrace.

Jackson, Mississippi: In "The Creepy Candy Coating Corollary" (3-5), Sheldon tells a sad tale about how he wore his Starfleet Academy costume on a ten-hour bus trek to get to a Dixie-Trek convention in 1995 at which Wil Wheaton was a guest of honor.

In point of fact, there was no Dixie-Trek convention ever held in this town; they were all held in Atlanta, Georgia. But Jackson, Mississippi, did host at least one *Star Trek* convention. In 2007, "Galaxy of Stars" featured Marina Sirtis (Counselor Deanna Troi from *Star Trek: The Next Generation*) and other actors from the franchise as guests of honor.

I can find no evidence of Wil Wheaton as a guest at any Dixie-Trek convention.

Bozeman, Montana: According to its Chamber of Commerce (bozemanchamber.com), Bozeman has a "small-town feel with big-city amenities." It's also the home of Montana State University. "Clean air, national forest access, and trails just minutes away, and moderate climate make this a perfect place for outdoor recreation."

In "The Bozeman Reaction" (1-13), after suffering a break-in at his apartment, Sheldon decides to relocate to a safer city elsewhere in the United States and telecommute. After looking at all the alternative locations, he settles on Bozeman. But he stays just long enough to buy a return ticket home after a "helpful" local steals his bags at the bus depot, proving to him that crime is a fact of life no matter where you live.

An Elemental Explication

According to the city-data.com, Bozeman's crime index in 2009 was 193, well below the U.S. average of 319. That year, Bozeman had 1 murder, 13 rapes, 6 robberies, 39 assaults, 141 burglaries, 1,029 thefts, 75 auto thefts, and 14 incidents of arson.

Omaha, Nebraska (ci.omaha.ne.us), the state's largest city, has a population of 427,872. That's minus one person, of course, after Penny moved away from her parents' farm to seek her fame and fortune on the golden, sun-drenched streets of California. In the first episode of the show ("Pilot," 1-1), Penny tells Sheldon and Leonard that she's "writing a screenplay. It's about this sensitive girl who comes to LA from Lincoln, Nebraska, to be an actress, and winds up a waitress at the Cheesecake Factory." It is not, as she tells Leonard, based on her life, because she's from Omaha.

Although we have seen Penny's father, Wyatt, and her friend Christy Vanderbell, we've yet to get a glimpse of Omaha. Known for being the largest meat processor in the United States back in the late 1950s, the city had to diversify after a restructuring of its railroad and meatpacking industries forced inevitable change. Today, information, not meat, is processed in Omaha. "The modern economy . . . is diverse and built on skilled knowledge jobs," states Wikipedia.

East Rutherford, New Jersey (eastrutherfordnj.net), is a small town with a population of ten thousand. Its industrial base is a blend of small and large businesses. In "The Work Song Nanocluster" (2-18), when Penny gets an order for Penny Blossoms, "a thousand sparkly flower barrettes with rhinestones" for "The Fifth Annual East Rutherford, New Jersey, Gay, Lesbian, Bisexual, and Transgender Alliance Luau," she recruits Sheldon to help her make them, and he drafts the others to pitch in. (Many hands make the work go faster.)

For anyone whose sexual orientation is other than straight, East Rutherford is not the best place to go for a GLBTI (Gay, lesbian, bisexual, transsexual, intersexual) event. For that, you'd go to **Ashbury Park, New Jersey,** which in 2011 hosted its 20th Annual GLBTI Pride Celebration. Sponsored by Jersey Pride Inc., (jerseypride.org), it's a parade, rally, and festival. According to the Jersey Pride website, "Highlights of this event will include a rally stage, exhibits, activities, entertainment, and of course a large marketplace offering food, beverages, and other merchandise."

For heterosexuals like Leonard, Howard, and Raj, who wouldn't be caught dead at a GLBTI event, the preference would be a trip to **Las Vegas** (lasvegasnevada.gov), for which Sheldon provides useful advice in "The Vegas Renormalization" (2-21). Vegas is where the disenchanted and dispossessed, and the forlorn and horny, go to satisfy polymorphously perverse desires. As Sheldon says, it's "designed specifically to help people like Howard forget their problems. Where you can replace them with *new* problems, such as alcoholism, gambling addiction, and sexually transmitted diseases."

Princeton University (princeton.edu) in New Jersey: Dr. Plimpton, a cosmological physicist from this Ivy League university, has come to Pasadena because, as Sheldon explains in "The Plimpton Stimulation" (3-21), "she's under consideration for a position at our university." As it turns out, Penny's got her number; she calls Plimpton "Dr. Slutbunny." Plimpton doesn't get the job at Caltech, but while there, she did assume several positions—in bed with Leonard, and soon thereafter she tried to do the same with Raj and Howard.

An Elemental Explication

If you're considering applying to Princeton to major in physics, be forewarned that it expects you to have a basic knowledge of:

1. Mechanics
2. Electromagnetism and wave phenomena

3. Quantum mechanics and its application in simple atomic physics
4. Kinetic theory, thermodynamics, and statistical mechanics
5. Experimental physics

11. INTERNATIONAL LOCATIONS

New Delhi: India's capital is located in its northern region. Though its summers are long and hot, its winters are short and cool. In "The Grasshopper Experiment" (1-8), Raj is finally able to communicate with his parents, who live in New Delhi, after they get broadband access, which allows real-time audio/video chat via his laptop computer's webcam.

The Heidelberg Institute for Theoretical Studies in Heidelberg, Germany, or HITS (www.h-its.org), concentrates on theoretical astrophysics using high-performance supercomputers. From its website: "Cosmology seeks answers to ... the origin and ultimate fate of our Universe ... the formation and evolution of galaxies, supermassive black holes, stars, and planets." In "The Pancake Batter Anomaly" (1-11), we learn that at age fifteen Sheldon was a visiting professor at the Heidelberg Institute.

Leningrad Politechnica (Leningrad, Russia): Now known as St. Petersburg State Polytechnic University, this university, founded in 1899, is one of the country's most advanced engineering schools, second only to the Moscow Institute of Physics and Technology. Wikipedia tells us that it "includes 23 Institutes and Faculties, 6 associated institutes outside Saint Petersburg ... and many scientific research laboratories."

In "The Bat Jar Conjecture" (1-13), Sheldon is pitted against his friends (Leonard, Howard, Raj) and his enemy (Leslie Winkle) in a physics bowl tournament. Sheldon is forced to play on a team with three other members, though he makes it explicitly clear that only he is going to answer the questions. But he's stumped with the final question, and the janitor, a former physicist from Leningrad

Politecnica, correctly answers the brainteaser whose answer eludes everyone else. ("Go polar bears!")

Geneva, Switzerland (geneva-tourism.ch): This city is many things to many people: a major European financial center, the headquarters of the Red Cross, the headquarters of many UN agencies, and a major diplomatic center. It's also known in the business community for its financial sector, which manages 1 trillion USD annually. But none of that is of interest to Sheldon and his posse, who have their eyes on a bigger prize: the **Large Hadron Collider** nearby, under the Franco-Swiss border. Built by CERN (European Organization for Nuclear Research), the LHC is a "synchrotron designed to collide opposing particle beams."

In "The Cushion Saturation" (2-16), Howard is slated to go to Switzerland to see the Large Hadron Collider, until Leslie Winkle, who arranged the invitation, retracts it because she's upset he won't attend her sister's wedding.

Also, in "The Large Hadron Collision" (3-15), there's a question as to whom Leonard will take on his trip to Switzerland. He wants to take Penny, but Sheldon thinks he should get to go instead.

Arctic Circle, North Pole: Sheldon, who gets an NSF grant "to detect slow-moving monopoles at the magnetic North Pole" ("The Monopolar Expedition," 2-23), spends three months with his posse in pursuit of the elusive monopole, only to come away empty-handed.

An Elemental Explication

In a 2009 interview with Ira Flatow on NPR ("Real-Life Physics Problems Star on TV," npr.org), Bill Prady shed some light on the monopole episode:

> Well, magnetic monopoles is something that Sheldon's been working on for a while, and it came out of our need to send him to the North Pole. So we asked Dr. Saltzberg [the show's science advisor] very specifically, "Give us an area of research that Sheldon is working on that he would work on at the Arctic Circle,

where he would need to bring along an experimental physicist, an engineer and an astrophysicist." And he said, "Well, that's a tough one. Let me think about it for a while." And he called up a couple of hours later, and he says, "I've got it. They're looking for magnetic monopoles, you know, predicted by string theory. And you would look for them up at the North Pole, and you'd need an engineer and you'd need an astrophysicist. It's perfect."

In this episode, we see the four boys up at the North Pole, living in a garage-size house whose interior curiously resembles the layout of Sheldon's apartment, while outside a blizzard rages. We can infer that the structure the boys are living in has other buildings nearby in a hive-like community, which provides necessary support functions. This is like **McMurdo Station**, the science facility for the United States at the North Pole.

Mumbai, India: A major metropolitan city once known as Bombay, located in western India, it's home to 12.5 million people, making it India's most populous city.

In "The Precious Fragmentation" (3-17), one of Raj's cousins in India, an inept attorney, negotiates via webcam with Sheldon, Howard, and Leonard, hoping to trade Raj's quarter interest in the One Ring replica for a jet ski or two. (No deal, said the other boys.)

An Elemental Explication

Just as the real One Ring in *The Lord of the Rings* had to go back to the place where it was forged so it could finally be destroyed, Leonard argues that the One Ring replica has to go back to its rightful owner—or to New Zealand, where it was manufactured.

The rings in the movie were not manufactured by Weta, the special effects company owned by Peter Jackson, but by Jens Hansen Gold & Silversmith (jenshansen.com). When first issued, a 14-ct replica ring cost $700; now it costs $1,927. Of all the ring replicas for sale, the

Jens Hansen ring is the only one with direct ties to the film; the others are merely licensed product.

New Zealand (newzealand.com), located eight hundred miles east of Australia, is home to Peter Jackson's film studio, which Leonard cites as the place where he returned the One Ring replica.

Weta Workshop (wetanz.com) is the special effects arm of Jackson's company that "houses a range of disciplines under one roof, including conceptual design, weapons, armour and chainmaille, specialist props, vehicles, specialty costumes, models and miniatures, special makeup and prosthetics, public art and displays."

Some of the movies Weta has worked on include (most notably) *The Lord of the Rings* (all three films), James Cameron's *Avatar*, *King Kong*, and *The Chronicles of Narnia*.

12. SPACE

In *The Big Bang Theory*, not all the action is terrestrial. In fact, some of the more memorable episodes take us off-planet, which makes sense since the show centers around a theoretical physicist, an experimental physicist, an astrophysicist, and an aerospace engineer. So let's strap ourselves in and head skyward, into the heavens, from the edge of Earth into deep space.

The International Space Station, or ISS (nasa.gov), is a research platform in space manned by an international crew. Among all their other concerns, the astronauts would run into a real-world problem if their waste collection system malfunctioned. The space toilets use "rotating fans to distribute solid waste for in-flight storage." There are two space toilets onboard the ISS, and they both see heavy use.

In "The Classified Materials Turbulence" (2-22), the fecal matter literally hits the fan. The Wolowitz Zero Gravity Waste Disposal System (presumably for solid waste, as Howard and coworker

Pishkin designed a liquid waste disposal system) fails, leaving the astronauts with few options.

The Moon: In 270 B.C., Aristarchus determined the distance from the Earth to the Moon to be R/r~60, "which fits the average distance of the Moon accepted today, 60 Earth radii," as noted on istp.gsfc.nasa.gov.

Today we don't have to estimate; we only have to measure. According to universetoday.com, at its closest point (the perihelion), the distance between the Earth and the Moon is 225,622 miles; at its most distant point (the aphelion), it's 252,088. "How do we know it so well? When the astronauts landed on the Moon during the Apollo program [in 1969], they left smaller reflective mirrors on the surface of the Moon. Astronomers point lasers at the Moon, which travel all the way to the Moon and then bounce off and return to Earth. By calculating the length of time light takes to make the return journey, and knowing the speed of light with incredible accuracy, they can calculate the Moon's distance."

In "The Lunar Excitation" (3-23), the boys engage in lunar ranging on top of their apartment building. They fire a laser that, as Leonard explained, takes "2.5 seconds for the light to return. That's the Moon! We hit the Moon!"

As Leonard says, the experiment conclusively proves that man landed on the moon—a fact contested by a community of conspiracy theorists who believe the landings were elaborate hoaxes perpetrated by NASA.

Beyond the Moon—*far* beyond it, actually—is Mars. Depending on their orbits, the closest point from the Earth to Mars would be 54.6 million kilometers, and the furthest point, 401 million kilometers, according to universetoday.com. There are no current plans by NASA to send a manned mission to Mars.

In "The Lizard-Spock Expansion" (2-8), Howard breaches security protocol by promising a woman he meets in a bar the opportunity to drive a Mars Rover. At the control room, Howard drives it into a ditch. It's one misstep for a small man, and one giant leap backward for nerd-kind.

THE STRAIGHT POOP ON SPACE TOILETS
· · · · · · · · · · · ·

In the real world, shit happens: in 2008, a Russian NPP Zvezda zero-gravity toilet failed, resulting in "a rush delivery of a replacement pump by the shuttle *Discovery*," according to blogs.discovermagazine.com.

In a worst-case scenario, there are two options. In *How Do You Go to the Bathroom in Space?*, William R. Pogue explains, "Each Shuttle mission carries two bags per day per crew member, with enough for a two-day mission extension. For backup urine collection the crew can use commercial adult diapers, which are very effective in absorbing the urine and protecting the skin from continued contact with moisture."

On this episode of *The Big Bang Theory*, after the Wolowitz toilet failed, the American crew on the ISS went on a space walk for an EVA (extra vehicular activity).

In the real world, as Pogue explains, "We had two devices to wear under our space suits. A UCD (urine collection device) for urine, and a FCS (fecal containment system) for solid waste." Women, he explains, used diapers for urine collection—an option the men can also use.

Beyond Mars one will find **trans-Neptunian objects**. Small planets orbiting the Sun, they are—in terms of distance from the Earth—beyond Neptune.

Raj studied these objects in "The Pirate Solution" (3-4) and, just a year earlier, in "The Griffin Equivalency" (2-4), he discovered what he called "Planet Bollywood," a planetary object beyond the Kuiper belt.

Part 4

FANDOM

Nerdvana: exploring worlds of imagination

THE NEWCOMER'S GUIDE TO FANDOM

*I*n the Sheldonian universe, the term "hippie" is derogatory; so is the term "muggle," which designates a person wholly bereft of imagination. J.K. Rowling coined "muggle" to characterize what science fiction fans have long termed ordinary people ("mundanes"). It's simply an acknowledgment that the person has no interest in fantasy or science fiction. "Reality," science-fiction fans say, "is for people who can't handle science fiction."

But since *you* can obviously handle science fiction and fantasy, here's how you can avoid the "muggle" label and be known as an insider, or a "tru-fan."

Longtime fans Robert and Juanita Coulson, in *The Neo-Fan's Guide to Science Fiction Fandom* (second edition, 1966), give a concise history of science fiction fandom:

> Science fiction fandom had its start between 1923 and 1929 when the first four successful pulp magazines, crammed with stories and letters from readers, were placed on sale: *Weird Tales* (March 1923), *Amazing Stories* (April 1926), *Science Wonder Stories* (June 1929), and *Air Wonder Stories* (July 1929) . . . The editors of those four magazines grew bold and invited letters from readers; they got

them in quantity. Soon the readers were writing to each other, and that led to "science [fiction] clubs," and then social and correspondence clubs centered on the magazines and their editorial personalities. [In the early thirties], some of the clubs published bulletins for their memberships, and the fan magazine ["fanzine"] was born. Those early bulletins were primarily concerned with magazine fiction, author and editor adulation, film comment and a little film chatter . . . The concept of fandom spread rapidly, in part sired by those early correspondence clubs . . . Fans and fan groups sprang up in big and little towns across the country, followed by the same in Great Britain . . . [The fans were] astronomers, geologists, physicists, chemists, rocketeers, teachers, physicians, attorneys, photographers, reporters, press agents, broadcasters, furnace salesmen, stock market personnel, electronics and medical technicians, actors, and a few bums.

The first science-fiction convention was held in conjunction with the New York World's Fair in 1939. Two hundred fans showed up for the three-day event. According to Isaac Asimov, in an essay for *F&SF* titled "The Feminization of Science Fiction," "Magazine science fiction had its beginnings in 1926, and for a third of a century—a full generation—it was a strongly masculine field. The readers were almost all young men, and, to a large extent, rather withdrawn young men, who had either not come to be at ease with members of the opposite sex or who were actively afraid of them."

Those were the first geeks, a word tinged with gentle criticism because they were socially inept. Introverted but exceptionally bright young men, they dreamt of rocketing off into deep space, battling aliens, and exploring new worlds, but became nervous and tongue-tied at the mere idea of asking a girl for a date.

Geeks. Nerds. Call them what you want (today the two words have somewhat diverging definitions), but it wasn't a compliment. As seen in the 1984 movie *Revenge of the Nerds*, their stereotyped portrayal was, as you'd imagine, deliberately conceived to provoke laughter. In that movie, the "in crowd" (the jocks and the cheerleaders at Adams

College) gang up on the nerds, who are easy to spot: a nerd wears thick glasses, a short-sleeve shirt with a pocket protector, dress slacks, and white socks, and looks, well, *geeky.*

Back then, Hollywood's purpose in making films about geeks was simply to make fun of them. *Revenge of the Nerds* says it all: unwilling to be put in their place by the popular crowd on campus, the nerds fight back—and prevail. They get their revenge against the jocks who are hell-bent on making their lives miserable, especially Ogre, a dim-witted but large and imposing loudmouth whose battle cry is, "I *hate* nerds!"

That was 1984.

This is 2011.

In the intervening twenty-seven years, the word "geek" has changed from an insult to a compliment, a badge of honor. What's also changed is that fandom has gone mainstream, and there's a large, and welcome, presence of girls and women in various fandoms, who fit right in with the Klingons and other burly males at comic conventions.

Print-Based Fandom

In the days before personal computers and the internet, fandom was largely a print-based world. Fanzines were published using ditto and mimeograph machines, requiring typewriters to set type. Professional printing via photo offset was only for those with deep pockets. These were called semi-prozines because of the upgraded production values, and usually had semipro art and text. Most fans used offset only for reproducing covers, especially if the artwork required it.

Because long-distance phone calls were expensive, fans most often typed letters to one another. The U.S. Postal Service was the main means of communication, supplemented by local, regional, and national get-togethers at conventions.

There were no retail stores that catered to fans, so buying collect-ibles meant shopping principally through mail order and providing "want" lists to booksellers or dealers, who'd check with other dealers to find what you wanted. This, of course, is why conventions were so popular; in addition to the socializing aspect, for most fans, they were virtually the only place to see the merchandise before actually buying it.

THE RISING COST OF COMICS
. . . .

These days, though, comics aren't cheap: even with a recent retail price drop, comic books cost up to several dollars each. But it wasn't always that way. As longtime fan and collector Danny Tyree says on his blog, the Cagle Post (blog.cagle.com), "Readers in the Great Depression got a 64-page comic for one thin dime. When I was the age of my son (that is, 7) my weekly allowance was based on the 12-cent price of a 32-page comic book. As recently as 1988, the average price at the spinner rack was 75 cents." The average comics price today is around $3.99, though in January 2011, citing the recession, DC Comics rolled back prices with their "Drawing the Line at $2.99" campaign.

Electronic-Based Fandom

With the advent of personal computers, desktop publishing software, inexpensive photocopying, and the internet, fans began communicating more efficiently. Fanzines could be professionally typeset, photocopied, or reproduced inexpensively with short-run litho-printings. Artwork was scanned and could be printed in short runs inexpensively, and with remarkable fidelity. E-mail, instant messaging, web pages, bulletin boards, blogs, social networking, and podcasts allow real-time communication for free—no postage stamps needed. The smart phone with voice, texting, tweeting, e-mail, Web access, and photographic capabilities became a fan's majordomo, an electronic manservant. Specialty stores can now be found virtually worldwide, carrying a wide range of comics and collectibles, and the computer allows for online shopping anywhere in the world, making even the rarest of items available through eBay, search engines, and databases of rare book dealers. The Web also allows multiplayer role-playing games that fans worldwide can engage in simultaneously.

What *hasn't* changed is that fans, regardless of age, sex, and location, share a common bond: in fandom we are one tribe. No matter what our interests—science fiction, fantasy, horror, comic books, anime, gaming, costuming, *Star Wars*, *Star Trek*, et al.—we find kindred spirits who share our enthusiasms. *That* is what fandom is all about.

A Short Fandom Glossary for the Neo-Fan

Convention • a collective meeting of fans, usually at a hotel or a convention hall, where there is formal programming, guests of honor, an art show, a dealers' room, costuming, and other activities of interest. It's supplemented with informal get-togethers, parties, and other social events. These can be small, one-day gatherings at a fan's house or local hotel, or weeklong events at a major convention center. (See "A Convention Primer for Muggles" on page 171.)

Fan • an aficionado, a devotee.

Fandom • a collective group of fans, either categorized by common interest or as a whole.

Fanfic • an abbreviation for "fan fiction." Most often exploring known writers' fictional worlds, sometimes with incongruous couplings, these are written by fans and usually published in printed or electronically distributed fanzines or online at message boards, communities like livejournal.com, and websites like fanfiction.net.

Fanzine • a publication usually written, edited, and produced by a fan for free distribution or at little cost.

Mundane • someone who doesn't participate in fandom and usually has little or no interest in imaginative fiction, movies, or related product. They are commonly referred to as "muggles," a word popularized by J.K. Rowling, author of the Harry Potter novels.

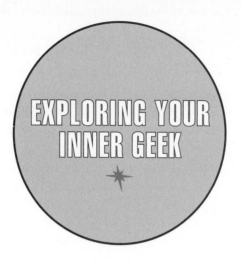

EXPLORING YOUR INNER GEEK

heldon, Leonard, Howard, and Raj are the quintessential geek squad. Here's a simplified guide on how to emulate them.

Comic Book Store

1. Action figures, limited edition books, limited edition prints, et al. can all be found here. Support your local comic book shop or it'll go the way of the independent bookstores!
2. Dress for success. Make a grand entrance wearing a T-shirt with an embedded audio speaker, preferably playing marching music, which strikes the right note.

COMIC BOOK DISTRIBUTION

• • • • • • • • • • • •

Comics are principally sold at specialty retail stores supplied by the industry's sole comics wholesaler, Diamond Comics Distributors (diamondcomics.com). There are approximately

(continued on next page)

(continued from previous page)

two thousand specialty stores, which receive new comics on Wednesdays. Marvel has approximately 42 percent of the market share, DC Comics has 32 percent, and Image has 6 percent, with the remaining 20 percent distributed among small independent publishers. The easiest way to find your local store is to use a specialized search engine, like comicshoplocator.com or the-master-list.com.

Communication

1. A smart phone with video capability is critical. You never know when a "Kodak moment" will occur, which will require recording and, as soon as possible, uploading to YouTube or Twitter.
2. Social networking online. You can't have too many friends. MySpace and Facebook are great ways to engage with people you know, and a lot of people you don't.

Computers

1. Laptop, not desktop. The boys of *The Big Bang Theory* prefer laptops. Desktops are best for office use. No Macs; Linux operating systems only.
2. Fractional T-1 bandwidth. It's the Flash of Internet connectivity. No wonder Sheldon and Leonard explored selling their seed in the pilot to get it for their apartment. ($450 per month is an average cost, according to bandwidth.com.)

Conventions

1. There's a plethora of conventions to choose from, but save up for the biggie: the annual Comic-Con in San Diego.

Electronics

1. Know where the local RadioShack is located. It's *the* hardware store for geeks.

Entertainment

1. Go with Blu-ray for eye-popping visuals.
2. Keep your eyes open for movie marathons at local theaters. *Star Wars, Star Trek, The Lord of the Rings, Planet of the Apes, The Terminator, Indiana Jones, The Matrix* (well, on second thought . . .). Great fun, especially if you show up appropriately attired. But keep the following at home: your Indiana Jones–inspired whips and swords and pistol, your four-foot-long Klingon *Bat'-leth*, your phasers and blasters, and your light sabers, to name the most obvious. (And absolutely no ninja-style weapons like stars, nunchucks, and knives.) A good rule of thumb: if it can't get past airport security, *leave it at home*. Alternately, put on a movie marathon at home—perfect for viewing on your new flatscreen television. Encourage people to dress up.
3. Keep your eye open for special editions, director's cuts, and other value-added DVD packages with extra bonus material not found in the vanilla edition. In other words, get *The Lord of the Rings EXTENDED EDITION* instead of the cheaper but less complete *THEATRICAL EDITION*.

4. Season-long DVD collections are a good bet. Much cheaper than buying DVDs individually. Especially when a series has ended, get the last boxed set with *all* the extras.

Gaming

1. All the major computer game manufacturers update their players on a frequent basis. Upgrade as necessary, since the technology's always getting better, which is important because the games are becoming more complex and graphics-heavy, and place bigger demands on the systems themselves.
2. You'll want to spend a lot of time playing online games with fellow fans around the world, so make sure you've got easy-to-use, durable controllers.

Get Out of the House

1. Sometimes it's good to get physical. Find your local paintball park and shoot to your heart's content. (Be sure to wear appropriate protective gear, though.)

Home Furnishings

1. In the bathroom, get a geeky shower curtain with something like the Periodic Table on it. Soak and learn at the same time!
2. You can't have too many whiteboards.
3. Position action figures in every nook and cranny of your home and office.
4. Frame comic books for the wall, like Sheldon did for his bedroom. Framed fantasy and science-fiction art are also in order. (Please, no velvet Elvis paintings or dogs playing cards.)

Personal Attire

1. Wear quirky T-shirts instead of polo shirts. Don't follow the latest clothing trends; make your own fashion statement.
2. Accessorize with the right belt buckle, which can say a lot about who you are and what you're interested in. To add a little more personal flair, sport an alien pin—but be mysterious and never explain why you wear it.
3. Carry props like phasers, Tricorders, etc. No member of a landing party would dream of beaming down without the bare essentials.
4. Have fun with costuming, but pick name-brand, iconic figures like Batman, Superman, the Flash, and Frodo Baggins. Eschew Peter Pan and Aquaman, who is b-o-r-i-n-g. For women: Wonder Woman or Supergirl and, if you've got the bod, Princess Leia in a metal bikini. But please, no semi-naked slave girls! Show a little more imagination and a lot less skin.
5. For those custom costume jobs, learn how to sew. It's a handy skill.

Reading Material

1. Subscribe to scientific journals, which are much classier to read on the bus than *Bombay Badonkadonks*.
2. Get all the latest comics and select back issues. Be sure to buy acid-free backing boards and plastic bags for protection. (For resale, comic book conditions significantly affect valuation.)

Star Trek

1. Star Trek over Star Wars. No debate.
2. Play Klingon Boggle, but be sure to have a copy of *The Klingon Dictionary* on hand to check answers. It's written by Marc Okrand and converts English to Klingon and vice versa.

THE INSIDER'S GUIDE TO GETTING IN FOR A LIVE TAPING OF *THE BIG BANG THEORY*

*T*he bad news: *The Big Bang Theory* is the hottest TV show in town, so the 250+ free tickets per episode are in high demand. Also, getting a ticket *does not* guarantee entry.

The good news: tickets are free and available on a "first-come, first-serve" basis. (If you aren't fortunate enough to get into a taping of *The Big Bang Theory*, which goes on hiatus from late April through mid-August, the alternative is to take a Warner Bros. studio tour, which is offered year-round.)

How to Get Tickets

It always helps to have connections in Hollywood. If you do, you can ask an insider to score you VIP tickets, which gets you to the head of the line and a private escort who guides you to stage 25 on the Warner Bros. studio lot. If you're an ordinary Joe, you've got to know how to strategize, because general tickets for the show are *only* available online and usually are gone in less than twenty minutes. Here's my strategy for scoring tickets:

1. Bookmark the website for ordering tickets: tvtickets.com/fmi/xsl/tickets/addrecord.xsl?.

2. At tvtickets.com/overview.htm, click on *The Big Bang Theory* logo to get a confirmed list of each episode's air date. Mark your calendar for thirty days prior to those dates, which is the day when tickets are available. (*Note:* If the date falls on a Saturday or Sunday, ticket availability moves to the following Monday.)

3. Tickets for the show are available online within a thirty-minute window starting at 8:30 A.M. PST. For this show, you can only order *one* ticket, so if you need two, open a second browser window, or have whomever you wish to go with on a second computer to score his/her own ticket.

4. The ticket ordering website requires you to fill in information, which is time-consuming. It helps if you're a fast typist, but it's better if you've entered default data in your computer that will auto-fill. The form requires: (a) selecting the show (*The Big Bang Theory*), (b) selecting the number of tickets (choose ONE ticket), and (c) personal information: first name, last name, address, city, state, zip code, country, phone, and e-mail address.

5. If at first you don't succeed . . . try, try again. The server is jammed for those thirty minutes, especially the first twenty, after which the tickets are usually all gone. (In that case, you'll see a "SOLD OUT" legend.)

6. If you're one of the lucky people who scored a ticket, follow the instructions. As explained on the website, "When you click the 'Submit' button below after completing the order form, your ticket and a studio location map will be generated for printing. We do not send anything to you, so please PRINT YOUR TICKET immediately after submitting your order."

On the Day the Show Airs

1. Carefully read the instructions you printed out when you ordered your ticket.

2. Eat before leaving for the studio. You'll be waiting in line for about two hours to get in, and the actual taping will take another three hours.

3. Stage 25 is brightly lit for filming purposes, and the room is air-conditioned. Bring a light jacket, sweater, or sweatshirt because it may be frigid. (If you want to simulate the environment, see if your friend at the Cheesecake Factory will let you try out their room-size freezer.)

4. Leave your camera/cell phone in your car. It will otherwise be confiscated by security during check-in.

5. Bring a picture ID—a driver's license is best. (Your JLA Membership Card won't cut it.)

6. TVtickets.com states that audience parking and check-in for Warner Bros. is at gate #3, at 4301 W. Olive Ave in Burbank. Located across from the main gate, "free audience parking is usually available in the structure no more than 2 hours prior to show time; however, this is controlled by WB security and may vary depending on how many shows are filmed on a particular day and/or studio personnel parking requirements. Each guest at Warner Bros. must have an individual ticket or be on our ticket list under his/her name with matching photo ID at check-in."

7. Like Sheldon and his posse waiting to get into the midnight showing of *Raiders of the Lost Ark* ("The 21 Second Excitation," 4-8), you'll have to wait in line. If you arrive *way* too early, the guard will tell you to come back. If you arrive too late, you won't get in, even if you have a ticket.

   Important comfort tip: pre-line urination. (Sheldon, as you know, always likes to schedule time for this before seeing a movie.) Additionally, I know it can be hot in Southern California, but you'll regret buying that 7-Eleven Xtreme Gulp with fifty-one ounces of Coke or your favorite sixteen-ounce Smoothie.

   Most people get there at 4:00 P.M. To be on the safe side, get there at 3:30 P.M., and you are practically guaranteed entry.

8. The show starts taping at 6:30 or 7:00 P.M., and they'll let you in an hour earlier.

9. You must first pass through several barriers, each more daunting than the last. Security point #1 is where they check for cameras, cell phones, and any other photographic/ recording devices with a magnetometer. Obviously they don't want you to secretly film the show before the air date and post it on YouTube.

   You will, by the way, get your hand stamped, which raises a question: on what authority are they permitted to mutilate patrons upon entry?

10. The actual filming will take place at stage 25, in the middle of the Warner Bros. lot. Realizing that you've probably waited in line for two hours or longer, they usually herd you to the bathroom for a preshow urination. (Yes, you can go during the show, as you would a movie, but isn't it smarter to take care of nature's call before the show?) If you're a guy, you have another option, though I heartily *don't* endorse it: Stadium Pal, which Howard recommended in "The 21 Second Excitation (4-8)." "Let me put it this way: it takes care of the bathroom problem, and it keeps your calf warm."

11. At the door to the soundstage, a final security check is done. The magnetometer is once again employed. Now you're "clean" and can get inside stage #25.

During the Taping

1. If you are a VIP, your seat is designated and marked, just as seats during rehearsal are marked for the Academy Awards. For everyone else, it's general seating.

2. An emcee named Mark Sweet will take the stage and introduce himself and then the cast individually. (You'll see him a lot

for the next three hours. In between takes, he's there to insure that audience enthusiasm doesn't flag.)

Important tip: Take your response cues from the emcee. Keep in mind that it's a *live recording*, not your living room or a stadium at a sporting event where you can whoop and holler whenever you wish. If that happens, it may require a reshoot, and you can expect to get the stink-eye from security and admonished—or kicked out.

3. Assuming you are a civilized person and not a *homo habilis* who just discovered his opposable thumb, settle in your seat, relax, and enjoy the show. There will be several retakes until they get the scene exactly right; three is average, but five or six is not uncommon, depending on how difficult the lines are. Don't expect the cast to ad-lib or joke too much when they flub up; they've got a job to do, and they don't want to be onstage, under those broiling lights, any longer than they have to be.

4. You will usually be fed pizza and given a water bottle sometime during the taping. Sweet! Just remember, the bathroom you passed halfway to the soundstage from the first security point is a trek, so you don't *have* to drink the entire bottle of water.

5. The taping should end between 10:00 and 10:30 P.M., but don't expect to hang around near the soundstage long afterward. By that time, the cast and crew want to go home. So getting autographs is problematic. If you can score one, why not get it on the playbill they distribute before the taping? That's a tangible piece of memorabilia to take home, in addition to your fond memories.

THE WARNER BROS. STUDIO VIP TOUR

*W*hat you will see on a typical tour: reconstructed New York–style buildings, Midwest-style buildings, a garage containing vintage cars seen on TV and film from WB productions, the set for *The Ellen Degeneres Show*, a permanent exhibition set for *Friends*, the props department, and the studio museum.

Note: This is a studio tour, not specifically a tour of *The Big Bang Theory*. Though soundstage #25 is where the show is filmed, there is no guarantee that you will be able to see it. But it doesn't hurt to ask your tour guide; if enough people express an interest, your group may be accommodated.

Tour Contact Information and Hours

WB Studio Tour
3400 Riverside Drive
Burbank, CA 01522
7:30 A.M. to 7 P.M., Monday through Friday
818-972-8687

The iconic WB tower

How to Get Tickets

Buy tickets online at vipstudiotour.warnerbros.com at least one day in advance to get your preferred tour time. Alternatively, go early to pick among the tour times available on any given day. Remember, tickets are given on a first-come, first-served basis.

The cost per VIP ticket is $49 plus a $3 service charge.

How to Get There

Parking is located at gate 6, across from the Warner Bros. office building in a secured lot, and costs $7.

After securing your car, go directly across the street. To your left, security will screen your personal belongings as you go through a metal detector.

Once inside, pass through the gift shop area. The ticket area will be to your right.

Tour Tips

1. Buy from the gift shop after the tour.
2. For the first two hours of the tour, you will not be able to go to the bathroom. So if you are not a master or mistress of your bladder, go *before* the tour starts.
3. Bring a bottle of water and headwear (a baseball cap is ideal), and wear comfortable shoes. You'll be walking and standing a lot in the hot California sun.
4. Bring a camera. There are plenty of photo opportunities. (Note: Your camera will be secured in a locked compartment on the tour vehicle at specified times, including during the tour of the garage with vintage cars, any soundstage or set, and the company museum.)
5. Freely engage the tour guide by asking questions. They know a lot more than they can possibly share on the tour and are eager to share their in-depth knowledge.

The Tour Itself

At the designated time printed on your ticket, you will be admitted to a small auditorium where a brief introduction will be given regarding the tour itself. It is followed by a ten-minute film clip showing the history of the studio along with highlights from famous movies.

Afterward, the audience breaks down into tour groups. Your ticket will indicate which guide to follow outside to the tour vehicle.

All ready? Now, on with the show!

Insider Tour Tip: Ride "shotgun" if you can. Sitting next to the driver/tour guide, you get the best view, the most seating room (everyone else is seated three across in a bench-style seat), and a place to store your bottled water. (No beverage holders are available in front of the other seats.)

Once seated, with your seat belt secured, you'll pass through the main gate to the back lot. There you'll disembark to listen to the tour guide explain the history of the studio, then take a walk through the New York environment, while stopping to listen to the tour guide recount highlights and specific scenes from popular movies.

Early on, there is a photo op for *The Big Bang Theory* fans: in the New York street environment is a classic movie theater, which was used in "The 21 Second Excitation" (4-8).

One other stop of note for *The Big Bang Theory* fans: at the two-hour mark, your tour group will be free to wander around the studio's two-story museum. While the second floor is all Harry Potter props, costumes, and statues, the first floor has memorabilia from other productions, including a display for *The Big Bang Theory*. It shows costumes worn by Leonard, Penny, and Sheldon, and displays a copy of Research Lab, the beta version of a physics board game designed by Sheldon in "The Guitarist Amplification" (3-7), complete with play cards. (*Note:* The museum will be your only opportunity to hit the water fountain or a bathroom during the tour, so take advantage of it.)

The tour ends where it begins: in the gift shop, where you can check out the display of licensed product (T-shirts, cups, baseball caps, key rings, etc.) from *The Big Bang Theory*.

A facade on the back lot used in "The 21 Second Excitation" (4–8)

TOURING WARNER BROS. STUDIO
• • • • • • • • • • • •

Warner Bros. offers two studio tours: the VIP Tour ($49), described above, and the Deluxe Tour ($225).

The rules:

1. Have a government-issued ID (driver's license or passport).
2. Photography is limited (a lockbox on each cart secures cameras in select areas), and no filming is allowed.
3. Your personal items are subject to search. (Count on it.)
4. You can order tickets online (vipstudiotourtickets.warner-bros.com) or by phone (818-972-8687).
5. You can get tickets in person at the VIP Tour Center outside the studio gates on weekdays from 7:30 a.m. to 7:00 p.m. The Tour Center has a refreshment stand where you can get Starbucks coffee and snacks; for more substantial fare, the adjacent Studio Plaza Café offers lunch/dinner fare. The Center also carries a full line of studio-themed memorabilia, which is also available online at wbshop.com.

VIP Tour (2 hours, 25 minutes; $49)
See pages 166–169.

Deluxe Tour (5 hours, $225)

Like the VIP tour, this tour also begins at WB's tour center. Unlike the VIP tour that runs several times a day, this tour only runs once daily for twelve people, and is two and a half hours longer. The tour starts at 10:20 a.m., but you should arrive at least twenty minutes earlier. It includes a more "behind the scenes" look at the prop department, a visit to the Foley Stage where sound creation and editing is done, and the costume department. Afterward you get to have lunch in the studio's Commissary "Fine Dining Room."

That's where, when *The Big Bang Theory* is filming, you may get a glimpse of some of the actors, according to fans who have taken the tour.

GETTING YOUR GEEK ON IN PUBLIC

A CONVENTION PRIMER FOR MUGGLES

*I*n "The Electric Can Opener Fluctuation" (3-1), Sheldon is thrice disappointed: his scientific experiment goes awry, thanks to his friends; he misses the new *Star Trek* movie; and worst of all, *he misses Comic-Con!*

Comic-Con: a convention so diverse that fans no longer call it by its original name, SDCC, or its full official name: San Diego Comic Con International. It's simply Comic-Con, and it is, as Howard likes to call it, Nerdvana.

Today, Comic-Con hosts one hundred and twenty-five thousand attendees from all over the world. The demand for tickets is so great that they sold out in seven hours for the 2011 convention.

Comic-Con, the granddaddy of all comic book conventions, is no longer about comics; in fact, comic books are just one of the many attractions. As John Rogers, the president of Comic-Con, explained in the 2010 program book:

> When we first started we were able to hold the entire convention in the basement of a hotel . . . But many don't realize that it was never our intention to be the largest event of its kind in the world. We . . . have always tried to put on the type of show we ourselves want to attend. That still holds true today. The difference is that over the years the general public has realized that this group of geeks and

nerds are on to something. While we may not have felt welcome at some of "their" events or parties, our doors have always been open to everyone . . . We're all friends at Comic-Con, regardless if your interest is comics or movie, games or toys.

Geeks of all stripes arrive in full force and often dress in costume, which is a Comic-Con tradition. But if you don't show up as a character from *Star Trek*, *Star Wars*, or another fictional universe, that's fine. The idea is to go, have fun, and get your geek on.

Though the Comic-Con is the biggest, baddest convention for geeks, it's not the one I'd recommend for newcomers because of its overwhelming size, the density of its crowd, and its three-ring-circus atmosphere. Moreover, parking near the convention center is problematic, hotel rooms are exorbitant (local hotels jack up the rates just for the convention period), it's literally wall-to-wall people within the convention center itself, and to get into the main hall to see the television and movie stars means standing in line for several hours; even then, you may, like Sheldon and his friends in "The 21-Second Excitation" (4-8), stand in line for all that time and then be denied entry because all the seats are taken. In an instance where life imitated art, during 2010's Comic-Con, at Hall H, which can seat sixty-five hundred people, hundreds were turned away when the petty functionary with the clipboard cut off the line for *The Big Bang Theory*.

Convention programming, even at the smallest conventions, offers a wide range of activities. Depending on the event, there may be panels at which authors, writers, actors, or others speak about their craft; an art show with professional and amateur (fan) art; a huckster's room where you can buy collectibles of all kinds and at all prices, including books, magazines, original artwork, and figurines; autograph signings; talks given by artists, writers, or actors; and costume contests.

Just as important, conventions offer the opportunity to meet fellow fans whom you've known only online, and long-distance friends you likely see only at events such as this.

Over the years I've attended numerous conventions—small one-day events, weekend events, and weeklong events—themed around science fiction, comics, J.R.R. Tolkien, and Harry Potter. I've also attended Renaissance Faires.

As a vendor, a pro, a guest of honor, and, most often, as a fan, I've enjoyed every minute of every convention, as will you. For the newcomer, here's a brief overview of the various conventions, organized by fandom.

Science Fiction

The big kahuna is the annual World Science Fiction Convention. Fan groups bid for the right to hold the convention internationally, as it's held in a different city each year. For fans who have only an interest in fantasy or science fiction, this is a good choice, especially if you know why fans are "Slans."

This Con tends to attract an older crowd, in their forties and up. The programming is extensive, and the partying lasts into the wee hours. The main website is worldcon.org, which will have links to the dedicated website for the current Worldcon.

An Elemental Explication

In A.E. van Vogt's novel *Slans*, Slans are in every way an improvement over mankind, so naturally these superintelligent beings, hated for their abilities, are hunted down by humans who want to exterminate them.

Science-fictions fans like to compare themselves to Slans. Fans, especially those with superior intellects, see themselves as outsiders, persecuted by the "mundanes" because of their apparent differences.

The key publication in this field is *Locus* magazine, which maintains an updated list of conventions, arranged chronologically, at locusmag.com/Resources/Conventions.html.

For your first convention, the Worldcon may be a bit overwhelming. Fortunately, there are many regional conventions hosted by experienced fan groups that have been around for many years, including NESFA (New England Science Fiction Association), which hosts Boskone, the Lunarians' Lunacon, and the Southern fans' Deep South Con.

For a good overview of SF (*not* "sci-fi") conventions, see Wikipedia's entry for "Science fiction convention."

Popular Arts

In the early years, comic book conventions were squarely focused on comics; however, as major media coverage of comics grew, the Cons also grew to include movies, television shows, and other subjects of pop culture interest.

The biggest of them, of course, is Comic-Con, which bills itself as a comic book convention and also a popular arts convention, an all-encompassing category that includes peripheral fields of interest.

New York Comic Con, NYCC (newyorkcomiccon.com)

For a predominantly comics-themed show, the big one is the New York Comic Con in the Big Apple, the home of Marvel Comics and DC Comics, the two biggest comic book publishers. This annual convention is held in October, and in 2010 drew over ninety-six thousand participants. Though the primary emphasis is comics, this Con does cater to related interests, much like its big brother in San Diego. "Our show floor plays host to the latest and greatest in comics, graphic novels, anime, manga, video games, toys, movies, and television," notes the New York Comic Con website.

Comic-Con in San Diego (www.comic-con.org)

The Comic-Con (as it's widely known) is the ultimate event, though its title belies its scope. In recent years, attendance has mushroomed due to the presence of nearby Hollywood, which shows up in full force with movie stars, elaborate booths, booth girls, and prop displays to help build early buzz on the web for its "tent pole" projects, the ones designed to financially hold up the major franchises.

Artist Donato Giancola, who began exhibiting at Comic-Con in 1998, said that in those days, DC Comics, Marvel Comics, and Dark Horse were the largest exhibitors; the show was then mostly oriented toward comic book fans. Today, comic artists, especially indie publishers, are a small but important part of the show. The Con's focus shifted to the "Mega Con" concept in 2001 when New Line Cinema put up a massive display to promote *The Lord of the Rings: The Fellowship of the Ring*. In 2004 Lucasfilm upped the ante and displayed a full-scale model of an X-wing fighter on the show floor. Since then, the sky's been the limit, as major studios compete to put up the biggest displays to catch the fans' attention.

An unadvertised bonus: Comic-Con's close proximity to Los Angeles means that there are always stars who show up to walk the floor, see the exhibits, and buy collectibles, just like any other carbon-based life form. Last year, for instance, as soon as I walked onto the convention floor, I saw John Cryer (of *Two and a Half Men*) buying original art, and had a brief conversation with him. He kindly signed my program book. So keep your eyes open. You'd be surprised who might be standing next to you—hey, is that *Jim Parsons*?

Bazinga!

For fans of *The Big Bang Theory*, the principal cast (Jim Parsons, Johnny Galecki, Kaley Cuoco, Simon Helberg, and Kunal Nayyar) have all shown up four years in a row (2008–2011) to appear on a panel, and will likely be in attendance for the foreseeable future. In 2010, the cast signed free photos.

Comic-Con's parent organization also runs two other, smaller

Cons: APE (Alternative Press Expo) in October, for comic book fans; and Wondercon in April.

Dragon*Con (dragoncon.org)

Held in Atlanta, Dragon*Con is similar in scope to the San Diego Comic-Con, with forty thousand plus attendees in 2011. It is held annually in September. For someone wanting to attend a large pop culture convention on the East Coast, this is a good choice. One of the most popular features is its half-mile parade downtown. The Con has all the usual attractions as well: autograph areas, an awards banquet, live music for after-hours dancing, readings by authors, and stars (TV and movie) signing photos and other memorabilia. For those who can't get to Comic-Con, this is a fun alternative.

Wizard World (wizardworld.com)

Billed as the "pop culture capital of the world," this is a franchise of themed conventions, with an emphasis on movie and television stars. There are conventions year-round principally in the U.S.

Creation Entertainment (creationent.com)

Run by longtime fans and convention organizers Gary and Adam Malin, these are official licensed conventions with unparalleled access to the movie and television stars. Located throughout the country, these Cons cater to fans of various movie and television franchises, including *Star Trek*, *Battlestar Galactica*, *Farscape*, *Smallville*, *Supernatural*, *Twilight*, *Sanctuary*, *Gossip Girl*, *UnDead*, *The Lord of the Rings*, and more.

If you're an autograph collector and are concerned about buying a bogus signature online from one of the popular auction websites where forgeries are rampant, Creation Entertainment offers an affordable alternative: they have authentic signed photos for sale at their events and on their website, which they guarantee.

Star Wars

Star Wars Celebration (starwarscelebration.com) is where the Wookies mix it up with Ewoks, Stormtroopers march down the street en masse in formation, and Boba Fett is fêted. This official Lucasfilm event is for "all things *Star Wars*, produced by fans for fans. 'Celebrations' are the largest *Star Wars* parties, featuring cast and crew celebrities, fans, costumes, music, live entertainment, autographs, collectibles, and panels—but mainly friends who gather to have fun and celebrate their love for the saga."

Safety note: All blasters must have their safeties engaged and be sheathed, unless you spy Greedo, in which case shoot *first.*

And FYI: Going to the Con wearing a T-shirt with a built-in speaker that plays the "Imperial March" from *Star Wars* is *strictly* optional.

Gaming

See page 183.

Anime

Anime Expo (anime-expo.org) is the place to be. In recent years, it's centered in the Southern California area; for 2011–2013, it will be at the Los Angeles Convention Center, which can hold the one hundred and five thousand plus fans who show up.

A good website to follow Anime activities worldwide is anime-newsnetwork.com.

Renaissance Faires

If you had a time machine like Leonard's ("The Nerdvana Annihilation," 1-14) or a holodeck from *Star Trek*, you could travel back to the colorful, courtly years of England's Queen Elizabeth I. If you lack them, you can still experience merry olde England by getting thyself to a Renaissance Faire, where period clothing, food, and activities are the order of the day.

Get into the spirit of things by dressing up in period clothing, as did Sheldon and his posse in "The Codpiece Topology" (2-2). *Note:* You will usually find costumes on sale by vendors at these events, if you prefer not to order by mail or online.

For information on Faires:
- renfaire.com/sites
- faires.com
- faire-folk.com

For period clothing:
- majesticvelvets.com
- renstore.com
- lords-n-ladies.com

TEN TIPS FOR CONVENTION NEWBIES

. . . .

by Kirsten Cairns

1. Take a shoulder bag or backpack. It should be big enough to carry a bottle of water, your money, camera, pen, and a notepad—you never know when you might want to get an autograph or make a note of something. You also don't want to have to keep heading back to your room, which can take a long time when queues are forming for the elevators, so carrying headache tablets, lip balm, etc. in that bag can be handy, too. Basically, plan to stay out of your room all day, and only go back to change and get ready for the evening parties.

2. Bring a sharpie pen and a poster tube. The pen is ideal for autographs, and the tube is the best way to get a photograph or picture safely home.

3. Pick a comfortable costume. If you are costuming, make sure your costume isn't going to cause you agony; you want to enjoy wearing it, not be crippled by it.

4. Bring lots of cash. Even though you can get cash from ATMs, the lines are very long, and sometimes the machines run out.

5. Save money by bringing your own food. Apples, nuts, cereal bars, chocolate, etc. can be kept in your hotel room and will do for breakfasts and lunches. I try to only buy one meal a day at the Con. Also, if you're lucky (and ask the reservation clerk way in advance), you may be able to get a fridge in your room, in which case you can even take things like yogurt and milk. Drinking the coffee in the hotel room also saves lots of money and time—lines for Starbucks get very long.

(continued on next page)

(continued from previous page)

6. Buy alcohol at a local store. If you like a drink at the Con, save money by taking a few beers or some such to have in your room, rather than paying for overpriced bar drinks. In addition, if you host your own room party, you'll have libations to offer guests.

7. Look at the schedule and make a rough plan for each day. Otherwise, the Con slips by and you realize you didn't make it to any of the panels you wanted to see. Be savvy about the popularity of panels; if a big star is appearing, you'll need to get in line at least an hour in advance. At bigger Cons, such as Comic-Con, you may need to be in the line several hours in advance. Plan with your Con-mates what your rough schedule will be each day; even with the wonders of cell phones, it can be hard to find each other unless you have some idea of where people are going to be.

8. Mix and match activities. Recharge your batteries by wandering around the art show or the dealers' room. Panels are fabulous, but a change of pace is as good as a rest. And you may miss something wonderful by never venturing beyond your chosen track.

9. Stop by the fan tables. Meeting like-minded people is one of the greatest things about Cons. It's a terrific chance to chat with people who are as passionate as you are, and maybe make lifelong friends.

10. Take business cards. No matter what your line of work, you never know when you may meet someone who is interested in what you do, or wants to hire you, or may be able to help you in your career. Having a business card ready to give is always a good idea.

Kirsten is a veteran conventioneer who especially enjoys attending Dragon*Con every year. She is the Director of Opera Studies at Boston Conservatory.

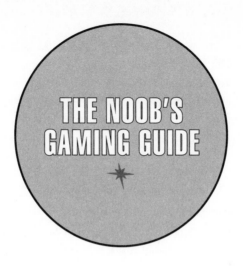

THE NOOB'S GAMING GUIDE

A newbie, or "noob," is self-explanatory. At the opposite end of the spectrum are gamers like Sheldon, Leonard, Howard, and Raj, all of whom are masters of their virtual domains.

We get a taste early on of their addiction to gaming in "The Fuzzy Boots Corollary" (1-3), in which we learn that the boys have prepped themselves for ninety-seven hours to storm the Gates of Elzebub and fight "a horde of armed goblins" to get the Sword of Azeroth in the MMORPG (massively multiplayer online role-playing games) game *World of Warcraft*. (*Note:* There is no Gates of Elzebub in *WOW*.)

A year later, in "The Barbarian Sublimation" (2-3), Penny gets a taste, then becomes hooked, on *Age of Conan*, another MMORPG, in which Sheldon's avatar is Sheldor the Conqueror. (Penny quickly adopts an avatar named Queen Penelope and, armed with a sword, sallies forth into author Robert E. Howard's fictional-turned-virtual world until Howard shows up as his avatar, Sir Howard of Wolowitz, and offers Queen Penelope "spirited questing" followed by "a flagon of ale" at the virtual tavern.)

Just *how* serious is Sheldon's interest in gaming? In "The Bozeman Reaction" (3-13), when his apartment is robbed, the laundry list of stolen hardware and software—game players, consoles, game cartridges, etc—is extensive. He obviously invests a lot of money in gaming, not to mention time: in "The Zarnecki Incursion" (4-19), after a thief has broken into his *World of Warcraft* account and absconded with his virtual goods, it's *three thousand hours* of game time down the drain. The mighty Sheldor got ripped big-time: "They got my enchanted weapons, my vicious gladiator armor, my wand of untainted power, and all my gold."

An Elemental Explication

Either Todd Zarnecki is a super hacker, or Sheldon's password was too easily guessed. Leonard likes to use "Kal-El" for his all-purpose password, but software company Agile Bits recommends, and generates with its software, passwords that are fifty characters/letters in upper/lowercase, which are virtually unbreakable.

All the boys are "hard-core" gamers who enjoy individual game play, "clan" gaming (in teams with others), "retrogaming" (playing older games principally on the computer using emulators to run them), and "mobile" gaming with handheld devices. But Sheldon, by virtue of his eidetic memory, is perhaps the most formidable. That explains why he disparages Penny ("The Dumpling Paradox," 1-7) when she innocently volunteers to substitute for Howard in *Halo 3*. Sheldon tells her, "This is a complex battle simulation with a steep learning curve, there are myriad weapons, vehicles, and strategies to master, not to mention an extremely intricate backstory." In other words: forget it, honey—men at work!

Though the boys enjoy all forms of game play, they devote the most time and attention to MMORPGs because these offer the greatest challenge. (*World of Warcraft*, for instance, has over 12 million subscribers worldwide.) Going online to fight in a graphically rich environment with sound, and doing so against dedicated players worldwide, is what separates the boys from the men. Only the best survive.

An Elemental Explication

Sheldon has a big advantage when playing any card-based game like Dungeons & Dragons: he's got an eidetic memory, so once he knows which cards have been played, he knows exactly what's left, and can anticipate the possible outcomes. In "The Creepy Candy Corollary" (3-5), we see his memorization skills put to good use. In a Mystic Warlords of Ka'a tournament at Stuart's comic book store, Sheldon demolishes every team he's up against and, finally, is pitted against his nemesis, Wil Wheaton. It's Sheldon's game to lose at that point, and he does just that by underestimating Wheaton, who proves to be nefarious.

Gaming Conventions

Gen Con (gencon.com)

This annual convention attracts over thirty thousand people annually to Indianapolis, Indiana, and principally caters to "traditional pen-and-paper, board, and card-style games, including role-playing games, miniatures wargames, board games, live action role-playing games, collectible card games, non-collectible card games, and strategy games," states Wikipedia. Convention statistics: thirty thousand attendees; three hundred exhibitors; eight thousand events with twenty-four hour programming.

Origins Game Fair (originsgamefair.com)

Held in Columbus, Ohio, Origins is run by GAMA (Game Manufacturers Association) and is "specifically chartered to serve gaming in general, including wargames and miniatures gaming . . . Board games, trading card games, LARPs, and role-playing games are also popular at Origins," states Wikipedia.

PAX (Penny Arcade Expo East conference) (east.paxsite.com)

By far the biggest gaming convention is PAX, which draws seventy thousand people annually. According to its website, it's for "tabletop, videogame, and PC gamers." It's the Comic-Con of gaming conventions.

For a detailed Con listing for gamers, go to: sjgames.com/con. Wikipedia also has a listing of gaming conventions worldwide at en.wikipedia.org/wiki/List_of_gaming_conventions.

Part 5

RELIANCE ON SCIENCE

In which we intrepidly explore the known universe, from the Big Bang and the history of our world, to the Singularity—and beyond

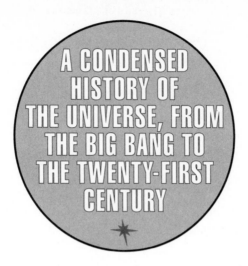

A CONDENSED HISTORY OF THE UNIVERSE, FROM THE BIG BANG TO THE TWENTY-FIRST CENTURY

*I*f, like Sheldon's mother, Mary, you are a Fundamentalist Christian, you believe that God created Heaven and Earth within a week. During that time, He created light, the sky, land, the seas, vegetation, celestial bodies, all manner of creatures, and finally man/womankind. Then, on the seventh day, known as the Sabbath, He rested.

This is what Mary would call the Word of God, as chronicled in the Bible. But it's what Sheldon would call a "creation myth," one of many that, depending on your religion, explains how the known universe was created by a Divine Being.

In "The Electric Can Opener Fluctuation" (3-1), we see Sheldon and his mother standing on opposite sides of the fence. When she thinks Sheldon is sassing her by saying that he plans on staying in Texas, "trying to teach evolution to creationists," she cautions him: "You watch your mouth, Shelly. Everyone's entitled to their opinion." Sheldon responds, "Evolution isn't an opinion—it's fact." To which she says, "And *that* is *your* opinion."

Sheldon is not swayed by her fiercely held convictions. He subscribes to the tenets of science, a discipline that subjects everything to the scientific method of inquiry, as articulated by S. Crawford and L. Stucki in "Peer review and the changing research record," from the *Journal of the American Society for Information Science and Technology* (1990):

1. Define a question
2. Gather information and resources (observe)
3. Form an explanatory hypothesis
4. Perform an experiment and collect data, testing the hypothesis
5. Analyze the data
6. Interpret the data and draw conclusions that serve as a starting point for new hypothesis
7. Publish results
8. Retest (frequently done by other scientists)

So let's put our faith in Sheldon's "opinion" (as his mother has it), and start with a simplified telling of the Big Bang itself as Sheldon himself might explain it to, say, one of Penny's boyfriends.

The Birth of the Universe

A long time ago, in a galaxy far, far away, a great cosmic event took place. "The universe began in a small, dense, hot state followed by an explosion that brought space and matter into existence approximately 13 billion years ago. The universe, today, still expands from this explosion." So stated professor Neil deGrasse Tyson in *My Favorite Universe.*

In the subsequent pre–solar system phase, a primal supernova exploded, triggering the formation of our solar system. After the formation of the Sun, its outer planets were formed, including Earth, around 4.5 billion years ago. Approximately 100 million years ago, the western margin of California began forming when the Pacific and North American plates deep below the surface collided; 25 million years ago they pushed offshore Pacific islands together to create its western coastal range. The collision of the two plates created what we now call the San Andreas Fault.

The Birth of Civilization

As for mankind: descending from apes and chimpanzees, the first men, genus *Homo habilis*, made their appearance approximately 2.5 million years ago. John Pickrell wrote, in *New Scientist*, early man's "face protrudes less than early hominids, but still retains many ape features. Hominids start to use stone tools regularly, created by splitting pebbles." Somewhere between 1.5 and 1.8 million years ago, Pickrell continues, "*Homo erectus* is found in Asia. First true hunter-gatherer ancestor, and also first to have migrated out of Africa in large numbers . . . Our own species *Homo sapiens* appeared on the scene—and shortly after begins to migrate across Asia and Europe."

As civilizations grew up around the world, and vast empires were established, Europe witnessed scientific and industrial revolutions. In 1492, Christopher Columbus failed to discover a new route to the Indies (India and China), but discovered the New World, which eventually led to the subjugation of the indigenous population in North America by Europeans.

In 1847, when Mexico surrendered California, it became a U.S. territory.

In 1887, the Santa Fe Railway was completed, and it was instrumental in bringing "wealthy people from the East Coast" who "began to spend the winter in the warmth and sunshine of Southern California," notes the *DK Eyewitness Travel: California* guidebook. "Many settled in Pasadena and were soon joined by artists and bohemians, who were also seeking the sun."

From 1886 to 1941, according to Wikipedia, Pasadena's growth spurred "the development of new neighborhoods and business districts, and increased road and transit connections with Los Angeles, culminating with the opening of the Arroyo Seco Parkway,

California's first freeway. By 1940, Pasadena had become the eighth largest city in California and was considered by many to be a twin city to Los Angeles."

In the aftermath of World War II, Pasadena saw an influx of high-tech manufacturing and scientific companies, eventually leading to the establishment of NASA's Jet Propulsion Laboratory in northern Pasadena.

In the 1970s, downtown Pasadena saw significant changes. Demographically, the prevalence of serious crime helped encourage an exodus to the suburbs. This caused a drop in urban property values, which, notes Wikipedia, encouraged "local artists and hipsters" to move back into the city.

In the early 2000s, the city, known architecturally for its art buildings, underwent an extensive beautification program. Rapid transit lines were reopened, and trendy, high-density condos went up in the downtown area.

The Birth of Homo Novus: The New Man

In 1973, Sheldon Cooper was born in Houston, Texas; in 2003, after rigorous courses of study that culminated in earning two doctorates, he began work at Caltech.

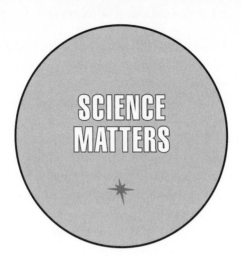

SCIENCE MATTERS

*7*he science of *The Big Bang Theory* is largely a backdrop. Though on occasion it takes center stage as a major plot point, for most of the show's 13+ million viewers, it's the interaction among the principal cast that they tune in to see. Viewers may not relate to the science, but they do relate to the people depicted in the show, and even take a bit of comfort in the fact that although these guys are geniuses, in many ways they aren't so different from the rest of us. They're supersmart but they're obviously, painfully human and handicapped with all the foibles that plague ordinary people.

But because there *is* science, though the show is obviously fictional, the cocreators have gone to great lengths to insure it has scientific verisimilitude. With the exception of Mayim Bialik, who has a doctorate in neuroscience, none of the cast members has a science degree. For that reason, Jim Parsons and Johnny Galecki met with physicists at the University of California, who gave them insight into what scientists do, how they think, and—most importantly from the actors' points of view—how they conduct themselves.

Because of the generally positive depiction of the show's geek squad, it has gotten a warm reception among the scientific community, who are more used to seeing banal stereotypes or, worse, misleading portrayals and characterizations that make scientists appear obtuse, objects of ridicule, or completely clueless around other people.

Saltzberg told an Australian fan website that "the response I have received is overwhelmingly positive. And strongly so. We had a positive full-page review in *Science Magazine*. I am very happy that the public relations people of the American Physical Society wrote to me that they loved the show, and they even sent the cast physics toys ... In this era of declining media coverage for science, here is a venue with over 15 million viewers to get the word out about modern scientific work."

Just as Indiana Jones led to increased archeology department enrollments, and *Star Trek* inspired large numbers of (mostly) young men to go into related technical fields, *The Big Bang Theory* has raised awareness about physics and its place in our universe, and also kindled enthusiasm among technically minded men and women who look skyward and see an entire universe waiting to be explored.

The Goddard Space Flight Center's website, "Blueshift: Bringing the Universe Closer to You" at astrophysics.gsfc.nasa.gov, even extols the virtues of the emphasis of science on the show: "We're avid readers of Dr. David Saltzberg's blog, The Big Blog Theory." Subtitled "the science behind the science," Saltzberg's blog makes it clear that what we see on the show isn't simply fabricated in the hope that most people won't know the difference.

There's a large body of scientists who would understand and, if it was wrong, would grumble and grouse to their contemporaries about how Hollywood, once again, didn't get it right. But this time, with *The Big Bang Theory*, the cocreators and writers *did* get it right, which means the show doesn't insult our collective intelligence. Though most people will not understand the physics references, those in the scientific community do, and it makes a big difference as to whether or not they give the show positive word-of-mouth recommendations.

The writers, and many viewers, may only consider the science to be a backdrop, but clearly the science matters.

The Quotable Dr. Saltzberg

Audience: I know a few professors who watch the show—more than I would have expected—and they like it. And I also get positive feedback from graduate students. Since it's taped in front of a live audience, and I go to every taping, I do get a lot of requests, and I always can get them seats. I'm also allowed to bring one special person with me—it's almost always a physicist—down to where the writers stand watching the show from the side. The writers call them the "geek of the week." (*UCLA Today*, 2010)

Science fiction: I unfortunately know next to nothing about science fiction and many other aspects of the "smart" dialogue, such as logic and just about any aspect of science other than physics. These are all real-life interests of the writers, and it comes from their lives. (The unofficial fan website, the-big-bang-theory.com)

An Elemental Explication

Though *The Big Bang Theory* could be set at any major university, there are distinct benefits to setting it at Caltech because of the hometown advantage. In this case, the actors, writers, producers, and science advisor are all in the greater Los Angeles area, which simplifies logistics tremendously. Moreover, Caltech's academic divisions encompass multiple fields that allow maximum flexibility in character and story creation: biology; chemistry and chemical engineering; engineering and applied science; geological and planetary sciences; social sciences and humanities ("Oh, the humanities!" as Sheldon opined); physics, mathematics, and astronomy; and interdisciplinary programs.

SCIENCE ADVISOR TO THE STARS

· · · · · · · · · · · ·

To insure the science is correct, the show's producers recruited an expert, Dr. David Salzberg, a professor of physics and astronomy at the University of California, Los Angeles (UCLA). According to his university bio (physics.ucla.edu/~salzbrg/bio. html), he checks scripts and meets with "producers, writers, actors, set decorators, prop masters, costume designers, etc., to help ensure scientific accuracy."

David Salzberg's blog, The Big Blog Theory: The Science Behind the Science (thebigblogtheory.wordpress.com), provides an in-depth explanation of each episode's science after it airs. As *The Big Bang Theory*'s science advisor, Salzberg is in the perfect position to do so: all of the show's science can be credited to him. He provides input on scripts and the formulas on whiteboards displayed at Sheldon's apartment and office. He also shows up at every taping to be on hand "just in case there is a last-minute science question, but there rarely is," according to an interview he did with a fan website, thebigbangtheory.com.ar.

He adds, "Some of the cast and crew have also visited our labs here at UCLA. They learned about a few modern experiments and also met real-life physicists who are passionate about their work. I think the cast had not met so many physicists before, so I think it was helpful to them."

He particularly lauds Parsons' performance: "I don't know how Jim Parsons does it. His lines are not only pronounced correctly, but really sound like a physicist saying them. Not just the pronunciation matters, but the whole rhythm of the language and the emphasis on words must be correct."

STELLAR SCIENTISTS STAR ON *THE BIG BANG THEORY*

*I*t's a testament to the show's popularity and its treatment of science that stellar scientists want to make appearances on *The Big Bang Theory*. The following scientists, listed alphabetically, have made cameo appearances on the show.

BRIAN GREENE
(columbia.edu/cu/physics/fac-bios/Greene/faculty.html)
On "The Herb Garden Germination" (4-20), Brian Greene appears at a major chain bookstore to give a talk. The background shows that he's just published a book, *The Hidden Reality: Parallel Universes and the Deep Laws of the Cosmos*. Sheldon takes the opportunity to needlessly needle Greene, who is flummoxed at the verbal attack, until Sheldon defuses the situation by saying he wasn't serious.

A link is provided to a video with Greene talking about string theory on ted.com, which explains that he is "perhaps the best-known proponent of superstring theory, the idea that miniscule strands of energy vibrating in 11 dimensions create every particle and force in the universe." Greene was a math prodigy and a Rhodes scholar, who has written several bestselling and nontechnical books, such as *The Elegant Universe*, a Pulitzer finalist, Aventis winner, and the basis for a three-hour Nova special. He is a professor at Columbia University's

Institute for Strings, Cosmology, and Astroparticle Physics. (From his brief cameo on *The Big Bang Theory*, it's also clear that he's an excellent lecturer and actor.) According to Green,

> My area of research is superstring theory, a theory that purports to give us a quantum theory of gravity as well as a unified theory of all forces and all matter. As such, superstring theory has the potential to realize Einstein's long-sought dream of a single, all encompassing theory of the universe. One of the strangest features of superstring theory is that it requires the universe to have more than three spatial dimensions. Much of my research has focused on the physical implications and mathematical properties of these extra dimensions—studies that collectively go under the heading "quantum geometry."

GEORGE SMOOT

(cosmos/lbl.gov/cobe.html)

In "The Terminator Decoupling" (2-17), Sheldon explains to Penny that "George Smoot is a Nobel Prize–winning physicist, one of the great minds of our time. His work in blackbody form and anisotrophy of the cosmic microwave radiation cemented our understanding of the origin of the universe." (The actual Nobel Prize in Physics citation reads: "for their discovery of the blackbody form and anisotrophy of the cosmic microwave background radiation.")

Sheldon, who bows to no one, considers Smoot to be his peer. Sheldon's goal, as he explains to Leonard, is to present to Smoot his paper on "astrophysical probes of M-theory effects in the early universe" and use that as an opportunity to suggest they collaborate on a paper, which Sheldon hopes will win him a Nobel Prize. It's a great plan, but Smoot isn't buying it. "With all due respect, Dr. Cooper," he retorts, "are you on crack?"

Smoot's 1992 announcement, at a meeting of the American Physical Society, "essentially silenced all the scientific critics of the Big Bang theory and helped change the course of future investigations into the origin and evolution of the universe," noted Lynn

Yarris, a PR spokesperson for DOE/Lawrence Berkeley National Laboratory.

Smoot, who shares the 2006 Nobel Prize with John C. Mather of NASA Goddard Space Flight Center, explained on his web page, Smoot Group: Astrophysics & Cosmology:

> The tiny temperature variations we discovered are the imprints of tiny ripples in the fabric of space-time put there by the primeval explosion process. Over billions of years, the smaller of these ripples have grown into galaxies, clusters of galaxies, and the great voids of space . . . People have contemplated the origin and evolution of the universe since before the time of Aristotle. Although cosmology has been around since the time of the ancients, historically it has been dominated by theory and speculation. Very recently, the era of speculation has given way to a time of science. The advance of knowledge and of scientific ingenuity means that at long last, we can actually test our theories.

NEIL DEGRASSE TYSON
(haydenplanetarium.org/tyson)

In "The Apology Insufficiency" (4-7), Sheldon is beside himself. After bolloxing up Howard's chances for a high-level security clearance, he's in a very foul mood and takes it out on Neil deGrasse Tyson when, in a hallway at Caltech, Raj introduces them. Sheldon snarkily responds, "I'm quite familiar with Dr. Tyson. He's responsible for the demotion of Pluto from planetary status. I liked Pluto. Ergo, I do not like you."

On Sheldon and deGrasse's second encounter in this episode, when Sheldon rebuffs a second apologetic overture, he is not merely miffed but genuinely pissed off. Again, it's Dr. Tyson who bears the brunt of his wrath. Dr. Tyson proffers an apology, and Sheldon barks back, "Oh, shut up."

In an e-mail, Tyson told me that the show's producers had approached him to appear on the show. Tyson, who has a doctorate in astrophysics, set off a firestorm with his views about Pluto. According to Wikipedia,

As director of the Hayden planetarium, Tyson bucked traditional thinking to keep Pluto from being referred to as the ninth planet in exhibits at the center. Tyson has explained that he wanted to look at commonalities between objects, grouping the terrestrial planets together, the gas giants together, and Pluto with like objects, and to get away from simply counting planets. He has stated on [several TV shows] that this decision has resulted in large amounts of hate mail, much of it from children. In 2006, the I.A.U. confirmed this assessment by changing Pluto to the "dwarf" planet classification. Daniel Simone wrote of the interview with Tyson describing his frustration, "For a while, we were not very popular here at the Hayden Planetarium."

In a 2007 article for *Spark*, a newsletter of the American Astronomical Society, Tyson wrote that he felt everyone had made a mountain of a molehill. "If my overstuffed e-mail index is any indication, this game of planetary enumeration remains a deep concern of elementary school students and the mainstream media." He concluded, "The fuss over Pluto doesn't have to play out as a death in the neighborhood. It could mark instead the birth of a whole new way of thinking about our cosmic backyard."

STEPHEN HAWKING
(hawking.org.uk)

Though Hawking doesn't appear on the show, because of his prominence in the field, he is acknowledged in several episodes.

In the first episode ("Pilot," 1-1), Howard rushes into Sheldon's apartment with Raj in tow and excitedly says, "Wait 'til you see this. It's a Stephen Hawking lecture from MIT in 1974. It's before he became a creepy computer voice."

In subsequent episodes, Howard makes many other references to Hawking, a theoretical physicist who, according to his official website,

has worked on the basic laws which govern the universe. With Roger Penrose, he showed that Einstein's General Theory of

Relativity implied space and time would have a beginning in the Big Bang and an end in black holes. These results indicated that it was necessary to unify General Relativity with Quantum Theory, the other great scientific development of the first half of the 20th century. One consequence of such a unification that he discovered was that black holes should not be completely black, but rather should emit radiation and eventually evaporate and disappear. Another conjecture is that the universe has no edge or boundary in imaginary time. This would imply that the way the universe began was completely determined by the laws of science.

Though I can find no record of Hawking giving a talk at MIT, he has lectured at Caltech. At one such talk, in 2009, tickets cost $10 and quickly sold out. A similar talk he gave at NASA, along with a transcript, is available at nasa.gov/50th/NASA_lecture_series/ hawking.html.

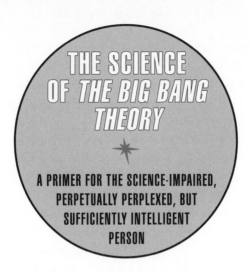

THE SCIENCE
OF *THE BIG BANG
THEORY*

A PRIMER FOR THE SCIENCE-IMPAIRED,
PERPETUALLY PERPLEXED, BUT
SUFFICIENTLY INTELLIGENT
PERSON

I understand if you snoozed during chemistry, biology, math, and physics in high school and college. Unless your brain is wired that way, the hard sciences are, well, hard. Fortunately, none of *The Big Bang Theory*'s episodes require an advanced degree to enjoy them. Still, knowing something about the most frequently highlighted scientific concepts will enhance your comprehension of the show. So here's a simplified, rocket-propelled ride, an overview of the key science concepts from the show for those of us who don't know what the heck topological insulators are.

The Big Bang Theory • Most scientists believe that originally the universe was in an extremely hot, dense state, and that approximately 13 million years ago, the universe as we know it formed in a gigantic explosion—a "big bang," as it were. The resultant explosion created all matter in space, and its effects are ongoing: the universe is still expanding and cooling. (See also page 188.)

Physicist Stephen Hawking, author of *The Grand Design*, dismisses the notion of a godlike cosmic creator who is responsible for the universe. "Because there is a law such as gravity, the Universe can and will create itself from nothing, why the Universe exists, why we exist . . . It is not necessary to invoke God to light the blue touch paper and set the Universe going."

For a technical discussion, go to scienceandreason.net/oq/oq-co008.htm. Additionally, NASA has a general discussion at science.nasa.gov/astrophysics/focus-areas/what-powered-the-big-bang.

The Big Bang theory is the connective tissue that holds the show together, not only as its leading scientific premise but the human dimension as well: our relationships with people, our circle of friends, are in a state of constant, simultaneous change, a state of expansion/entropy.

Doppler Effect • In "The Middle Earth Paradigm" (1-6), at a Halloween party at Penny's, the boys all dress up as fictional characters, except (who else?) Sheldon; he dresses as the Doppler Effect, which confuses the muggles. Sheldon's black-and-white costume with vertical bands visually represent the effect, but only his posse gets it.

In 1842 Austrian physicist Christian Doppler noticed the change in wave frequency relative to oneself, and termed it the Doppler Effect. As Sheldon explains, "It's the apparent change in the frequency of a wave caused by relative motion between the source of the wave and the observer." His explanation, however, fails to shed light on the phenomenon, and so he resorts to vocalization: he simulates an approaching, then diminishing, sound, but even that fails to convey the meaning of the term.

For a visualization of this effect, see chair.pa.msu.edu/applets/doppler/a.htm.

Drake Equation • In "The Hofstadter Isotope" (2-20), when Howard asks Sheldon if he's familiar with the Drake Equation, Sheldon—in one of his most memorable demonstrations of verbal expression—rattles off the equation. It's a pure Sheldon moment.

Frank Drake, Emeritus Professor of Astronomy and Astrophysics at the University of California, Santa Cruz, derived this equation to determine the number of detectable extraterrestrial civilizations in the Milky Way Galaxy. By his calculations, that would be only ten out of many millions.

The late Dr. Michael Crichton dismissed it, saying at a Caltech lecture in 2003, "The Drake equation is meaningless, and has nothing to do with science. I take the hard view that science involves the creation of testable hypotheses. The Drake equation cannot be tested and therefore SETI [Search for Extraterrestrial Intelligence] is not science." Booyah!

Experimental Physics • This is Dr. Leonard Hofstadter's field of study. It focuses on observing physical phenomena to get data about the universe. Recommended textbooks: *The Art of Experimental Physics* by Preston and Deitz, and *Experiments in Modern Physics* by Melissinos.

Kuiper Belt • In "The Griffin Equivalency" (2-4), it's Raj's time to shine. An astrophysicist, he discovers a "little planetary object . . . spotted beyond the Kuiper belt," which he informally names "Planet Bollywood." Its discovery launches Raj into a new, albeit temporary, high orbit, eclipsing his envious friends.

The area of space from Neptune's orbit, which is 30 astronomical units (AU) from the Sun, out to 55 AU, comprises the Kuniper belt. (An "AU" is equal to 92,955,807 miles, or the mean distance from the Earth to the Sun.) It's composed mostly of frozen volatiles such as methane, ammonia, and water.

Large Hadron Collider • A seventeen-mile tunnel located six hundred feet underground beneath the Franco–Swiss border near Geneva, Switzerland, the Large Hadron Collider is a subatomic particle accelerator. On its website, the European Organization for Nuclear Research (public.web.cer.ch) explains that the Collider is "used by physicists to study the smallest known particles—the fundamental building blocks of all things. Physicists will use the LHC to recreate the conditions just after the Big Bang, by colliding the two beams head-on at very high energy."

A good resource on the Collider for the general public is at public. web.cern.ch/public/en/lhc/lhc-en.html.

In "The Large Hadron Collision" (3-15), Sheldon assumes Leonard is going to take him to see the Collider, when Leonard in fact plans to take his then-girlfriend Penny. This episode is a collision of sensibilities and assumptions, and, as is often the case, the resultant collision produces unexpected results.

Magnetic Monopole • In "The Monopolar Expedition" (2-23), Sheldon and his posse head off to the North Pole in search of the elusive magnetic monopole. Sheldon sees it as his ticket to the fame he feels he is due—or, more accurately, long *over*due. "If I'm able to detect slow-moving magnetic monopoles there, I will be the scientist to confirm string theory," he says. "People will write books about me." Unfortunately for Sheldon, his elation proves to be premature, and deflation sets in when he realizes he's been punk'd by his own posse. (They cite self-preservation as their justification.)

First theorized by Pierre Curie in 1894, the magnetic monopole, according to Wikipedia, is a "hypothetical particle in particle physics that is a magnet with only one magnetic pole ... Within theoretical physics, some modern approaches predict the existence of magnetic monopoles. Joseph Polchinski, a prominent string-theorist, describes the existence of monopoles as 'one of the safest bets that one can make about physics not yet seen.'"

Jennifer Quellette, in *Discovery News*, explained that:

> [Sheldon] figures finding a magnetic monopole would put him on the fast track for a Nobel Prize. And he would be right. But he shouldn't count on finding one right away; magnetic monopoles have eluded our best scientists for centuries ... Sheldon is a string-theorist, and string theory also predicts the existence of magnetic monopoles. So their discovery would provide a key piece of experimental evidence for this contender for a Grand United Theory meshing general relativity with quantum mechanics.

Neuroscience • In "The Bat Jar Conjecture" (1-13), when Howard, Leonard, and Raj need a fourth for their physics bowl team, Raj suggests Mayim Bialik, "the girl who played TV's Blossom. She got a PhD in neuroscience or something."

The Society for Neuroscience (sfn.org) defines the field as "the study of the nervous system," which "advances the understanding of human thought, emotion, and behavior."

Parallel Universes • In "The Desperation Emanation" (4-5), Sheldon says, "It just occurred to me, if there are an infinite number of parallel universes, in one of them there's probably a Sheldon who doesn't believe parallel universes exist." Also, in "The Gothowitz Deviation" (3-3), Sheldon asserts that, "While I subscribe to the many worlds theory, which posits the existence of an infinite number of Sheldons in an infinite number of universes, I assure you that in none of them am I dancing." Later, though, Sheldon changes his tune. In "The Agreement Dissection" (4-21), the girls take him out dancing, as he and Amy catch Saturday-night fever. (And, yes, it turns out that Sheldon *can* dance.)

Coined in 1895 by American philosopher and psychologist William James, the theory of parallel universes postulates the existence of other universes, or multiverses, which have been hypothesized in fiction, religion, philosophy, and the sciences. A popular theme in comic books, the presence of parallel universes in contemporary fiction is extensive. Among many others, Stephen King's Dark Tower series postulates multiple worlds, as does Philip Pullman's His Dark Materials trilogy, in which a "subtle knife" is used to cut out windows to other worlds.

M Theory (also known as string theory) • In "The Einstein Approximation" (3-14), Sheldon goes job hunting and, when asked what his last job was, he explains that he was a "senior theoretical particle physicist at Caltech, focusing on M theory, or, in layman's terms, string theory."

In "The Jerusalem Duality" (1-12), a Korean child prodigy named Dennis Kim sees formulae on a whiteboard in Sheldon's office and says, "The string theory research being done here is nothing but a dead end." Sheldon, of course, defends his turf and hotly protests, but Kim shrugs it off. "Well, obviously you don't see it, but trust me, you will."

Dr. Patricia Schwarz, who received her PhD in physics from Caltech, simplifies the definition of string theory for those of us who don't have a science background. On her website (super-stringtheory.com), she begins her explanation:

> Think of a guitar string that has been tuned by stretching the string under tension across the guitar. Depending on how the string is plucked and how much tension is in the string, different musical notes will be created by the string. These musical notes could be said to be excitation modes of that guitar string under tension.
>
> In a similar manner, in string theory, the elementary particles we observe in particle accelerators could be thought of as the "musical notes" or excitation modes of elementary strings.

For another explanation of M theory, go to PBS' Elegant Universe page (pbs.org/wgbh/nova/elegant). And for an authoritative, book-length explication of string theory, read Andrew Zimmerman Jones' *String Theory for Dummies.*

STRING THEORY FOR DUMMIES

· · · · · · · · · · · ·

Explaining the mysteries of string theory is no easy task, but Andrew Zimmerman Jones tackles it in *String Theory for Dummies*. Zimmerman, who had an undergraduate degree in physics from Wabash College, also holds a master's degree in mathematics education from Purdue University.

(continued on next page)

(continued from previous page)

In the book's introduction, he explains why string theory is important: it may hold the key to unlocking many secrets of the universe.

"Understanding the implications of string theory means understanding profound aspects of our reality at the most fundamental levels. Are there parallel universes? Is there only one law of nature or infinitely many? Why does our universe follow the laws it does? Is time travel possible? How many dimensions does our universe possess? Physicists are passionately seeking answers to these questions."

The 384-page book helps unravel the mysteries of string theory to laymen, who aren't scientists but, like them, are consumed with curiosity about the big questions the universe poses.

Quantum Mechanics • Per Wikipedia, quantum mechanics is "the body of scientific principles that explains the behavior of matter and its interactions with energy on the scale of atoms and atomic particles."

When Sheldon first meets Penny ("Pilot," 1-1), she sees the whiteboard at his apartment and says, "This is really impressive." Sheldon preens and explains, "Yeah, well, it's just some quantum mechanics, with a little string theory doodling around the edges."

Schrodinger's Cat • In "The Tangerine Factor" (1-17), Sheldon explains to Penny that her dilemma about Leonard—should she go out with him or not?—could be considered in light of Schrodinger's Cat. The comparison is lost on her, but Leonard, who also solicits Sheldon for advice, immediately gets it. "Wow," says Leonard, "that's brilliant."

Schrodinger's Cat doesn't refer to an actual cat, but a fictional one in a hypothetical situation. In *Black Holes and Baby Universes*, Stephen Hawking sheds light on this dark matter: "In the case of Shrodinger's Cat, there are two histories that are reinforced. In one the cat is shot, while in the other it remains alive. In quantum theory both possibilities can exist together. But some philosophers get themselves tied in knots because they implicitly assume that the cat can only have one history."

Singularity • In "The Cruciferous Vegetable Amplification" (4-2), Sheldon works out a timeline of his life, taking into account his family history. He concludes, "In order to live long enough to fuse my consciousness with cybernetics, I need to change my diet." He changes it, but only temporarily. Cruciferous vegetables, as he discovers, have a particularly noisy and noxious side effect. And, besides, he dearly loves Indian food, Chinese food, and fast food, which he refuses to give up.

In that episode, Sheldon was referring to technological, not gravitational, Singularity. Vernor Vinge came up with the term. He theorized that the exponential growth in technology means that in the future, possibly in as soon as a few decades, superhuman artificial intelligence will appear.

Futurist Ray Kurzweil, who has written extensively about technological Singularity, postulates that once it occurs, the dominant life form on Earth will no longer be mankind but sentient artificial intelligences, or humans who have been cybernetically modified— a fusion of man's consciousness with a machine, which will allow him to live forever, free from the biological constraints of being human.

For some mind-stretching reading, check out Kurzweil's *The Singularity Is Near: When Humans Transcend Biology* (2005), an updated synthesis of two of his previous books published in 1990 and 1999. Additionally, a documentary on his life and work, *Transcendent Man*, explicates his vision of technological Singularity. The promise: mankind will soon be able to live forever!

Part 6

THE EPISODE TITLE EXPLICATION

A chronological episode guide

SEASON ONE

1. Pilot (September 24, 2007)

Plot: Penny, a pretty girl who moves in next door to Sheldon and Leonard, stirs things up. Leonard volunteers himself and Sheldon for a knight's errand: to retrieve Penny's TV from her former boyfriend, the muscle-bound Kurt.

Title: none

2. The Big Bran Hypothesis (October 1, 2007)

Plot: Sheldon sneaks into Penny's apartment at night while she's sleeping to clean up, which freaks her out. After Sheldon and Leonard laboriously move a heavy box of unassembled furniture components upstairs to Penny's apartment, Howard and Raj pitch in and take over—or think they do.

Title: Sheldon, in the kitchen, must choose between low-fiber and high-fiber breakfast cereal, and, after hearing Penny rage against his whackadoodle cleaning expedition at her apartment, he opts for high fiber.

3. The Fuzzy Boots Corollary (October 8, 2007)

Plot: Leonard goes out on a "date" with Penny. Leslie gets more than Leonard's hopes up, but ultimately leaves him high and dry.

Title: Leonard contemplates adopting a cat, whom he considers naming "Fuzzy Boots."

4. The Luminous Fish (October 15, 2007)

Plot: Sheldon's honesty with his new boss gets him fired. Trouble looms as he careens from activity to activity to keep himself occupied.

Title: Sheldon conducts an experiment that enables him to make luminescent goldfish, which he keeps in a bowl by his bed.

5. The Hamburger Postulate (October 22, 2007)

Plot: Leslie seduces Leonard and, after they make the beast with two backs, abruptly abandons him.

Title: Sheldon has a dilemma: he usually eats a Big Boy hamburger on Tuesday nights, but should he switch to eating a hamburger at the Cheesecake Factory instead?

6. The Middle Earth Paradigm (October 29, 2007)

Plot: Penny invites Sheldon, Leonard, Howard, and Raj to a Halloween costume party.

Title: Leonard dresses up as an inhabitant of Middle-earth: a hobbit named Frodo who hails from the Shire in J.R.R. Tolkien's epic quest novel *The Lord of the Rings*.

7. The Dumpling Paradox (November 5, 2007)

Plot: Howard gets it on with Christy, Penny's friend from back home who's visiting. Penny, to the boys' astonishment, excels at *Halo*.

Title: Howard's absence from dinner at a local Chinese restaurant upsets Sheldon: "Our entire order is predicated on four dumplings and four entrees divided among four people."

8. The Grasshopper Experiment (November 12, 2007)

Plot: Raj reluctantly goes on a blind date arranged by his parents. Penny practices her bartending skills on the boys.

Title: A reference to the alcoholic drink Penny serves Raj, a Grass-hopper. "It's a sweet, green miracle," he tells her.

9. The Cooper-Hofstadter Polarization (March 17, 2008)

Plot: Sheldon and Leonard's friendship temporarily unravels when the two come to blows after an argument about an academic paper; Leonard wants to present it at a talk, but Sheldon forbids it. Penny helps Leonard prune his outdated wardrobe in the hopes they can find something appropriate for him to wear to the talk.

Title: Sheldon and Leonard have an academic dispute and occupy opposite poles.

10. The Loobenfeld Decay (March 24, 2008)

Plot: In an elaborate effort to avoid attending Penny's workshop production of *Reds*, Leonard tells a white lie, and Sheldon builds it to ludicrous heights.

Title: Sheldon recruits a colleague at work who poses as Toby Loobenfeld.

11. The Pancake Batter Anomaly (March 31, 2008)

Plot: When Sheldon gets sick, Leonard, Howard, and Raj batten down the hatches and hide out at a *Planet of the Apes* movie marathon.

Title: Leonard mixes pancake batter in the measuring cup that Sheldon uses to measure his "fluid intake and output," i.e., his urine. Leonard, of course, is pissed off.

12. The Jerusalem Duality (April 14, 2008)

Plot: Think *Survivor*, in which Sheldon must outwit, outplay, and outlast a child prodigy his boss is wooing to join the school. With the help of the other boys, Sheldon prevails.

Title: Sheldon cooks up a chimerical plan to establish a "Nuevo Jerusalem" in the Senora desert of Mexico, in an attempt to win a Nobel Peace Prize.

13. The Bat Jar Conjecture (April 21, 2008)

Plot: Sheldon forms his own team named AA (Army Ants) for the physics bowl competition. The other boys recruit Leslie Winkle as the fourth for their team, named Perpetual Motion Squad (PMS), to go up against Sheldon's.

Title: Leonard gives Sheldon a Batman cookie jar as a gift to cushion the blow that will inevitably come when Sheldon is kicked off the team.

14. The Nerdvana Annihilation (April 28, 2008)

Plot: The boys chip in to buy a life-size movie prop that dominates Leonard and Sheldon's living room and, temporarily, their lives. Leonard is distraught when Penny disparages him for collecting comic book memorabilia.

Title: Howard attempts to change Leonard's decision to sell a box of his prized collectibles to Stewart, the owner of a local comic book store, because of Penny's derisive comments. Howard objects: "You can't do that. Look at what you've created here. It's like Nerdvana!"

15. The Pork Chop Indeterminacy (May 5, 2008)

Plot: Sheldon's sister visits him at work, and the other boys do their best to woo her. Raj becomes a test subject at the School of Pharmacology and takes new drugs designed to combat panic attacks and social disorders. The drugs have unexpected side effects and work temporarily, but they wear off at the worst possible time.

Title: Howard to Sheldon: "I'd kill my rabbi with a pork chop to be with your sister."

16. The Peanut Reaction (May 12, 2008)

Plot: Howard makes a big sacrifice at the hospital to buy time, getting Leonard out of his apartment so the others can surprise him with a birthday party—his first ever. Sheldon, who is with Penny at a retail electronics store to buy Leonard a gift, becomes sidelined when befuddled customers ask him for advice on computer-related equipment.

Title: Howard's big sacrifice is deliberately inducing an allergic reaction to peanuts.

17. The Tangerine Factor (May 19, 2008)

Plot: About to go on their first date, Penny and Leonard each seek help from Sheldon, who gives both of them the same advice. Penny has boyfriend problems, which Leonard aggravates in the process of trying to help.

Title: Sheldon wants to learn how to speak Mandarin because he's convinced that Szechuan Palace is playing fowl—er, foul—with his food order.

SEASON TWO

1. The Bad Fish Paradigm (September 22, 2008)

Plot: Sheldon can't keep a secret, and is prepared to take draconian actions to keep from spilling the beans. The boys discuss Leonard's chances of successfully dating Penny.

Title: Leonard explains to Howard and Raj that his relationship with Penny is slowing down, for which he serves up a food analogy: "I'm really enjoying this meal. I'm going to slow down and savor it." But Howard disagrees: "No, it's like 'this fish tastes bad, so I'm going to slow down and spit it out.'" After Penny puts him off for a second date, Leonard reluctantly agrees that he is indeed the "bad fish."

2. The Codpiece Topology (September 29, 2008)

Plot: Leonard finds a new girlfriend (or thinks he has) when he once again hooks up with Leslie Winkle, who, in a confrontation with Sheldon, draws a line in the sand. She forces the issue and puts Leonard on the spot—choose between her viewpoint or Sheldon's. Also, Sheldon debates whether or not to return to the local Renaissance Faire, and he does so in a new costume.

Title: Sheldon, who is upset at the historical inaccuracies he's observed at the Renaissance Faire, explains to the other boys that it's "More of a Medieval/Age of Enlightenment/any-excuse-to-wear-a-codpiece fair."

3. The Barbarian Sublimation (October 6, 2008)

Plot: Unsatisfied with how things are going in her life, Penny seeks semipermanent refuge in the virtual world of *Age of Conan*.

Title: The title refers to *Age of Conan*, an online multiplayer role-playing game exploring the virtual world of the Hyborean Age in Robert E. Howard's Conan story cycle. This is the game that Sheldon is playing while Penny sits in his apartment waiting for a locksmith.

4. The Griffin Equivalency (October 13, 2008)

Plot: Raj finds fame too intense a brew and, after being singled out by *People* magazine, lets it go straight to his head, alienating the other boys in the process. Penny escorts an inebriated Raj to a reception in his honor, as he's one of the thirty people under thirty who has made a difference in his field.

Title: As a child, Sheldon considered his ideal pet to be a griffin, a mythological beast that's half eagle, half lion. He humorously suggests they create a griffin to take Raj's place: "My point is, if Koothrappali is moving on to a new life of shallow, undeserved fame, perhaps this is an opportunity to create a better cohort."

5. The Euclid Alternative (October 20, 2008)

Plot: After Sheldon's backseat driving drives his friends to complete exasperation, they urge him to get a learner's permit so he can drive himself to work. Also, Sheldon, who is highly skilled at computer games, curiously proves incapable of driving a simulated car.

Title: Euclid Avenue is a road that Penny takes when she is pressured to drive Sheldon to work, which she does with great reluctance.

6. The Cooper-Nowitski Theorem (November 3, 2008)

Plot: A female graduate student not-so-gently injects herself into Sheldon's life, becoming a Yoko Ono to his John Lennon.

Title: Sheldon is joined at the hip, so to speak, with a graduate student named Ramona Nowitski, who is obviously impressed with Sheldon's most magnificent organ—his brain.

7. The Panty Piñata Polarization (November 10, 2008)

Plot: Penny strikes back after Sheldon bans her from his apartment. The uncivil war that results escalates, until Penny plays a trump card: she calls Sheldon's mother, who intercedes.

Title: At opposite poles, Sheldon and Penny are both stubborn and refuse to give an inch. Sheldon raises the bar, so to speak, by hanging her lingerie on a nearby telephone pole. When Penny asks how she's supposed to retrieve her clothes, Sheldon says, "I suggest you get a very long stick and play panty piñata."

8. The Lizard-Spock Expansion (November 17, 2008)

Plot: Howard tries to impress Dr. Stephanie Barnett, whom he's picked up in a bar, by promising to let her drive the Mars Rover. She's smitten, but not by him; she wants Leonard.

Title: A variation of the classic hand game "rock, paper, scissors," to which has been added: "lizard, Spock."

9. The White Asparagus Triangulation (November 24, 2008)

Plot: Sheldon does everything he can to stack the deck in Leonard's favor with Dr. Stephanie Barnett, even if it means perpetuating ruses that, in the end, backfire.

Title: The title refers to a jar of white asparagus that Sheldon pretends he can't open, so as to allow Leonard to open it and thus show a feat of strength that he thinks will impress Dr. Barnett.

10. The Vartabedian Conundrum (December 8, 2008)

Plot: Leonard's relationship with Stephanie hits turbulence when Leonard realizes she's making inroads into his life—specifically, his bedroom. He wants her in his life, but not *living* with him. Fortunately, Penny offers useful advice that he takes to heart. Also, Sheldon, a hypochondriac, is convinced he's sick, and he pesters Stephanie until she's forced to shut him up by performing a "Sheldondectomy."

Title: Mrs. Vartabedian, a tenant in Sheldon's apartment complex, is cited by Leonard as a person with whom he takes breakfast—a white lie.

11. The Bath Item Gift Hypothesis (December 15, 2008)

Plot: Sheldon is on the horns of a dilemma. It's Christmas, and when Penny tells him that she got him a gift, he's distressed because social protocol requires he must reciprocate. So he goes shopping with Howard and Raj to buy an appropriate gift. Also, a one-sided bromance develops between Leonard and a new colleague, Dr. David Underhill, who recently won a MacArthur genius grant. Things get complicated when a romance develops between David and Penny.

Title: Howard and Raj help Sheldon buy a gift for Penny at a Bath & Body Works–type store.

12. The Killer Robot Instability (January 12, 2009)

Plot: Tired of Howard's unsolicited and unwelcome personal comments, Penny opens up with both barrels and demolishes his self-esteem, humiliating him in front of the other boys. Also, Howard's killer robot named M.O.N.T.E. (Mobile Omnidirectional Neutralization and Termination Eradicator) proves to be outmatched by the aptly named Kripke Killer robot.

Title: Leonard tells Penny that what she saw burst through his apartment door as she was walking up the stairs was a "killer robot. We built it."

13. The Friendship Algorithm (January 19, 2009)

Plot: Sheldon goes out of his way to befriend Kripke, because he needs access to the open science grid computer, to which he mistakenly believes Kripke is key.

Title: Sheldon wants to write an algorithm that he hopes will yield a "friendship" with Kripke, but it's a friendship of convenience, not of substance, and eventually backfires.

14. The Financial Permeability (February 2, 2009)

Plot: As a result of covering her ex-boyfriend's bills (notably, a large court fee), Penny is strapped financially and reluctantly takes a loan from Sheldon to tide her over.

Title: Penny experiences temporary financial difficulties.

15. The Maternal Capacitance (February 9, 2009)

Plot: When Leonard's psychologist mother, Dr. Beverly Hofstadter, comes to visit, her invasive ways stir things up with everyone, except for Sheldon, who becomes her new BFF.

Title: Leonard's mother has a connection to everyone *but* her son.

16. The Cushion Saturation (March 2, 2009)

Plot: Leslie Winkle seduces Howard, whom she treats as a stud puppet. There's a great disturbance in the Force, not once but twice, when Sheldon's seat cushion is sent away for repairs and he also discovers that his Chinese food comes from a new restaurant.

Title: A sofa cushion in Sheldon's living room is saturated with green ink from a paintball pellet fired from a rifle that Penny accidentally discharged.

17. The Terminator Decoupling (March 9, 2009)

Plot: The boys catch a train to San Francisco to attend a symposium, and everyone but Sheldon is surprised and delighted to find that Summer Glau is seated nearby. Also, Sheldon hatches a chimerical plan to meet Nobel Prize–winning scientist Dr. George Smoot at the conference, in an attempt to collaborate with him on a paper.

Title: A reference to actress Summer Glau, who plays Cameron, a female cyborg/Terminator, in *Terminator: The Sarah Conner Chronicles*.

18. The Work Song Nanocluster (March 16, 2009)

Plot: After Penny enlists Sheldon to help in her new part-time business, they dragoon Leonard, Howard, and Raj into pitching in during an all-nighter to fill a large order of Penny Blossom hair barrettes.

Title: The work song is a sea chantey Penny and Sheldon sing together to make the time pass more quickly as they construct the Penny Blossoms.

19. The Dead Hooker Juxtaposition (March 30, 2009)

Plot: When beautiful blonde Alicia moves in upstairs, she rocks Sheldon's world, and everyone else's, too—especially Penny's, who becomes protective when she sees Alicia taking advantage of Howard, Leonard, and Raj.

Title: Alicia, an aspiring actress, scores a gig on the television show *CSI* as a dead hooker.

20. The Hofstadter Isotope (April 13, 2009)

Plot: On a trip to the comic book store to buy a gift for her nephew, Penny meets Stuart, the store owner, and is charmed; she agrees to goes out on a date with him, to Leonard's obvious distress. Depressed, Leonard goes to a bar with Howard to drown his sorrows and pick up women; they predictably return home empty-handed.

Title: Leonard is jealous of Stuart's budding relationship with Penny, and can't understand her interest in him.

21. The Vegas Renormalization (April 27, 2009)

Plot: The boys go to Las Vegas to cheer up a morose Leonard, but it's Howard who is clinically depressed and tweets his despair, prompting Leonard and Raj to gift him with a "Jewish girlfriend experience." Meanwhile, Sheldon, with his heart set on spending a quiet weekend alone, accidentally locks himself out of his apartment without his spare key, which Penny left in his apartment. He must stay with Penny until the others come home.

Title: The boys go to Vegas, baby!

22. The Classified Materials Turbulence (May 4, 2009)

Plot: The boys pitch in to help Howard, whose toilet on the International Space Station (ISS) will fail after its installation. Also, Leonard deliberately sabotages Stuart's budding relationship with Penny.

Title: A critical component on the ISS, the space toilet is classified, and everything about it is on a "need to know" basis. Its failure after a repair is made creates turbulence—all the American astronauts go for an unscheduled space walk to relieve themselves.

23. The Monopolar Expedition (May 11, 2009)

Plot: The boys' jubilation at Sheldon's announcement that he has accepted an invitation to go to the North Pole is premature: he has no plans to go alone, and persuades them all to come along as his support team. Also, Penny's true feelings for Leonard, long submerged, finally come to the surface. She cares more for him than she's let on, which Leonard already knows because of what happened on Penny's date with Stuart: in a make-out session with him in his car, she reveals what's *really* on her mind when she says the "L" word: *Leonard*. It's a deflating moment for Stuart, but an inflating one for Leonard, who is jubilant.

Title: It refers to the summer-long trip the four boys take to the North Pole after Sheldon's proposal to detect magnetic monopoles, submitted to the National Science Foundation, is approved.

SEASON THREE

1. The Electric Can Opener Fluctuation (September 21, 2009)

Plot: Sheldon resigns from the university after prematurely, and erroneously, informing his colleagues via e-mail that he's confirmed string theory. Leonard brings back a snowflake frozen in resin from the North Pole for Penny.

Title: An electric can opener used to produce spurious data adversely affects Sheldon's experiment.

2. The Jiminy Conjecture (September 28, 2009)

Plot: Sheldon, bugged by Howard's assertion that a cricket in his apartment is a common field cricket and not, as he believes, a snowy tree cricket, agrees to a bet and loses big-time. Also, Leonard's relationship with Penny hits a little unexpected turbulence.

Title: Sheldon names the cricket in his apartment Jiminy.

3. The Gothowitz Deviation (October 5, 2009)

Plot: Howard hatches a plot: he and Raj dress up in goth clothing with the hope of meeting goth chicks at a nightclub. To Leonard's annoyance, Sheldon uses behavioral modification techniques associated with psychologist B.F. Skinner on Penny.

Title: Goth + Wolowitz = Gothowitz.

4. The Pirate Solution (October 12, 2009)

Plot: After pursuing a dead-end project to predict the composition of trans-Neptunian objects, and with no other fields of study to explore, Raj is concerned he'll lose his job and get deported.

Title: Sheldon suggests piracy as an alternate vocation for Raj.

5. The Creepy Candy Coating Corollary (October 19, 2009)

Plot: Leonard persuades Penny to fix Howard up, and the two of them go on a double date with Howard and Penny's friend Bernadette. Sheldon takes on Wil Wheaton in a Warlords of Ka'a tournament at the local comic book store.

Title: Penny compares Howard's personality to a "creepy candy coating" because he's sweet inside but he comes across as skeevy.

6. The Cornhusker Vortex (November 2, 2009)

Plot: Wanting to be a bigger part of Penny's world, Leonard, to everyone's dismay, watches football with her "peeps," with whom he has absolutely nothing in common. Howard and Raj's friendship temporarily unspools when they have a lovers' spat.

Title: Penny's home team is the Nebraska Cornhuskers.

7. The Guitarist Amplification (November 9, 2009)

Plot: Leonard is upset and argues with Penny who has invited her hometown friend Justin to sleep on her couch.

Title: Justin is a guitarist.

8. The Adhesive Duck Deficiency (November 16, 2009)

Plot: An injured Penny badgers a reluctant Sheldon to help get her to the emergency room. The other boys go off to the high hills of Whittier, California, to watch the Leonid meteor shower.

Title: Penny's tub has no traction to minimize slippage, like the adhesive ducks that line Sheldon's; that deficiency lands Penny in the hospital.

9. The Vengeance Formulation (November 23, 2009)

Plot: Sheldon is made the laughingstock at work after Kripke executes a well-planned practical joke; Sheldon swiftly retaliates with overwhelming force. Bernadette and Howard are at an impasse in their fledgling relationship because he's clueless that she's ready to take it to the next level.

Title: After Kripke's practical joke, Sheldon strikes back with a vengeance.

10. The Gorilla Experiment (December 7, 2009)

Plot: Wanting to be able to talk with Leonard about his work, Penny beseeches Sheldon to teach her the basics of physics, with predictable results. Also, Howard flaunts his new girlfriend Bernadette at the university's cafeteria.

Title: Sheldon compares teaching rudimentary physics to Penny to teaching sign language to Koko the gorilla.

11. The Maternal Congruence (December 14, 2009)

Plot: Dr. Beverly Hofstadter pays Leonard a visit around Christmastime, but there's not much to celebrate: she's psychoanalyzing Penny and everyone else. Beverly bonds with Penny over drinks, and lowers her inhibitions.

Title: She's b-a-a-c-k!

12. The Psychic Vortex (January 11, 2010)

Plot: Penny and Leonard agree to disagree about the validity of her psychic's predictions, which she didn't see coming (ironic, right?). Raj and his new wingman Sheldon mix in at a university mixer.

Title: Penny believes in psychics, but Leonard clearly does not.

13. The Bozeman Reaction (January 18, 2010)

Plot: Sheldon's apartment is broken into and ransacked, leaving him to conclude that it's time to move to a safer city.

Title: A reference to Bozeman, Montana, where Sheldon moves, albeit temporarily.

14. The Einstein Approximation (February 1, 2010)

Plot: Sheldon's intellectually stuck and can't unstick himself until he sees the problem he's attempting to solve in a new light. Disco roller skating is the order of the day for everyone but Sheldon.

Title: Einstein's perfunctory bureaucratic job gives Sheldon food for thought.

15. The Large Hadron Collision (February 8, 2010)

Plot: Leonard lucks out at work and gets to go to Switzerland to attend a conference and visit the Large Hadron Collider. For the trip, he can bring whomever he wishes, and he chooses Penny. But Sheldon, who sees himself as a more logical choice, is dead set on going, which results in an inevitable collision.

Title: A reference to the Large Hadron Collider near Geneva, Switzerland.

16. The Excelsior Acquisition (March 1, 2010)

Plot: The boys are jazzed at the prospect of meeting Stan Lee at a local comic book store, especially Sheldon, whose plans are foiled when he's ordered to appear in traffic court on the same day.

Title: Stan Lee's autobiography is called *Excelsior!*

17. The Precious Fragmentation (March 8, 2010)

Plot: At a garage sale, the boys buy a box containing pop culture memorabilia that appears to be miscellaneous junk. But a golden treasure lies therein: a valuable prop ring from Peter Jackson's film adaptation of *The Lord of the Rings*.

Title: The obsessed character Gollum, from *The Lord of the Rings*, calls the One Ring "my Precious."

18. The Pants Alternative (March 22, 2010)

Plot: Sheldon's got stage fright but has to accept the university's Chancellor's Award. Fortunately, his friends all pitch in to help, though he turns out to be his own worst enemy after drinking too much wine.

Title: Sheldon "drops trou" and then kicks his pants off—in public, onstage, in front of his peers. (No wonder they think he's a little strange.)

19. The Wheaton Recurrence (April 12, 2010)

Plot: Bowling team leader Sheldon is determined to win a match against Stuart's team, whose last-minute substitution of Wil Wheaton inflames Sheldon.

Title: Wil Wheaton returns to bedevil Sheldon.

20. The Spaghetti Catalyst (May 3, 2010)

Plot: In the wake of Leonard and Penny's recent breakup, Sheldon must decide to whom he owes his principal allegiance.

Title: Sheldon eats a spaghetti dinner at Penny's.

21. The Plimpton Stimulation (May 10, 2010)

Plot: Sheldon plays host to Dr. Elizabeth Plimpton, a respected physicist from Princeton, when she's in town to visit Caltech.

Title: Dr. Plimpton has more on her mind than academics: she is sexually aggressive with Leonard, Raj, and Howard.

22. The Staircase Implementation (May 17, 2010)

Plot: A flashback: the story of when Leonard met Sheldon.

Title: Sheldon insists that if a staircase is off by two millimeters, a person will trip—an experiment he tried out on his father during his youth.

23. The Lunar Excitation (May 24, 2010)

Plot: The boys set up a laser on Sheldon's apartment rooftop to bounce its beam off a reflector left by the *Apollo 11* astronauts. Also, Sheldon goes on a blind date—something he could never have imagined happening anywhere in the multiverse.

Title: The boys literally shoot for the Moon.

SEASON FOUR

1. The Robotic Manipulation (September 23, 2010)

Plot: Howard gets in a pickle with his salami, and Penny reluctantly drives Sheldon and Amy to their first date.

Title: Howard invents a robotic hand to give him a hand.

2. The Cruciferous Vegetable Amplification (September 30, 2010)

Plot: Sheldon is adamant that he's going to live long enough to witness, and be part of, the Singularity, when his consciousness can be integrated with a machine and make him immortal. In the meantime, he's got to protect his too-fragile biological body from possible injury.

Title: Sheldon plans to forgo pizza, his usual Thursday-night meal, for a cruciferous vegetable: Brussels sprouts.

3. The Zazzy Substitution (October 7, 2010)

Plot: Amy commits an unforgivable sin against Sheldon, prompting him to immediately dump her and adopt a clowder as a substitute.

Title: He names one of the cats "Zazzy."

4. The Hot Troll Deviation (October 14, 2010)

Plot: Raj and Sheldon go to war when, while sharing Sheldon's office, Raj deliberately provokes him by bringing in, as Sheldon terms it, a "giant, big-ass desk."

Title: Howard is *so* busted! Bernadette catches him red-handed (well, maybe chafed) having virtual sex with a "hot troll" avatar online, who proves to be a male janitor at Caltech.

5. The Desperation Emanation (October 21, 2010)

Plot: Invoking his pact with Howard, Leonard gets fixed up on a blind date through Bernadette; meanwhile, Sheldon's got women problems: Amy wants to introduce him to her mother.

Title: Leonard is desperate for a girlfriend.

6. The Irish Pub Formulation (October 28, 2010)

Plot: When Raj's baby sister Priya comes to town, he's overly protective and wants to keep the other boys away lest they have impure thoughts, which Leonard does.

Title: Sheldon perpetuates a ruse that involves an Irish pub to help cover up Leonard's white lie.

7. The Apology Insufficiency (November 4, 2010)

Plot: Howard is up for a new job that requires security clearance, and he asks his friends for their help, since the FBI will be interviewing all of them. But they prove to be more of a hindrance, especially Sheldon, and Howard doesn't get the clearance.

Title: Sheldon tries, in his own unique way, to apologize to Howard, but it's not enough.

8. The 21-Second Excitation (November 11, 2010)

Plot: The boys stand in line to get into a theater showing *Indiana Jones and the Raiders of the Lost Ark*, only to be thwarted by Sheldon's nemesis, Wil Wheaton. Meanwhile, a slumber party for the girls turns out to be contentious.

Title: George Lucas adds twenty-one seconds of new footage to *Indiana Jones and Raiders of the Lost Ark*.

9. The Boyfriend Complexity (November 18, 2010)

Plot: Penny's father, Wyatt, visits her, and she tells him what he wants to hear: that she and Leonard are still a couple, even though they aren't.

Title: Leonard poses as Penny's active, not former, boyfriend.

10. The Alien Parasite Hypothesis (December 9, 2010)

Plot: After a girls' night out, when Amy spies Penny's former boyfriend Zack Johnson, she has an uncharacteristic response: she's hot for him. Sheldon dutifully steps in to help arrange an assignation, since he's a boy who's a friend but not a boyfriend.

Title: A reference to one of several theories postulated by Sheldon regarding Amy's behavior.

11. The Justice League Recombination (December 16, 2010)

Plot: To win "Best Group Costume" at Stuart's comic book shop competition, the boys enlist the help of Zack and Penny, who come dressed, respectively, as Superman and Wonder Woman to round out their team, the Justice League of America.

Title: The boys dress up in superhero costumes.

12. The Bus Pants Utilization (January 6, 2011)

Plot: Leonard comes up with a physics application (or "app") for mobile phones, and as usual, Sheldon wants to be the leader.

Title: When Sheldon rides the bus, he wears a separate pair of pants to protect himself from the effluvium often found on the seats.

13. The Love Car Displacement (January 20, 2011)

Plot: The boys (Sheldon, Leonard, Howard, and Raj) and the girls (Penny, Bernadette, and Amy) go to a resort hotel at Big Sur, twenty-six miles south of Carmel, California. The purpose: to speak at the Institute of Interdisciplinary Studies' symposium on "current scientific research on societal interactions."

Title: With Bernadette driving and Howard riding shotgun, it's the "love car" as far as Howard is concerned.

14. The Thespian Catalyst (February 3, 2011)

Plot: After receiving unexpected negative feedback from graduate students after his lecture, Sheldon asks Penny for help. Meanwhile, Raj has fantasies about Bernadette—it was bound to happen after she flattered him earlier.

Title: Sheldon takes acting lessons from Penny.

15. The Benefactor Factor (February 10, 2011)

Plot: The university president drafts the boys to show up and strut their intellectual stuff at a fund-raising dinner, hoping to raise millions. Sheldon makes a belated (and soon to be regretted) appearance, and Leonard gets taken for a ride: one wealthy donor, old enough to be his mother, has designs on him.

Title: The president of Caltech courts wealthy donors at the fund-raising dinner.

16. The Cohabitation Formulation (February 17, 2011)

Plot: It's a game of musical chairs: as the relationship between Howard and Bernadette heats up, he moves in with her—and soon moves out, when she makes it clear that she's not going to be his substitute mother.

Title: Howard temporarily cohabits with Bernadette.

17. The Toast Derivation (February 24, 2011)

Plot: Sheldon, whose apartment has traditionally been the gathering place for the boys, assumes he's the leader of the pack, the one who calls the shots, but Amy explains, "I think it's time to face the fact that Leonard is the nucleus of your social group. Where he goes, the group goes." Oh, the horror!

Title: In lieu of the boys' Thursday-night get-together at Leonard and Sheldon's for pizza, a long-standing tradition of eight years, Leonard decides to go to Raj's place because Priya is there.

When a toast is proposed, Priya asks why it's so called, and Leonard, in Sheldon's absence, matter-of-factly explains its Roman origin, to which Howard says, "Sheldon tells it better."

18. The Prestidigitation Approximation (March 10, 2011)

Plot: Sheldon goes bonkers when he can't figure out one of Howard's card tricks.

Title: "Prestidigitation" means "sleight of hand" and refers to magic tricks. Howard uses this technique to stymie Sheldon, who goes to great lengths to replicate it using science, but fails.

19. The Zarnecki Incursion (March 31, 2011)

Plot: After Todd Zarnecki breaks into Sheldon's *World of Warcraft* account and steals all his virtual goodies, the posse saddles up and heads to Carlsbad, California, to recover the goods and teach him a lesson. The much-needed lesson is taught not by Sheldon's hand but via Penny's well-placed foot.

Title: Zarnecki is a virtual thief.

20. The Herb Garden Germination (April 7, 2011)

Plot: Curious about meme propagation, Amy and Sheldon release pairs of rumors simultaneously to see which one takes root within their social circle; one rumor is mundane, the other racy. Amy tells Penny that she's thinking of starting an herb garden and that she and Sheldon are having sex. Of course the sex news makes the rounds quickly, as the garden rumor dies on the vine.

Title: The mundane meme of the herb garden fails to germinate (i.e., propagate).

21. The Agreement Dissection (April 28, 2011)

Plot: Priya slices and dices Sheldon's legally confusing roommate's agreement, to his growing frustration, giving Leonard the upper hand. But drawing on wisdom from *Star Trek: The Original Series*, in a last-minute maneuver, Sheldon takes back the conn.

Title: Held hostage for years by Sheldon's one-sided roommate's agreement, Leonard is delighted when Priya reads it and uses its ambiguity to hamstring Sheldon.

22. The Wildebeest Implementation (May 5, 2011)

Plot: At Amy's insistence, Bernadette infiltrates the Priya/Leonard camp to glean information. Priya, asserts Amy, is "testing B's loyalty to [Penny] and the group." Despite Amy's misgivings, she's a reluctant spy, and finally confesses all in front of Priya and the others when she can't maintain the pretense any longer.

Title: Amy says that a cheetah goes after the vulnerable prey, like the wildebeest, likening Priya to the cheetah and Bernadette to the wildebeest. As Amy points out, Bernadette has "a trusting nature and a teeny, tiny body." In short, she's pretty prey.

23. The Engagement Reaction (May 12, 2011)

Plot: Leonard becomes increasingly stressed out while Penny and Priya bond over his annoying habits, and Howard finally summons the courage to tell his mother about himself and Bernadette: they're more than a couple; they're engaged.

Title: Howard's mother, who is in the bathroom, falls off the toilet after Howard shares the news, and she is rushed to the emergency room.

24. The Roommate Transmogrification (May 19, 2011)

Plot: Bernadette gets her doctorate and a high-paying job, eclipsing Howard's accomplishments. Increasingly irritated by Leonard and Penny pointing out that he's now the only one in the group without a doctorate, Howard's frustration comes to a head when Bernadette gives him a Rolex.

Title: Raj ingratiates himself with Sheldon, his new, temporary roommate; soon Sheldon realizes there's a world of difference in the preferential treatment he gets from Raj, as opposed to Leonard's perfunctory ways.

Part 7

SHEDDING LIGHT ON DARK MATTER

In which we come to an annotated glossary of science fiction, fantasy, popular culture, and other miscellany mentioned on The Big Bang Theory

28 Days Later • A horror film in which zombies ravage London after the inadvertent release of a virus. Directed by Danny Boyle, released in 2002.

In "The Benefactor Factor" (4-15), Leonard mentions this film to Raj, who defends it; he takes Leonard's comments as criticism against Sandra Bullock.

52 • After the conclusion of DC Comics' seven-issue Infinite Crisis, they published a weekly comic book for a year, hence fifty-two issues, with "each issue detailing an actual week chronicling the events that took place during the missing year after the end of Infinite Crisis."

In "The Hofstadter Isotope" (2-20), Sheldon explains to Penny, looking to buy a comic for a nephew, that her random pick is "a superb choice" if he's already read "Infinite Crisis and 52, and is familiar with the reestablishment of the DC Multiverse."

A

A Beautiful Mind • Actor Russell Crowe stars in this film as real-world John Forbes Nash, Jr., a Nobel Laureate in economics. Soon after the film was released, the phrase "beautiful mind" came into common usage to signify a person with a genius-level IQ.

In "Pilot" (1-1), the whiteboards in Sheldon's apartment catch Penny's attention. She realizes her new neighbors are *different*. "So you're like one of those beautiful mind genius guys?" she asks Sheldon, who smiles and says, "Yeah."

Acting textbooks • In "The Thespian Catalyst" (4-14), Sheldon decides he has to take acting lessons to improve his lecturing skills, so he buys four books: *An Actor Prepares* by Stanislavski, *The Technique of Acting* by Stella Adler, *Respect for Acting* by Uta Hagen, and the fictitious *Heyyy, I'm an Actor* by Henry Winkler, who in real life has written a series of children's books centered around a character named Hank Zipzer.

Sheldon tells Penny he'd like "perhaps two" acting lessons because he'd "like to master the craft." In real life, Jim Parsons has a master's degree in acting, and told an interviewer that he would have liked to pursue a doctorate.

Admiral Ackbar • A character from *Star Wars: Return of the Jedi*, who commands a small fleet of ships from the Rebel Alliance in a concerted assault on the second Death Star, located near the planet Endor. When the ships come out of hyperspace, Admiral Ackbar sees a massive fleet of Imperial Cruisers waiting for them, and yells, "It's a trap!"

In "The Dead Hooker Juxtaposition" (2-19), Sheldon says Ackbar's line repeatedly because, as he explains to Penny, "I enjoy mimicry." Given that Sheldon is a master of verbal locution, his interest in mimicry is understandable.

Affleck, Ben • Among many other acting credits, actor Ben Affleck, dressed in skintight red leather, appeared in a 2003 film adaptation of the Marvel Comics series *Daredevil*. Fan reaction to Ben's performance was mixed; some credit his acting as being a factor in the movie earning a 45 percent Tomatometer rating on rottentomatoes.com. Adding insult to injury, on the fan website grouchoreviews.com, a reviewer wrote, "Affleck's lanky, offhand softness hardly suits the superheroic archetype, and his acting ability isn't enough to overcome the basic miscasting."

In "The Spaghetti Catalyst" (3-20), Leonard is moping over his relationship with Penny. When Raj explains that Leonard is "trying to invent that memory-wiper gizmo from *Men in Black*," Sheldon asks, "Is he making any progress? Because I'd like to erase Ben Affleck as Daredevil."

Age of Conan • Best described as a MMORPG (massively multiplayer online role-playing game), this game's full title is *Age of Conan: Hyborian Adventures*. Conan is a barbarian who lives during the Hyborian Age; he hails from Cimmeria, a bleak northern environment. The brainchild of Texas writer Robert E. Howard, who churned out pulp stories for numerous publications, mostly notably *Weird Tales*, Conan's popularity remains undiminished since his first appearance in June 1932, in "People of the Dark" from *Strange Tales of Mystery and Terror*. In 2011, Jason Momoa starred in a remake, *Conan the Barbarian*, directed by Marcus Nispel. (The original, in 1982, starred Arnold Schwarzenegger and was directed by John Milius.)

In "The Barbarian Sublimation" (2-3), Penny learns that Sheldon's alter ego is "Sheldor the Conqueror." As he tells her, "I'm playing *Age of Conan*, an online multiplayer game set in the universe of Robert E. Howard's *Conan the Barbarian*." As he explains more about the game, Penny gets interested and soon becomes obsessed with it. Lacking the positive reinforcement she seeks in real life, Penny finds solace in the fantasy world of *Age of Conan* as "Queen Penelope"—that is, until Howard's avatar shows up for a virtual date and she realizes her addiction has gotten *way* out of hand.

Alf • The extraterrestrial nicknamed ALF (Alien Life Form) was the titular character in a sitcom from 1986 to 1990. Recalling *My Favorite Martian* (1963–1966, a sitcom featuring an alien who crashes and is stranded on Earth), Alf lives in the garage of the Tanner family in suburbia. He hails from the planet Melmac.

In "The Precious Fragmentation" (3-17), a box of auctioned goods from a storage unit yields a touchstone to Howard's past—an Alf doll. It evokes a painful memory long submerged: at age eleven, Howard, abandoned by his father, took solace in the Alf doll his mother bought him, which helped him fall asleep at night. "I used to pretend that my dad had moved to the planet Melmac, and Alf was going to bring him back to me. But he never did. Where's my daddy, puppet? Where is he?"

Amazing Spider-Man #193 • The most popular character in the Marvel Comics universe, Spider-Man's exploits, adventures, and misadventures are recounted in many comic books. In this issue, Peter Parker's girlfriend Mary Jane rejects his marriage proposal.

In "The Guitarist Amplification" (3-7), at Stuart's comic book store, Howard points out to Sheldon that in #193, "Spider-Man loses a big fight and then his girlfriend breaks up with him." It mirrors Leonard's concerns about his ongoing relationship with Penny, because he feels threatened by a former boyfriend crashing on her couch. The worst part is that Howard had offered to buy the comic for Leonard because "it'll help take your mind off things."

AnaMantle HC Cream • According to drugs.com, this medicine is used for "treating pain, itching, soreness, and discomfort due to hemorrhoids" and works by decreasing inflammation around affected areas.

In "The Irish Pub Formulation" (4-6), Sheldon offers some to Leonard, thinking he's afflicted with a bad rash, when in fact it's merely Priya Koothrappali's lipstick.

Android • Not to be confused with robots (mechanical constructs) or George Lucas' droids, androids are staples in science fiction, most notably from the Star Trek universe. In *Star Trek: The Next Generation*, the android Data is a cybernetic Mr. Spock. More machine than man, Data is caught between two worlds but wonders what it would be like to be a man. In *Star Trek: Generations*, Data has a human emotion chip implanted, with predictable results. (For a brilliant take on machine-to-man transformations, read Roger Zelazny's novella, *For a Breath I Tarry*.) Androids also figure prominently in *Blade Runner*, a movie adaptation based on the Philip K. Dick novel *Do Androids Dream of Electric Sheep?*, and in the *Alien* movies, in which Bishop 341-B is a key character.

In "The Cruciferous Vegetable Amplification" (4-2), Sheldon yearns to live long enough to become an android-like being, his consciousness protected by a mechanical shell that can be repaired or replaced, unlike his fragile human body that will eventually grow old and die. To Leonard it's an unfathomable prospect, and he asks Sheldon, "So, you're upset about missing out on becoming some sort of freakish self-aware robot?" To which Sheldon replies, "By *this* much," pointing out a minuscule gap of time on a whiteboard between his current life and "the earliest estimate of the Singularity, when man will be able to transfer his consciousness into machines and achieve immortality."

Apple Computer • Literally started in Steve Jobs' bedroom and then migrated to the garage of his adopted parents' home at 2066 Crist Drive in Los Altos, California, Apple Computer is now Apple Inc., with a market valuation second only to Exxon. (Apple eclipsed its long-standing rival Microsoft in 2010.)

In "The Cruciferous Vegetable Amplification" (4-2), Sheldon, in the form of a mobile virtual presence device, is at the Cheesecake Factory with his friends when he spies one of the Apple cofounders, Steve Wozniak. "Sheldon" rolls over and thinks he's complimenting Wozniak by saying, "I just want to say I'm a big fan. You're my fifteenth favorite technological visionary . . . One of my proudest possessions is a vintage 1977 Apple II."

Sheldon, though, doesn't have an Apple for day-to-day usage; he's been seen with a Dell XPS laptop and also an Alienware M17x Nebula Red laptop.

Apple Genius Bar • Computers aren't toasters. No matter how much you simplify them, they aren't going to be as user-friendly as kitchen appliances. Realizing that, when Apple opened up its line of retail stores, they installed a bar where you can reserve time or walk in with your Apple product to get help with setup, software and hardware issues, peripherals, etc. Especially helpful to baby boomers and older folks who are intimidated by computers, it's a giant leap forward in customer service.

In "The Terminator Decoupling" (2-17), Leonard invites Sheldon to go with him and the other boys to the nearby Apple Store to "make fun of the guys at the Genius Bar," but he declines. "Oh, I always enjoy that, but I'm a little busy." Later, in "The Desperation Emanation" (4-5), we learn that Leonard and Howard have gone to the Genius Bar, dressed in employee T-shirts, in an attempt to pass themselves off as Apple experts to young women whom they want to pick up.

Aquaman • A comic book superhero from the DC Comics universe. He first appeared in *More Fun Comics* #73 in November 1941. Hailing from the legendary city of Atlantis, his powers include healing, telepathy, enhanced senses, and superhuman strength. He is, as his name suggests, especially adept underwater.

In "The Spaghetti Catalyst" (3-20), Raj tells the other boys, "If we were the Justice League, I'd be Aquaman." He later has a change of heart, though, and in "The Justice League Recombination" (4-11), says, "I don't want to be Aquaman. He sucks." We have no idea what caused such a radical change of heart, though having to wear a ridiculous-looking Aquaman costume, replete with a seahorse, is not likely to endear the aquatic superhero to Raj.

Arkham Asylum for the Criminally Insane • From the DC Comics universe, Arkham Asylum is a psychiatric hospital that is a wretched hive of scum and villainy. Its name is a nod to New England horror writer H.P. Lovecraft, who set many of his own tales in the fictional Massachusetts town of Arkham. (It's also the name of a small press, Arkham House, that published Lovecraft's first story collection, as well as Ray Bradbury's and Robert E. Howard's first books.)

In "The Vengeance Formulation" (3-9), after Kripke plays a practical joke on Sheldon, Leonard likens the situation to the Joker's need for revenge after Batman put him in the Arkham Asylum. The prank Sheldon pulls is admittedly classic, though it backfires on him: the trickster tricked!

Asimov's Three Laws of Robotics • In 1942, science-fiction writer Isaac Asimov established these laws in his short story "Runaround":

1. A robot may not injure a human being or, through inaction, allow a human being to come to harm.
2. A robot must obey any orders given to it by human beings, except when such orders would conflict with the First Law.
3. A robot must protect its own existence as long as such protection does not conflict with the First or Second Law.

In "The Fuzzy Boots Corollary" (1-3), Howard and Sheldon are discussing whether or not Sheldon would want to be told if he were a robot, which leads Howard to the conclusion that the laws actually fit Sheldon very well as is.

Atomic clock in Boulder, Colorado • A cesium atomic clock that sets the official time for the United States. It's so accurate that in 60 million years, it will neither gain nor lose one second of time.

In "The Loobenfeld Decay" (1-10), after Sheldon repeatedly bangs on Penny's apartment door late at night, she asks him, "Do you have any idea what time this is?" He takes the rhetorical question literally and explains that of course he knows *exactly* what time it is, citing the accuracy of his atomic watch.

Avatar • James Cameron's visually gorgeous 2009 movie that has earned more money than any other film in motion picture history. The story is set on a fictional world called Pandora, and the mining colony from Earth is hell-bent on exploiting its mineral assets, despite the impact that would have on Pandora's indigenous population, the Na'vi.

The battle scene between the high-tech Earthlings and low-tech Na'vi recalls the similarly technologically unbalanced battle between a garrison of Imperial Troops as they fight the teddy bear–like Ewoks in *Star Wars VI: Return of the Jedi.*

Despite the obvious symbolism in naming the planet Pandora (remember your Greek myths?), *Avatar* is a cautionary tale, perhaps drawing inspiration from Ursula K. Le Guin's novel *The Word for World Is Forest.*

"The Pants Alternative" (3-18) opens with Raj discussing *Avatar*: "Okay, in *Avatar*, when they have sex in Pandora, they hook up their ponytails, so we know their ponytails are junk [genitalia]."

B

Babylon 5 • A science-fiction TV series created by J. Michael Straczynski about a space station called Babylon 5. The first regular series episode aired on January 26, 1994. It ran 110 episodes.

In "The Staircase Implementation" (3-22), a flashback episode, Sheldon's new roommate Leonard invites two of his friends from work, Howard and Raj, over to watch *Babylon 5.* They're sitting down on a new couch Leonard bought for $100, but Sheldon hotly protests the viewing. "We don't watch *Babylon 5* in this apartment," he states. His roommate's agreement with Leonard backs him up.

Baggins, Frodo • The central figure in J.R.R. Tolkien's *The Lord of the Rings*, an epic quest novel in which Frodo, accompanied by his manservant and friend Samwise Gamgee, the other members of the Fellowship of the Ring, and, later, Gollum, journeys on foot to Mount Doom, deep in Mordor, where the evil lord Sauron holds sway. Frodo has to take the über-powerful One Ring back to the Cracks of Doom where it was forged, and destroy it. Frodo lives in a world called Middle-earth; his small corner of the world is colloquially known as the Shire, and formally known as Hobbiton, where he resides at Bag End, a comfy home built into the side of a hill.

In "The Middle Earth Paradigm" (1-6), Leonard dresses up as Frodo Baggins for Penny's Halloween party. Leonard, who is five feet, five inches tall, assumes the identity of Frodo in order to suggest that his self-worth is not tied to his height but to his identity and achievements.

Also, in "The Large Hadron Collision" (3-15), Leonard is about to enjoy dining on Frodo-shaped pancakes until Sheldon whisks his breakfast away. (The specially prepared breakfast was merely a bribe.)

Bat'leth • A four-foot Klingon "sword of honor," the Bat'leth is a steel blade favored among warriors.

In "The Zarnecki Incursion" (4-19), Sheldon and his friends travel to Carlsbad, California, to confront a virtual thief who broke into Sheldon's *World of Warcraft* account. Sheldon shows up with this weapon in hand, which the thief promptly steals.

Had Sheldon actually used it, the "sword of honor" would more properly have been termed "assault with a deadly weapon," which is a felonious charge. In the right hands, a Bat'leth could do a lot of damage, and in the wrong hands, like Sheldon's, it could do even more. (In fact, it has been used in two holdups at 7-Eleven stores in Colorado.)

Batman • Along with Superman, Batman is one of the crown jewels in the DC Comics universe. From his initial appearance in *Detective Comics* #27 (May 1939), Batman—created by artist Bob Kane and writer Bill Finger—has never flagged in popularity. He's a stark contrast to the traditional superhero who relies on a special power to fight crime. Superman, with his biblical overtones, is practically invulnerable, but Batman is human and, thus, more relatable to us mere mortals. Batman uses his brains, his brawn, and his high-tech tools to fight crime in Gotham City. DC has built a formidable media empire around this internationally iconic figure, with comic books, merchandising, a television show, movies, and product tie-ins.

In "The Justice League Recombination" (4-11), Leonard says that for the costume competition at Stuart's comic book store, he wants to be Batman. Who wouldn't? A masked avenger who sallies forth under cover of darkness to wreak havoc on the criminals in Gotham City, Batman has always been cool. Unlike, say, Aquaman, who swims with the fishes.

Batmobile • From the DC Comics universe, the Batmobile is Batman's principal means of automotive transportation (he also has a bad-ass motorcycle). The Batmobile originally appeared as a red sedan in *Detective Comics* #27 (May 1939), and has since evolved into a super-stealth, low-slung, super-fast, heavily armored and intimidating vehicle that produces shock and awe—and involuntary defecation—in most of Batman's enemies.

In "The Euclid Alternative" (2-5), when Howard sets up a computerized driving simulation for Sheldon, whose ongoing need for transportation to work drives everyone crazy, it's no surprise that Sheldon wants his computer vehicle to be the Batmobile. Wonder Woman may have her invisible flying jet, but the Batmobile is da bomb.

Bat-Signal • From the DC Comics universe, this searchlight with the outline of a bat is Gotham City's means of contacting Batman. The Bat-Signal first made its appearance in *Detective Comics* #60 (February 1942). Though Batman surely has a bat-shaped cell phone nowadays, the silhouetted searchlight has psychological value: it foreshadows Batman's imminent arrival.

In "The Vartebedian Conundrum" (2-10), Leonard is horrified at the prospect that he is actually living with his girlfriend Stephanie. Refusing to accept the obvious, Penny points out what's new in his bedroom and what's missing, like his coveted Bat-Signal. Its absence is an obvious and unmistakable sign that Stephanie has indeed taken up residence in Leonard's sanctum sanctorium, his Bat Cave.

Battlestar Galactica • A science-fiction television show that originally aired in 1978, with a spin-off in 1980 and a new reimagining in 2003. The original show, produced by Glen Larson, was inspired by the success of George Lucas' *Star Wars*. It pitted mankind against a race of robots, Cylons. In real life, ILM (Industrial Light & Magic) worked on both, which led to a war of words (a lawsuit) over a war of worlds (their respective fictional universes). In the 1978 version, the space fighter pilot "Starbuck" was played by Dirk Benedict. In the 2003 version, "Starbuck" was played by Katie Sackhoff, as Captain Kara Thrace—a significant casting improvement.

Sheldon's a big fan of *Battlestar Galactica* (the newer version), as is Howard, who is fixated on Captain Thrace—that is, Katie Sackhoff. Specifically, he wants her to climb into his cockpit. Leonard, too, is smitten with the show: he's got an original *Battlestar Galactica* flight suit hanging up in his closet, to Penny's amusement ("The Cooper-Hofstadter Polarization," 1-9).

"Beast with two backs" • In Shakespeare's play *Othello*, Iago says: "I am one, sir, that comes to tell you your daughter and the Moor are now making the beast with two backs." In other words, they're having coitus.

Though Amy Farrah Fowler has no respect for the liberal arts, she's well read enough to be able to cite noteworthy literary references. In "The Alien Parasite Hypothesis" (4-10), Amy, while at a bar with Penny and Bernadette, has her eyes glued to Zack's gluteus maximus at a bar; she's feeling uncharacteristically aroused. When she tells him that they should "make Shakespeare's metaphorical beast with two backs," Zack is understandably confused: a stranger to metaphor, the literary allusion goes *way* over his head.

Beetlejuice • A 1988 film by Tim Burton that starred Michael Keaton as manic "bio-exorcist" Betelgeuse (it's pronounced "Beetlejuice") who bedevils the new family that moves into his home. To summon Betelgeuse, one must say his name three times (which is also how you get rid of him).

In "The Toast Derivation" (4-17), Howard, hearing Sheldon's repetitive knocking at Raj's apartment door, says, "I think it's like Beetlejuice. We said his name too many times."

Berry, Halle • A former beauty queen and model, she's best known as an actress in roles like Jinx, a James Bond girl in *Die Another Day* (2002) with Pierce Brosnan, and Catwoman in a movie of the same name in 2005, for which she won the Golden Raspberry Award for Worst Actress.

Halle Berry has been mentioned in several episodes of *The Big Bang Theory*. Raj dislikes her Catwoman costume, though he's later forced to wear it when their bowling team loses to Stuart; Sheldon, on a sleepover with Howard in his bedroom, finds the large poster of her "a little unnerving," though he admits she's his fifth favorite Catwoman; and Howard calls her a "delicious caramel" when he attempts to explain why he's so attracted to movie stars over the local female talent (i.e., Bernadette) in "The Vengeance Formulation" (3-9).

Bert and Ernie • Two Muppets created by Jim Henson, from the television show *Sesame Street*. Ernie is the troublemaker and Bert is his foil.

In "The Creepy Candy Coating Corollary" (3-5), Penny tells Leonard that she and a friend "made a pact to marry Bert and Ernie. You know, from *Sesame Street*?"

Betty and Veronica • Two characters from the Archie Comics universe. Betty Cooper (the blonde) and Veronica Lodge (the brunette) are both girlfriends of Archie Andrews (lucky dude).

In "The Justice League Recombination" (4-11), the boys take Zack to the local comic book store, where he feasts his eyes and intellect on Archie comics. Sheldon feels that Archie is children's fare that specifically belongs "in the bedrooms of ten-year-old girls." But to each his own; Zack is happy with his "score. I got an Archie, Betty and Veronica, and a Jughead."

Beyoncé • Singer, songwriter, model, and actress Beyoncé Knowles is best known for being the lead singer of all-girl R&B group Destiny's Child; she went on to become a solo artist, and has sold over 75 million records on her own.

In "The Zarnecki Incursion" (4-19), as the boys head to Carlsbad, California, to confront the audacious Todd Zarnecki, Raj offers up music on a compact disc labeled "Beyoncé's Bootylicious Dance Mix." But it's not bootylicious at all; it's a recording of Wagner's "The Ride of the Valkyries," which was used in *Apocalypse Now* (1979) when an air-assault unit used helicopters to attack a Vietnamese village.

Bifurcated uvula • This sounds vaguely obscene, but it isn't. It's also called a "bifid uvula," and is located in the back of the throat. A normally shaped uvula looks like a stalactite, but when bifurcated it looks, oddly, like an upside-down heart.

In "The Irish Pub Formulation" (4-6), Sheldon reveals that he's got an "oddly shaped uvula" and worries that when he yawns, people will see it and ridicule him. Though Sheldon could care less what people *think* about him—they don't even register on his radar, for the most part—he's very conscious about anything that would cause people to ridicule him, because it recalls his painful childhood when bullies would constantly torment him for real or imagined differences.

Big Sur • A famous resort area on the central California coast, twenty-six miles south of Carmel.

In "The Love Car Displacement" (4-13), the boys (Sheldon, Leonard, Howard, and Raj) and the girls (Penny, Bernadette, and Amy) go to Big Sur in a two-car caravan. At a symposium, all seven are on a panel, with Sheldon attempting to moderate a discussion about scientific research on societal interactions, which soon degenerates into a verbal free-for-all about small and large projectiles.

Binks, Jar Jar • From the Star Wars universe, Binks, a Gungan from the planet Naboo, first appeared in *Star Wars Episode 1: The Phantom Menace* (1999). His chief trait is his clumsiness, which nearly gets him killed. He inadvertently plays a crucial role in a force-on-force engagement between his people and the Trade Federation. Jar Jar, to put it mildly, is not a universally beloved character.

In "The 21 Second Excitation" (4-8), Sheldon sees his archnemesis with his friends, waiting to get in at a movie theater, and remarks, "Well, if it isn't Wil Wheaton, the Jar Jar Binks of the Star Trek universe." It's the harshest insult that Sheldon can imagine.

Black-Eyed Peas • Edible beans often used in soul food. Or not.

Actually, it's an American hip-hop supergroup.

In "The Guitarist Amplification" (3-7), Leonard, who is in a relationship with Penny, is upset that she has invited a former boyfriend to sleep on her couch. Leonard ups the ante and suggests, "Why don't you rent some bunk beds and invite the Black-Eyed Peas?"

Given Leonard's petulance, we would not be surprised if Penny gave him a pair of black eyes, because he's being such a huge Dickensian.

Blade Runner • A Ridley Scott film based on the Philip K. Dick novel *Do Androids Dream of Electronic Sheep?* The film stars Harrison Ford as Rick Deckard, a policeman known as a "blade runner," someone who tracks down renegade replicants that, originally designed for menial and/or dangerous work off-world, have illegally returned to Earth.

In "The Peanut Reaction" (1-16), Howard suggests to Leonard that they go to the New Art Theater to see "the revised, definitive cut" of the movie *Blade Runner*, which has eight seconds of new footage. Leonard passes, but interestingly, all four boys are willing to camp out in a long line to see the first *Indiana Jones* movie because twenty-one seconds had been restored. (In real life, though, there has been no such restoration.)

Blogosphere • A blog, or web log, consists of commentary posted on websites or through dedicated sites like Blogger, owned by Google. The collective universe of these blogs, with linkbacks to other websites, forms an international community. There are an estimated 156 million blogs in the blogosphere.

In "The Hamburger Postulate" (1-5), Howard tells Leonard, "The blogosphere is a-buzzing with news of you and Leslie Winkle making . . . bang-bang music." A curious Leonard asks how that happened, and a nonapologetic Howard admits he was the culprit. (He usually is.)

Blue Man Group • An organization that puts on avant-garde, performance art–based shows worldwide. Each performance is composed of three members, who are visually distinctive, with blue skin, no hair, no ears, and no voice. From the official website: "Blue Man Group is best known for its widely popular theatrical shows and concerts that combine music, comedy and multimedia theatrics to produce a totally unique form of entertainment. The blissful party atmosphere created at the live events has become the trademark of a Blue Man Group experience."

In "The Vegas Renormalization" (2-21), Howard is depressed because, though he's in Vegas, his well-laid plans have gone awry: coitus ain't in the picture, as he had hoped. Hoping to raise his spirits, Raj suggests to Leonard that they take him to see the Blue Man Group. But after they see Howard's most recent tweet—a threat to commit suicide by eating peanuts, which he's allergic to—they decide what he needs isn't to see a show but to get relief from his epididymal hypertension (informally known as blue balls).

Bob's Big Boy • A restaurant chain started in 1936 by Bob Wian in Glendale, California, originally named Bob's Pantry. At the request of a customer who wanted something different, Wian "went to work, and the first double-decker hamburger was born." Bob's burger, taste-wise, is far superior to its imitator, the McDonald's Big Mac.

A favorite of Sheldon's, Bob's Big Boy is a classic burger. In "The Irish Pub Formulation" (4-6), Sheldon says that Priya ate a Bob's Big Boy burger for the first time at Toluca Lake, Los Angeles, in 2005.

Bridget Jones's Diary • A book by Helen Fielding published in 1996 and made into a film starring Renée Zellweger in 2001.

In "The Love Car Displacement" (4-13), Raj is in his hotel room at a resort in Big Sur and is settling in for the evening, box of tissues in hand, to watch this movie. "Oh, my God, I'm crying already," he says to himself, before he's interrupted by Sheldon. (Raj has decidedly odd tastes: chick flicks, chick books, and chick TV shows like *Sex in the City*.)

Brobdingnagian • A reference to Jonathan Swift's novel *Gulliver's Travels*. In Brobdingnag, the people are giant, as is everything else. The word has come to refer to anything of abnormally large size.

In "The Hot Troll Deviation" (4-4), egos clash when Sheldon and Raj share an office at work, and Raj moves in what Sheldon terms "a Brobding-nagian monstrosity," a too-large desk. In a case of "mine's bigger than yours," the two size each other up and engage in intraoffice warfare.

Bullock, Sandra • An actress best known by many for her role as a passenger-turned-impromptu bus driver in *Speed* (1994), she also appeared in an Oscar-winning film directed by Clint Eastwood, *Million Dollar Baby* (2004). In her personal life, she is known for having taken leave of her senses when she married Jesse James; when she regained her sanity, she promptly divorced the cheater.

In "The 21 Second Excitation" (4-7), Raj mentions a "new Sandra Bullock movie" as an alternative to seeing *Raiders of the Lost Ark*, if they can't get in. Raj, though, is mistaken because in November 2010, Sandra had no new movie out. Her last movie was 2009's *The Blind Side*.

C

C-3PO • A popular character from the Star Wars universe who first made his appearance in the original *Star Wars* movie (1977). C-3PO is a protocol droid, and his sidekick is R2-D2, a smaller droid. C-3PO, who has the mannerisms of a fussy British butler, hails from the planet Tatooine and was designed to be fluent, as he says, "in over six million forms of communication."

In "The Vegas Renormalization" (2-21), in Sheldon's apartment, while playing a word game, Raj correctly deduces that Leonard is thinking of C-3PO, or, as Raj calls him, "a shiny Sheldon." Sheldon dismisses that comparison, saying, "That's preposterous. I do not resemble C-3PO. Don't get me wrong, I'm flattered, I just don't see it." But, Sheldon, the *rest* of us do . . .

Caligula • A Roman emperor from A.D. 37–41. According to the Encyclopedia Britannica Online, "Accounts of his reign by ancient historians are so biased against him that the truth is almost impossible to disentangle." In films and books, he's most often mad and sexually perverse, due in large part to Malcolm McDowell's portrayal of him in the 1979 film by the late *Penthouse* publisher Bob Guccione.

In "The Toast Derivation" (4-17), Sheldon likens the experience of hanging out at Raj's apartment with Priya to "the last days of Caligula" because "Raj put on reggae music and his sister took off her shoes." Penny's comment: "Oh, the horror."

Camarillo State Mental Hospital • Located in Camarillo, California, this hospital housed mentally ill and developmentally disabled patients. It closed in 1997.

In "The Thespian Catalyst" (4-14), Sheldon imagines seeing it after Penny suggests he improvise during the acting lessons she's giving.

Caprica • A science-fiction television show that airs on Syfy Channel. It's a prequel to the rebooted *Battlestar Galatica*, set fifty-eight years before the Diaspora, in the wake of the Cylon attack.

In "The Irish Pub Formulation" (4-6), Raj expresses surprise that Leonard, a regular viewer, missed an episode. In truth, Leonard took a pass on the show to make time with Raj's hot sister Priya.

Captain America • A superhero from the Marvel Comics universe, whose long lineage dates back to March 1941. When an experimental serum turns Steve Rogers from sickly to superb, he dons a red, white, and blue costume and carries a starred shield bearing the same colors. (He appeared on the silver screen in 2011 in *Captain America: The First Avenger*, starring Chris Evans.)

In "The Boyfriend Complexity" (4-9), the boys are discussing "who's got to be the bravest person in the Marvel universe," as Raj puts it. Howard volunteers: "You want to talk brave, how about Captain America's undocumented Mexican gardener?" At a time when INS is wrestling with a terrestrial alien problem and has no realistic policy in place, Howard has a point; but so does Raj, who concludes that the discussion is becoming inane. "We're having a conversation about probing the heinies of superheroes." Like Wolverine, who is also mentioned in the conversation, Raj has a point.

Captain Marvel • Here's a bit of odd comic book history: both DC Comics and Marvel had claim to this character, but a lawsuit in the late sixties gave Marvel the trademark. DC Comics' superhero of the same name was renamed Shazam, after the word used by Billy Batson to turn himself from a sickly boy to an adult man with marvelous powers. The letters from "Shazam" are an acronym for the legendary figures whose attributes he shares: Solomon (wisdom), Hercules (strength), Atlas (stamina), Zeus (lightning bolts), Achilles (courage), and Mercury (speed).

In "The Codpiece Topology" (2-2), Sheldon explains to Penny that Leonard is having coitus with Leslie Winkle. Sheldon considers her to be "the Doctor Doom to my Mr. Fantastic, the Doctor Octopus to my Spider-Man, the Doctor Sivana to my Captain Marvel." In other words, she's malevolent, diabolical, and indisputably Sheldon's archnemesis at work, just as ill-willed Wil Wheaton is his archnemesis away from the job.

Capybara • A herbivorous, semiaquatic mammal from the order *Rodentia* that can weigh up to 140 pounds. Known for their friendliness, they are excellent swimmers.

In "The Apology Insufficiency" (4-7), Sheldon, over lunch at the university cafeteria, attempts to interject the animal into the conversation because he'd rather not discuss Leonard's ongoing problem with women. Sheldon, who is utterly disinterested in human interactions, is more excited to tell the boys about this mammal that eats its own excrement.

Carney's • A family-owned business established in 1975, this restaurant has two locations in West Hollywood and Studio City. Housed in a yellow converted railroad car, it is best known for heavenly hamburgers and hot dogs.

In "The Irish Pub Formulation" (4-6), Sheldon speaks lovingly of the restaurant, which marries two of his favorite interests: railroad cars and hamburgers.

Cat on a Hot Tin Roof • One of Tennessee Williams' best-known works, this play is about the relationships between family members, notably how everyone deals with Maggie, the "cat."

In "The Thespian Catalyst" (4-14), Penny selects a scene from this play to rehearse with Sheldon, but he doesn't like it. Instead, he opts to dramatize his own work, a dreadful "*Star Trek* fan fiction novella I wrote when I was ten."

Cathy • A newspaper comic strip by cartoonist Cathy Guisewite that ran from November 22, 1976, to October 3, 2010. Available from the Universal Press Syndicate, this humorous, autobiographical strip is about a young woman who is overwhelmed by the many demands of modern life.

In "The Wheaton Recurrence" (3-19), Sheldon brings Penny ice cream as comfort food, saying that he got the idea from *Cathy*, because of its insights into female behavior.

Chamomile tea • According to adagio.com, this tea's name comes from the Greek word for "ground apple." "Considered a remedy for all ills by the ancient Egyptians, this golden herb remains a modern favorite to promote calm and relieve anxiety."

In "The Zarnecki Incursion" (4-19), Sheldon is so upset over the loss of the fruits of his *World of Warcraft* labor—three thousand hours on the computer as a Level 85 Blood Elf, in the guise of Sheldor of Azaroth—that even this tea, which he prefers, cannot "quell the rage in my heart." Sheldon, in other words, is teed off.

Clarinet • A black woodwind instrument that is sometimes called the "licorice stick."

In "The Herb Garden Germination" (4-20), Priya explains to Leonard that her family was worried that Raj was going to be the "clarinet enthusiast," which translates to homosexual—not that there's anything wrong with that. (The bromance between Raj and Howard has merely confused matters for Raj's family.) The sexual symbolism of the clarinet is beyond the scope of this entry, but suffice to say that Raj, who has a crush on Bernadette, wants her to play *his* "clarinet."

Classic text-based computer games from the eighties • A long time ago, computers ran CP/M and DOS, with line-command codes instead of a point-and-click graphical user interface (GUI). The computer games of that era were, of course, also text-based. Now a footnote in the history of computers, text-based games are curiosities; they are a far cry from the sophisticated, graphics-heavy games of today.

In "The Irish Pub Formulation" (4-6), Sheldon explains to Leonard that he's "found an emulator online that lets you play classic text-based computer games from the eighties." Though primitive compared to current games, the text-only games provide Sheldon with fond memories of his early exposure to computers. Even Leonard admits, "That's pretty cool."

Clone Wars • Set in the Star Wars universe, this animated series was originally developed for TV and ran from 2003 to 2005, then returned to TV on October 3, 2008. Creator George Lucas plans for it to run one hundred episodes.

In "The Lizard-Spock Expansion" (2-8), Sheldon refuses to see the *Clone Wars* show because he hasn't yet seen the movie version. He says, "I prefer to let George Lucas disappoint me in the order he intended."

Code of Manu • Not a law but a social tradition inherent in Hinduism, the Code of Manu puts women on the bottom rung. The male-centric code, in part, states:

No act is to be done according to her own will by a young girl, a young woman, or even by an old woman, though in their own houses. In her child- hood a girl should be under the will of her father; in her youth, of her husband; her husband being dead, of her sons; a woman should never enjoy her own will. She must never wish separation of her self from her father, husband, or sons, for by separation from them a woman would make both families contemptible. She must always be cheerful and clever in household business, with the furni- ture well cleaned, and with not a free hand in expenditure.

Like the devil citing scripture, Sheldon brings up the Code of Manu, buttressing Raj's concerns about Priya's relationship with Leonard, in "The Cohabitation Formulation" (4-16). Raj is quick to agree with Sheldon's pronouncements, though Raj is hardly a devout Hindu—he is, in fact, a "real Yankee Doodle boy!" ("The Apology Insufficiency," 4-7).

Comic-Con (SDCC) • An annual geekfest held in San Diego each July, this is the largest pop culture convention in the world, with a self-imposed limit of one hundred and twenty-five people. (See "Getting Your Geek On in Public: A Convention Primer for Muggles" on page 171.)

In "The Electric Can Opener Fluctuation" (3-1), Sheldon expresses his great disappointment in sacrificing his summer to go to the North Pole to do research. He missed out on many things, "and I didn't even get to go to Comic-Con!" he cries.

Connor, Sarah • A character from the *Terminator* movie and television series. This role was played by Linda Hamilton (*Terminator 1* and *2*) and Lena Headley (*Terminator: The Sarah Connor Chronicles*).

In "The Robotic Manipulation" (4-1), Sheldon observes Howard's mechanical arm/hand and urges caution. When asked why, he explains, "Today, it's a Chinese food retrieval robot. Tomorrow, it travels back in time and tries to kill Sarah Connor."

Country Bear Jamboree • A show in which audio-animatronic bears perform country music at Walt Disney's Resort in Orlando, Florida, and in Tokyo.

In "The Robotic Manipulation" (4-1), Sheldon is not overly impressed with Howard's mechanical arm/hand. He considers it only a "modest leap forward from the basic technology that gave us Country Bear Jamboree." And he's probably right. Audio-animatronics is state-of-the-art, and Howard's mechanical arm is impressive but not revolutionary or evolutionary.

Crusher, Wesley • From the Star Trek universe (specifically, *The Next Generation*), Wesley is the son of Dr. Beverly Crusher; she served on the *Enterprise* as its Chief Medical Officer under Captain Picard, who initially found Wesley's presence discomfiting. Wesley's intelligence, however, impressed Picard, who came to accept him and subsequently appointed him the rank of acting ensign.

Wesley was played by American actor Wil Wheaton, whose popular blog, wilwheaton.net, marked him as a Geek of the First Order. Wheaton, who lives in Pasadena, has published several books, including *Memories of the Future: Volume 1*, in which he gives a blow-by-blow account of his time on *Star Trek: The Next Generation*.

In "The Creepy Candy Coating Corollary" (3-5), Sheldon refuses to join a Mystic Warlords of Ka'ah tournament, until he finds out that Wil Wheaton will be competing. As a young boy, Sheldon looked up to, and identified with, the character of Wesley Crusher. As he explains to Stuart, "Growing up, I idolized Wil Wheaton. Wesley Crusher had an eidetic memory just like me." But after failing to show up at a convention that Sheldon traveled to by bus, Wheaton was relegated to sixth place on Sheldon's "all-time enemies list," and now Sheldon wants revenge. Quoting Khan Noonien Singh from a *Star Trek* movie, Sheldon swears eternal vengeance. It is the start of a beautiful friendship between Sheldon and Wheaton.

Bazinga!

CSI • An international television franchise currently airing on CBS, *CSI* has popularized forensic science to such an extent that today's jurors now regularly have unrealistic expectations as to what forensics is capable of.

And so does Sheldon, in terms of when CSI investigators are likely to show up—in the case of a homicide, and not because of a simple robbery, no matter how much swag was bagged. In "The Bozeman Reaction" (3-13), Sheldon asks a policeman investigating a theft, "When does the CSI team get here?"

Sorry, Sheldon, they've got other priorities.

Also, in "The Dead Hooker Juxtaposition" (2-19), Penny has a new nemesis, a beautiful, tall blonde named Alicia who's getting acting jobs, including "a callback to audition for *CSI* to play a hooker who gets killed." Alicia gets the job, which prompts Penny to comment, "Well, dead whore on TV, live one in real life."

D

DC Multiverse • The fictional universe of DC Comics is well established, but by postulating the existence of other worlds, it opens up the possibilities for infinite story lines.

In "The Hofstadter Isotope" (2-20), Penny is shopping for a comic book for her nephew, and when Sheldon helps her out, she is puzzled by his reference to the DC Multiverse. Sheldon realizes she's out of the loop when it comes to DC comic book history, and he says, "Get her out of here."

Deep Space 9 • From the Star Trek universe, this show's title refers to a space station designated DS9. The United Federation of Planets uses it as the base for further exploration of the Gamma Quadrant by way of an adjacent wormhole.

In "The Lizard-Spock Expansion" (2-8), at Sheldon's apartment, Raj wants to watch *Star Trek: Deep Space Nine* instead of *Saturn 3*, which took a drubbing from critics. Sheldon also likes *Deep Space Nine* and, in "The Hofstadter Isotope" (2-20), expresses disappointment when Leonard turns off the TV showing "the classic *Deep Space Nine/Star Trek: The Original Series*, 'Trouble with Tribbles' crossover episode."

Discovery Channel • On television and the web, this heavily science-based channel is a favorite of Zack's, whose low intelligence is a stark contrast to that of Sheldon and his posse, who mercilessly gang up on him in "The Justice League Recombination" (4-11) when he tells Penny that he wants to "talk science with the science dudes." Howard's first with a cutting response, which sets the tone, and then it's a free-for-all as the boys pile up on Zack, just as others had done to them when they were growing up. They're lucky that Zack didn't kick their collective asses. (Penny, though, gives them a piece of her mind.)

Doctor Doom • From the Marvel Comics universe, this supervillain is the enemy of the Fantastic Four, originally comprised of Mr. Fantastic (Reed Richards), the Invisible Girl (Sue Richards, his wife), the Human Torch (Sue's brother, Johnny Storm), and the Thing (Benjamin Jacob "Ben" Grimm). Doctor Doom, the counterpart to Mr. Fantastic, is the ruler of Latveria and a malevolent genius and inventor. He first appeared in *Fantastic Four* #5.

In "The Codpiece Topology" (2-2), Sheldon says Leslie is "Doctor Doom to my Mr. Fantastic." In other words, his archenemy.

Doctor Octopus • From the Marvel Comics universe, "Doc Ock," as he's informally known, is one of Spider-Man's earliest and most formidable villains. Dr. Otto Gunther Octavius is a scientist who was the victim of a lab accident, which permanently welded his physical body to four mechanical, octopus-like arms. He controls the arms telepathically, and they are as versatile as they are deadly. Doc Ock first appeared in *The Amazing Spider-Man* #3 (July 1963), and he was portrayed by Alfred Molina in the second Spider-Man movie (2004).

In "The Codpiece Topology" (2-2), Sheldon says Leslie Winkle is, among other things, "The Doctor Octopus to my Spider-Man." In other words, his archenemy.

Doctor Sivana • Initially from the Fawcett Comics universe, and now part of the DC Comics universe, this evil villain is Captain Marvel's nemesis. Short and bald with a big head, he's famous for saying, "Curses! Foiled again!"

In "The Codpiece Topology" (2-2), Sheldon says Leslie Winkle is, among other things, "The Doctor Sivana to my Captain Marvel." In other words, his archenemy.

Doctor Who • An extremely popular British television show. According to the show's official website (bbc.co.uk/doctorwho/dw), the titular character is "an excited explorer of the universe, with a keen intelligence that means he often notices what everyone else has missed." Doctor Who travels through time and, in the grand tradition of superheroes, though he is not one himself, sets things straight by righting wrongs. As of April 2011, there have been 771 episodes on BBC, making it the longest-running sci-fi show in the world.

In "The Dumpling Paradox" (1-7), Sheldon tells Penny and Leonard that his Saturday-morning routine is unvarying: "I have awakened at 6:15, poured myself a bowl of cereal, added a quarter cup of 2% milk, sat on *this* end of *this* couch, turned on BBC America, and watched *Doctor Who*."

Dolbear, Amos • Amos Emerson Dolbear was a physicist and inventor in the late nineteenth century. In addition to studying electrical spark conversion and sound waves, he published an article in 1897 called "The Cricket as a Thermometer," positing the correlation between a cricket's chirp and temperature.

In "The Jiminy Conjecture" (3-2), Sheldon explains that Dr. Dolbear "determined that there was a fixed relationship between the number of chirps per minute of the snowy tree cricket and the ambient temperature." Sheldon is sure that a snowy tree cricket is in his apartment, whereas Howard is just as adamant that it's a common field cricket. The result? Howard, 1; Sheldon, 0.

Doodle Jump • A computer game from Lima Sky. According to Wikipedia, "Game play consists of guiding a four-legged creature known as 'Doodler' up an unending series of platforms without falling, in an attempt to gain a high score."

In "The Zarnecki Incursion" (4-19), Sheldon explains to Penny that *Doodle Jump* is just a game, whereas *World of Warcraft* is several orders of magnitude more than a game. (He also adds *Angry Birds* to the mix, lumping it with *Doodle Jump*.)

Dungeons & Dragons (D&D) • A fantasy role-playing game invented by Gary Gygax and Dave Arneson that is now a billion-dollar industry fueled by 20 million fans. As Wikipedia explains, "D&D departs from traditional wargaming and assigns each player a specific character to play instead of a military formation. These characters embark upon imaginary adventures within a fantasy setting."

In "The Middle Earth Paradigm" (1-6), Penny invites the boys over to her Halloween party, and Sheldon, unsure as to potential costume restrictions, gives her a list of possibilities: "TV, film, D&D, manga, Greek gods, Roman gods, Norse gods . . ." But he finally chooses to appear as a scientific principle, the Doppler Effect.

E

Elvish • In the context of *The Lord of the Rings*, it refers to a race of elves, who are tall, noble, long-lived, handsome/beautiful, and brave.

In "The Middle Earth Paradigm" (1-6), Penny's ex-boyfriend Kurt confuses elves with hobbits, until Leonard, dressed as a hobbit named Bilbo Baggins, clarifies: "A hobbit is a mortal halfling inhabitant of Middle-earth, whereas an elf is an immortal, tall warrior."

Ephron, Zac • American actor, singer, and dancer best known for his role as Troy Bolton in *High School Musical* (2006) and its sequels.

In "The Bath Item Gift Hypothesis" (2-11), the boys are in the university cafeteria and Raj and Howard are debating who is more handsome. Howard says he's "more of a Zac Ephron kind of guy."

Ewok • Creatures from the Star Wars universe, the teddy-bearish Ewoks are second only in aggravation to Jar Jar Binks. These irresistibly cute tree-dwellers use their wits and little else to defeat a technologically superior force. Standing only about three feet tall, these feisty, courageous creatures first appeared in *Star Wars Episode VI: Return of the Jedi*.

In "The Irish Pub Formulation" (4-6), after Sheldon discovers that Leonard has pulled the wool over his eyes by sneaking Priya in his bedroom for the night—a violation of the roommate agreement, not to mention an agreement made years ago in which Leonard promised Raj he would never romantically pursue Priya—Sheldon tells Leonard, "You're far too short to be Darth Vader. At best, you might be a turncoat Ewok."

The height joke is a sore point with Leonard, who stands five feet, five inches. Because Sheldon towers over him (at six feet, two inches), he makes height jokes about Leonard with about the same frequency that he teases Howard about his lack of a doctorate degree.

F

Fabergé egg • These exquisite, handmade, egg-shaped *objets d'art* are encrusted with jewels and precious metals. Many thousands were made by the House of Fabergé from 1885 to 1917, each worth a princely sum. (In 2002, Christie's sold "The Winter Egg" for $9.58 million.)

In "The Roommate Transmogrification" (4-24), Sheldon makes a comparison between the fragility of the neck holding up the important "payload" of the head and "balancing a Fabergé egg on a Pixy Stix."

Fantastic Four #48 • A Marvel comic book, this issue features the first appearance of the Sentinel of the Spaceways (aka, the Silver Surfer) and the omnipotent Galactus, who literally has an appetite for planets—specifically, their life energies.

In "The Jiminy Conjecture" (3-2), Howard puts his money where his mouth is and offers up a prized copy of this comic as a bet, insisting that the cricket at large in Sheldon's apartment is a common field cricket and not, as

Sheldon asserts, a snowy tree cricket. Turns out Sheldon's barking up the wrong tree; he loses the bet and admits to Leonard, "In a moment filled with biblical resonance, pride wenteth before my fall, causing my *Flash* #123 to goeth to Wolowitz."

Mr. Fantastic • A fictional character in the Marvel Comics universe, Richard Reed is a scientist with interdisciplinary interests and the leader of the Fantastic Four. Mr. Fantastic invented the spaceship that took him, Sue Storm, her brother Johnny, and Ben Grimm into a cosmic radiation storm, which gave them each different superpowers. Mr. Fantastic's power is the ability to stretch his body in any shape; he's a giant rubber man, like Pixar's Elastic Girl.

In "The Codpiece Topology" (2-2), Sheldon tells Penny that Leslie Winkle is, among other things, "the Doctor Doom to my Mr. Fantastic." In other words, his archenemy.

Well, maybe that's a bit of a *stretch* . . .

Fiddler on the Roof • A musical that inspired the film of the same name, *Fiddler* is based on the book *Tevye and his Daughters* by Sholem Aleichem. According to Wikipedia, "The story centers on Tevye, the father of five daughters, and his attempts to maintain his family and Jewish religious traditions while outside influences encroach upon their lives. He must cope with both the strong-willed actions of his three older daughters . . . and with the edict of the Tsar that evicts the Jews from their village."

In "The Grasshopper Experiment" (1-8), in which Raj is fixed up on a blind date that he thinks will lead to a loveless marriage, Howard explains that the "entire premise of *Fiddler on the Roof*" is that, as Sheldon stated, "arranged marriages were the norm, and it served society quite well." But this is the twenty-first century, and Raj has no compulsion to date, much less marry, a childhood acquaintance—that is, until he sees Lalita Gupta as a grown woman. She's lovely, well spoken, and catches Raj's eye, even though she's actually casting *her* eyes at (of all people) Sheldon.

Flash • A superhero from the DC Comics universe, Flash first appeared in *Flash Comics* #1 (January 1940). As his name suggests, his power is superspeed. Over the years, in various incarnations, he's been part of super teams such as Teen Titans, the Justice League, and the Justice Society of America. In *Flash* #123, "The Flash of Two Worlds," he meets and becomes friends with himself from a parallel world. That issue is highly collectible, and in June 2004, a copy sold for $23,000 at Heritage Auctions (Dallas, Texas).

In the pantheon of pop culture superheroes, some are cool and some are not. Not so cool: Aquaman and Fartman (Howard Stein's alter ego). Cool: Batman and Flash. In "The Middle Earth Paradigm" (1-6), for a costume party, all four boys initially show up dressed as the Flash because they all want to be, as Raj explains, "the fastest man alive!" It's Sheldon, though, who is most readily identified with Flash, not only because he often wears a Flash T-shirt, but also because in "The Justice League Recombination" (4-11) he's dressed as the Flash, and actually looks the part. It requires someone with long legs and arms, and Sheldon fits the bill.

In his imagination and in the real world, Sheldon does see himself as the Flash. After knocking on Penny's door rapidly, he explains that he's knocked "thirty thousand times." And when Leonard frustrates him, to work off his ire, Sheldon "runs" all the way from Pasadena to the Grand Canyon and back in seconds, just as the Flash would have done.

Flatland • The full title of this satirical 1884 novella by Edwin Abbott is *Flatland: A Romance of Many Dimensions.* Per Wikipedia, the novella is about "a two-dimensional world referred to as Flatland which is occupied by geometric figures, line-segments (females) and regular polygons with various numbers of sides."

In "The Psychic Vortex" (3-12), Sheldon tells a disenchanted Raj, "One of my favorite places to visit is the two-dimensional world described in Edwin Abbott's mathematical fantasy, 'Flatland.'" Raj is unconvinced; he wants to go to a university mixer so he can meet real women, not "a sexually attractive line segment."

Force Choke • From the Star Wars universe, Darth Vader's Force Choke is similar to Spock's nerve pinch, with one essential difference: Vader uses it to kill. This technique was first used in *Star Wars* (1977).

In "The Electric Can Opener Fluctuation" (3-1), Sheldon learns that the results of his three-month experiment in the North Pole are worthless because the other boys deliberately tampered with them. The result: Sheldon feels they have abandoned him, and when he sees them in the university cafeteria, he uses the Darth Vader Force Choke to "kill" them off, just as he's tried to use the "scanner" technique to make people's heads explode. Neither move works, of course, but if nothing else, the Force Choke does get the message across symbolically: he wants his enemies dead.

Leonard got an early clue that Sheldon was a little upset. He told the others, "He came out of his room this morning wearing his Darth Vader helmet and tried to choke me to death with the Force."

Fortress of Solitude • Superman's hidey-hole in the Arctic where he goes to be alone, surrounded by mementos from his home planet of Krypton. Though Superman (aka, Clark Kent, a mild-mannered reporter from Metropolis) keeps an apartment in the city, he maintains a separate residence where he need not worry about mortals discovering his alter ego. In recent years, Superman's Fortress of Solitude has been located in several other remote spots. Since he can fly, his terrestrial fortress can be situated anywhere on Earth.

In "The Vegas Renormalization" (2-21), Sheldon tells Penny that he's looking forward to a rare weekend alone in his apartment, his "Fortress of Solitude." Alas, Sheldon's Fortress of Solitude remains barred for the weekend because he has locked himself out. He has to take refuge in Penny's apartment, which turns out to be a rare opportunity for them to spend time together without the others around.

Fox, Megan • The aptly named American actress is best known for her appearances in two *Transformers* movies, which starred Shia LaBeouf. But who would notice him with foxy Megan running around in the same flick? She's won several awards, including "Choice Female Hottie" (Teen Choice Award) two times, "Choice Summer Movie Star Female" (Teen Choice Award), "Best Sci-Fi Actress" (Scream Award), "Best Performance by a Human Female" (Spike Video Game Awards), and "Choice Movie Actress: Horror/Thriller" (Teen Choice Awards).

In "The Vengeance Formulation" (3-9), Howard is having doubts about making any kind of commitment to Bernadette, because he's holding out for a fantasy—a superhot girl like "Megan Fox from *Transformers*, or Katee Sackhoff from *Battlestar Galactica*." Having spent years in his bathtub and bed playing tug-of-war with himself to images of starlets, no ordinary woman is good enough, which prompts Penny to ask, "Are you high? . . . Howard, you're going to throw away a great girl like Bernadette because you're holding out for some ridiculous fantasy?"

Franklin Mint collectible plates • The Franklin Mint is a private company based in Exton, Pennsylvania, that issues manufactured collectibles—coins, books, knives, figurines, plates, etc.—for sale to the public. Critics complain that some of their commemorative plates, which are hawked as collectibles, aren't likely to appreciate in value because of their high manufacturing runs, sometimes up to one hundred thousand pieces.

In "The Guitarist Amplification" (3-7), Sheldon tells Penny and Leonard about his parents' loveless and combative marriage, which often forced him to seek refuge in his bedroom while his father was "on the roof skeet-shooting her Franklin Mint collectible plates."

G

George Foreman grill • A line of electric grills licensed under the name "George Foreman Healthy Cooking." "With over 100 million grills sold worldwide," says the official website, georgeforemancooking.com, "there's never been a better time to enjoy flavorful, healthy food by cooking with George."

In "The Robotic Manipulation" (4-1), Amy makes a deal that involves her being able to use her mother's Foreman grill, which "seals in the flavor without the fat."

Ghostbusters II • A 1989 sequel to the marvelously inventive *Ghostbusters* (1984), this one was originally titled *Ghostbusters II: River of Slime*, referring to a bubbling pink muck that flowed deep underground in the sewers beneath New York City.

In "The Precious Fragmentation" (3-17), the boys get excited when they find, in a box of auctioned goods from a storage facility, "an original draft *Ghostbusters* script with actual slime stains!" as Leonard exclaims. But their excitement turns to disappointment when they realize it's actually a script for the forgettable sequel, prompting Leonard to add: "Never mind."

Glau, Summer • An American actress who is best known for playing a Terminator named Cameron in the TV series *Terminator: The Sarah Connor Chronicles*. Just like a Terminator, Glau is trained in kung fu and kickboxing. She also played River Tam in the TV series *Firefly*.

In "The Terminator Decoupling" (2-17), the boys, en route to a conference in San Francisco, are amazed to find out that Summer Glau is onboard their train. This gives them each an opportunity to make fools out of themselves, especially Howard. Of course, each fails to impress Summer—except a tongue-tied Raj, who then beats a fast retreat after discovering the beer he's drinking is nonalcoholic.

Godzilla • The largest Japanese movie monster, Godzilla ran amok through Japan's most populous cities in twenty-eight different films. He even has his own star on the Hollywood Walk of Fame. (What? No star for Mothra?)

In "The Pants Alternative" (3-18), Sheldon explains to Raj that he is the mayor of the fictional city Sheldonopolis, and is urging his citizens to run for cover because "a Godzilla-like monster is approaching the city."

Godzilla prefigures largely in Sheldon's life; there's even a clause in the roommate agreement that addresses what Leonard should do in the event Godzilla makes an appearance.

Goldberg, Whoopi • An African American comedienne and actress. In the second season of *Star Trek: The Next Generation*, she played Guinan, a bartender and advisor to Captain Picard.

In "The Wheaton Recurrence" (3-19), Howard has an opportunity, during a lull in a bowling competition, to ask Wil Wheaton a question. Of all the possible questions he could have posed, he asks, "I'm sure you're probably sick of *Star Trek* questions, but . . . Whoopi Goldberg, you ever hit that?"

Goodall, Jane • Best known for her work as a primatologist, Goodall has spent forty-five years at the Gombe Stream National Park in Tanzania studying chimpanzees, specifically the Kasakela chimpanzee community. Her eye-opening research has shown remarkable similarities between humans and chimpanzees, which is not surprising: the genome of the chimpanzee, catalogued in 2005, showed that we are a 96 percent match with them genetically. (More recent studies have shown that we are actually even closer to the Orangutan, approximately a 97 percent match.)

Just as Leonard's parents eschewed the normal activities associated with major holidays to take the opportunity to study their sociological aspects, so, too, does Sheldon at a party Penny throws. In "The Middle Earth Paradigm" (1-6), he compares himself to Goodall observing the apes. He observes the party's attendees, who clearly have their own distinct patterns of interaction. For example, "How wasted am I?" is met with the response, "Dude."

Goonies • An adventure-comedy movie from 1985, written by Chris Columbus, about a group of children living in the "Goon Docks" neighborhood of Astoria, Oregon. As they go on a final "Goonie adventure" before their neighborhood is lost to the depredations of the Astoria Country Club, they find a map that leads them to an underground cavern, where they find treasure onboard an old galleon, *The Inferno*.

In "The Pirate Solution" (3-4), the boys celebrate Christopher Columbus Day (in early October) by honoring the film director, not the explorer. Thus, they watch *Goonies*, *Gremlins*, and *Young Sherlock Holmes*, all films Columbus has written.

Gordon, Barbara • From the DC Comics universe, she was originally Batgirl. She's now known as Oracle, and is a computer expert who lends her hacking expertise to superheroes. Think Sherlock Holmes crossed with

Stieg Larsson's Lisbeth Salander with a PhD in library science, and you've got the general idea.

In "The Irish Pub Formulation" (4-6), Sheldon tells Leonard that Barbara Gordon is, in fact, Batgirl, which he offers as proof that he can't keep a secret.

Gorn • From *Star Trek: The Original Series*, he's a biped alien creature resembling an alligator/reptile, who fought Captain Kirk one-on-one in the episode "Arena" (1-19).

In "The Apology Insufficiency" (4-7), guilty Sheldon's dreams are haunted by Gorn after he unwisely and unwittingly volunteers information to an FBI agent about Howard that results in his being denied a higher security clearance.

Graphic novels • Just as Mark Twain observed that cauliflower is a cabbage with a college education, a graphic novel (or album, as it's sometimes called) is a comic published in book form. Because they offer a better value for the money, these compilations have cut deeply in the sales of individual comic books, which now cost up to $4 each.

In "The Guitarist Amplification" (3-7), Sheldon takes refuge in the graphic novel section at Stuart's comic book store, unable to endure the constant bickering in his apartment between Penny and Leonard, which evokes memories of the contentiousness between his parents when he was growing up in East Texas.

Grayson, Dick • From the DC Comics universe, Richard John "Dick" Grayson was Batman's sidekick, Robin. Just as Batman (Bruce Wayne) watched his parents gunned down during a robbery, Grayson saw his parents murdered by the mafia. When Grayson grew older, he became his own superhero, Nightwing.

After a date with Penny, Stuart gets into a lengthy discussion with Sheldon about Dick Grayson, in "The Hofstadter Isotope" (2-20).

Great Power • "With great power comes great responsibility" • A homily often attributed to Peter Parker's Uncle Ben, this oft-quoted phrase was first used in *Amazing Fantasy* #15, which also marked the first appearance of Spider-Man. The phrase can be found in the last panel of the comic book.

It's a line Sheldon uses in "The Panty Pinata Polarization" (2-7) after Penny bests him in competition, which earns her his begrudging admiration.

Green Goblin • From the Marvel Comics universe, the Green Goblin (Norman Osborn) and Spider-Man are bitter enemies. Per Wikipedia: "Norman Osborn was originally an industrialist who took a serum that enhanced his physical abilities and intellect but also drove him to insanity. He adopted a Halloween-themed appearance, dressing in a goblin costume, riding on a bat-shaped Goblin Glider, and using an arsenal of high-tech weapons."

In "The Wheaton Recurrence" (3-19), Sheldon sees Wil Wheaton and says that he's "The Green Goblin to my Spider-Man," among other comparisons. In other words, his archenemy.

Green Lantern • From the DC Comics universe. He originally appeared in *All-American Comics* #16 (July 1940). Wearing a green power ring charged by a lantern created by the Guardians of the Universe, today's Green Lanterns are intergalactic cops on the beat, like the Jedi Knights from the Star Wars universe. In "The Psychic Vortex" (3-12), Sheldon quotes Green Lantern's oath to Martha, who is visibly impressed. "In brightest day, in blackest night, no evil shall escape my sight."

A favorite superhero among the boys, Green Lantern is way cool. In "The Justice League Recombination" (4-11), Leonard dresses up as him. In "The Psychic Vortex" (3-12), Sheldon wears the power ring and carries the lantern, and it turns out to be a chick magnet, drawing Martha, who introduces her friend Abby to Raj. The girls go home with them to Sheldon's apartment, where Raj makes out with Abby, and Martha looks forlornly on as she waits for Sheldon to make a move.

Gremlins • A horror comedy from 1984 directed by Joe Dante, in which a pet called a mogwai spawns nasty, evil creatures that run amok in Kingston Falls.

In "The Pirate Solution" (3-4), the boys watch *Gremlins*, along with *Goonies* and *Young Sherlock Holmes*, to celebrate Columbus Day, because they were all written by Chris Columbus.

Grisham, John • A former lawyer turned bestselling legal-thriller novelist, Grisham's books feature formulaic plots and cardboard characters in which the little guy inevitably triumphs over the big bad one.

In "The Gothowitz Deviation" (3-3), Raj tells Howard that he's "kind of on a John Grisham kick right now," having read *The Pelican Brief* and *The Client*.

H

Halo • A science-fiction video game published by Microsoft Game Studios, playable on Xbox, Xbox 360, and Windows/Mac computers. It centers around an interstellar war between humanity and an alliance of aliens collectively known as the Covenant. The plot unfolds through the eyes of the Master Chief, a cybernetic human aided by Cortana, his artificially intelligent companion.

In "The Bozeman Reaction" (3-13), Sheldon is distraught because a break-in occurs at his apartment; the thieves abscond with their collection of computer games, including *Halo 1*, *Halo 2*, and *Halo 3*, among numerous other titles.

Harry Potter • Having grossed over $6 billion worldwide, the movie franchise, based on the novels by J.K. Rowling, is the highest-earning film series of all time.

In "The Jiminy Conjecture" (3-2), when Leonard says that the sex he had the night before with Penny was "just fine," Raj counters, "Oh, dude, the fourth Harry Potter movie was 'just fine.'"

Hellblazer • Also known as *John Constantine: Hellblazer*, this series from DC Comics is about the adventures of a streetwise magician. From Wikipedia: "The main character of *Hellblazer* is portrayed as a kind of confidence man who does morally questionable things, arguably for the greater good."

In "The Hofstadter Isotope" (2-20), Penny randomly picks up a copy of *Hellblazer* as a gift for her nephew and asks Stuart what it's about. He responds, "A morally ambiguous confidence man who smokes, has lung cancer, and is tormented by the spirits of the undead."

Hellboy • Published by Dark Horse Comics and created by writer-artist Mike Mignola, the comic book is centered around "a creature summoned, in the final months of World War II, by Grigori Rasputin on Tarmangant Island, off the coast of Scotland, having been commissioned by the Nazis to change the tide of war." The Wikipedia entry continues, "Proving not to be a devil in the traditional sense but a devil-like creature with red skin, horns, and a disproportionately large right hand made of red stone, he is dubbed 'Hellboy' by Professor Trevor Bruttenholm." Hellboy is the primary agent for BPRD (Bureau for Paranormal Research and Defense), a U.S. government agency formed to combat occult threats.

In "The Classified Materials Turbulence" (2-22), Stuart pulls a copy of *Hellboy* from his most recent shipment of comics to give to Sheldon, who is upset because Stuart already told him that it's "mind-blowing," thus spoiling his surprise.

Hippie • During the counterculture youth movement of the 1960s and 1970s, hippies, or "flower children," espoused an alternative lifestyle, rejecting the materialistic ethos of "the establishment." Their nirvana was the 1969 Woodstock Music and Art Fair, which drew a half million hippies who gathered to celebrate their "free" lifestyle and counterculture ethos. Their symbol was a peace sign and their message was "make love, not war."

A running joke on the show, Sheldon uses the term "hippie" to describe anyone he considers touchy-feely or New-Agey, people who are intuitive as opposed to being objective, pragmatic, and a believer in the scientific process. It's Sheldon's term of undearment.

Homunculus • A scale-model of the human body.

In "The Gothowitz Deviation" (3-3), Sheldon tells Penny that Leonard's a homunculus. At five feet, five inches, he's short for a man, but he's obviously not *that* diminutive.

Hoth • An ice planet featured in the second Star Wars movie, *The Empire Strikes Back*. In the film, Han Solo and Luke Skywalker are at the Rebel Alliance's new base. When Luke is attacked by a furry creature called a Wampa, he's down for the count. With night falling along with the temperature, Han saves Luke's life by using a light saber to open up a deceased Tauntaun (a riding beast, like a horse) and stuff him inside. Han erects a temporary shelter to survive the night, keeping Luke safe in the belly of the beast. They are saved the next day.

In "The Monopolar Expedition" (2-23), when the boys gather under Sheldon's supervision in a freezer at the Cheesecake Factory, the frigid air takes a toll. Leonard, unable to accomplish his task, admits defeat. "Okay, I can't do this." But Sheldon bucks him up by citing the example of Han Solo saving Luke's life on Hoth.

I

Ice Station Zebra • This action film from 1968, based on Alistair MacLean's novel of the same name, is about the captain of an American nuclear-powered submarine who is ordered to go to Ice Station Zebra, a research station in the Arctic, to check out an incident.

In "The Monopolar Expedition" (2-23), the boys are in the North Pole and, for entertainment, have to decide whether or not to see a suspense thriller (*Ice Station Zebra*) or a John Carpenter movie (*The Thing* [1982]). Given the circumstances—they're essentially alone for three months, and without women—wouldn't more, um, exciting visual stimuli be in order? Doesn't Howard have a stash of porn, or perhaps a Feynman tape for Sheldon?

Ikea • A Swedish manufacturer of self-assembled, inexpensive furniture. From Sheldon's apartment, the nearest location is in Burbank, eleven miles away, at 600 N. San Fernando Blvd.

In "The Big Bran Hypothesis" (1-2), Penny orders a "cheap Swedish media center" and has it delivered to the lobby of her apartment building. In fact, Sheldon and Leonard didn't need to drag/push it up four flights of stairs because, as Ikea explains, if you buy from one of their retail stores, "we delivery your new products directly to the room of your choice."

Imagineers • WDI (Walt Disney Imagineering) is principally responsible for the creation and construction of Disney's theme parks worldwide. Coining the word "imagineers"—combining imagination with engineering, or imaginative engineering—there are 140 job titles within this division, bringing together a wealth of world-class creative talent across multiple disciplines.

In "The Griffin Equivalency" (2-4), Sheldon, vexed that Raj's rapid ascension to fame has made him unbearable, suggests combining Japanese research with Imagineering techniques, which would produce a more suitable friend.

And in "The Robotic Manipulation" (4-1), when Howard creates a robotic arm to pleasure himself, he should have consulted with Imagineering, which could have created the whole package, and not just the arm.

The Incredibles • A 2004 Pixar movie directed by Brad Burt, this computer-animated full-length feature stars a family of superheroes who are trying to keep a low profile in the suburbs, until they must pull together as a super-family to fight a disgruntled fan-turned-villain named Syndrome.

In "The Spaghetti Catalyst" (3-20), it's Raj, as usual, who offers up the off-the-wall speculations. This time, he wonders if "the elastic woman" (Elastigirl, one of four Incredibles) "needs to use birth control, or can she just be a diaphragm?"

Incredible Hulk • Banner, Bruce • From the Marvel Comics universe. Scientist Bruce Banner morphs into a huge green monster when angered—the aptly named Hulk. The Hulk originally appeared in the comic book in *The Incredible Hulk* #1 in May 1962. "The madder Hulk gets, the stronger Hulk gets," as we've been told. Largely impervious to physical harm, he stands almost seven feet tall and weighs approximately six hundred pounds. He also serves as a metaphor for insane jealousy.

In "The Killer Robot Insanity" (2-12), Leonard tells Penny, "When you get angry, you kind of turn into, like, you, know grrrrr!" It's an allusion that Penny doesn't understand. "Seriously?" Leonard says. "Gamma rays? Bruce Banner? You didn't get the *Incredible Hulk* from that?" Ironically, when the shoe is on the other foot—when Leonard is insanely jealous because Penny has invited an ex-boyfriend to stay at her apartment and sleep on the couch—it's Leonard's turn to go from a mild-mannered scientist into the metaphorical green beastie, showing his own out-of-control, raging jealousy.

Infinite Crisis • A sequel to *Crisis on Infinite Earths* (1985), this seven-issue limited-series comic book was published beginning in October 2005. From Wikipedia: "It revisits characters and concepts from that earlier Crisis, including the existence of DC's Multiverse. Some of the characters featured were alternate versions of comic icons, such as an alternate Superman named Kal-L, who came from a parallel universe called Earth-Two."

In "The Hofstadter Isotope" (2-20), Sheldon suggests that the comic Penny picked up to give to her nephew is a good choice, but only if he's "already read *Infinite Crisis* and *52*, and is familiar with the reestablishment of the DC Multiverse."

J

Jack in the Box • A fast-food restaurant chain with twenty-one thousand locations in the United States. The first location was opened in San Diego, California, in 1951. It principally serves burgers and fries but, like McDonald's, has branched out with a more diverse menu.

In "The Benefactor Factor" (4-15), when Leonard tells Sheldon that Mrs. Latham, a wealthy benefactor, is taking him out to dinner to discuss his research, Sheldon—always ready with a quip to take Leonard down a notch or two—suggests that his research could be discussed during the time it takes to go through the drive-thru at a Jack in the Box.

Jackson, Peter • A New Zealand film director best known for his work on *The Lord of the Rings*, Jackson has taken the helm for *The Hobbit*, which will come out in 2012. His other recent projects have included a remake of *King Kong* (2005) and, as producer, the inventive *District 9* (2009).

In "The Precious Fragmentation" (3-17), the discussion at hand is whether or not to return the replica One Ring to its original owner, Peter Jackson. In the end, that's what Leonard says was done, after the other three boys fell asleep in a contest that was supposed to resolve who got to keep it. But the ring didn't go back to New Zealand; instead it stayed in Leonard's bedroom, in a hidden box under his bed.

Jacuzzi • This company makes a full line of hot tubs, bath and shower products, and mattresses.

Sheldon, in "The Toast Derivation" (4-17), makes a distinction between a hot tub, which he says is generic, and Jacuzzi, which is not. The matter came up during a ski trip in Colorado, when Barry Kripke is telling a story about being in a hot tub with a beautiful babe who's drunk and disrobing, and Sheldon's curiosity extends only as far as to ask whether it was merely a hot tub or a real Jacuzzi.

Jamba Juice • A company that sells fruit-based smoothies, with over seven hundred franchises in the United States. Founded in 1990 in California, it's the Starbucks of the blended-fruit-drink industry.

In "The Hot Troll Deviation" (4-4), Leonard says Raj and Sheldon working together is about as agreeable an arrangement as the science-fiction creatures Alien and Predator deciding "to go partners in a Jamba Juice" franchise.

Leonard's perception bears fruit because, in "The Pirate Solution" (3-4), Sheldon and Raj work together in Sheldon's office with (predictably) comical results. They're oil and water—or, more accurately, gas and a match.

Jenga • Derived from the Swahili verb *kujenga*, meaning "to build," this is a game using fifty-four wooden blocks to construct a tower that eventually must fall.

In "The Zazzy Substitution" (4-3), Sheldon alludes to "the great Jenga tantrum of 2008," in which if Leonard is to be believed, Sheldon pulled a Captain Kirk/*Kobayashi Maru* by bumping the table and causing the tower to collapse, thus prematurely ending the game.

Johansson, Scarlett • American actress who appeared in *Iron Man 2* (2010), among many other films.

In "The Vengeance Formulation" (3-9), after Howard alienates Bernadette and then doesn't call her for a week, he goes to the Cheesecake Factory to win her back. Penny tells him that she has been "talkin' some smack about ya," and takes the opportunity to cut him down a few notches, adding, "Scarlett Johansson and Wonder Women were just in here trolling around for neurotic little weasels."

In "The Boyfriend Complexity" (4-9), a drunken Raj calls an observatory in Hawaii and asks that they reposition the telescope to "Scarlett Johansson's house."

John and Yoko • Refers to the late musician John Lennon and his soul mate Yoko Ono, a controversial figure in the Beatles' history because of her purported role in breaking up the legendary group.

In "The Zazzy Substitution" (4-3), when Leonard sees Amy and Sheldon approach their lunch table, Leonard opines, "Oh, no . . . John and Yoko." To which Howard replies, "More like Yoko and Yoko."

Joker • Batman's archnemesis, from the DC Comics universe. "The original and currently dominant image is of a highly intelligent psychopath with a warped, sadistic sense of humor," notes Wikipedia. He first appeared in *Batman* #1 (Spring 1940).

In "The Vengeance Formulation" (3-9), Leonard suggests to Sheldon that, in repayment of Kripke's prank on him, he must retaliate "like how the Joker got back at Batman for putting him in the Arkham Asylum for the Criminally Insane." In other words, the ante has to be upped, and the repayment should be especially diabolical in nature.

Jones, Indiana • Created by George Lucas as an homage to 1930s pulp action heroes, Henry Walton "Indiana" Jones, Jr., is an adventurous archaeologist who travels the world in search of rare antiquities for the university at which he teaches, Marshall College in New England. He's a hugely popular character, from television (*The Young Indiana Jones Chronicles*) to the big screen (four movies to date). Indy is played by Harrison Ford, although the original casting choice was Tom Selleck, who had to decline because he was then signed to the TV series *Magnum, P.I.* (1980–1988).

In "The 21 Second Excitation" (4-8), a midnight showing of *Raiders of the Lost Ark*, with twenty-one seconds of restored footage, is the subject of interest and controversy. Sheldon and his posse are refused admittance after the theater capacity is reached, but if Wil Wheaton and his three friends had not been allowed to cut in line, our boys would have made it in.

Joplin, Scott • African American composer and pianist best known for his 1899 composition, "Maple Leaf Rag."

In "The Zazzy Substitution" (4-3), Joplin and his famous composition are cited by Sheldon in a word game he and Amy invented called Counterfactuals, in which an alternate world is postulated, and the other person responds and then must defend his answer.

Journey into Mystery #83 • From the Marvel Comics universe, this issue is noteworthy because it's the first appearance of Thor Odinson. As drawn by Jack "King" Kirby, Thor practically explodes off the page.

In "The Excelsior Acquisition" (3-16), when Stan Lee is scheduled to make an appearance at Stuart's comic book store, Leonard is torn between having him sign this comic or *Fantastic Four* #5.

Justice League of America • Usually called "JLA," from the DC Comics universe, this team of superheroes fights for truth, justice, and the American way. Members come and go, but have included Superman, Batman, Wonder Woman, Flash, Aquaman, Green Arrow, Hawkman, and many others.

In "The Excelsior Acquisition" (3-16), Stan Lee is signing at Stuart's comic book store, and the boys debate which comic to bring for his signature. Leonard's on the horns of a dilemma: should he bring *Journey into Mystery* #83 or *Fantastic Four* #5?

Also, Sheldon has a JLA card, which he carries in his wallet; he mentions it to an FBI agent as non-proof of identification when he challenges hers. In "The Justice League Recombination" (4-11), Sheldon and his friends dress up as Justice League members for a New Year's party at Stuart's. Sheldon is the Flash, Leonard is the Green Lantern, Howard is a diminutive Batman, Raj is a ludicrous Aquaman, Penny is a spectacular Wonder Woman, and Zack is a super Superman.

K

Kal-El • When Superman was born, this was his given name on the planet Krypton. (His father's name was Jor-El.)

In "The White Asparagus Triangulation" (2-9), Sheldon reveals that Leonard uses "Kal-El" as his password for everything. When Leonard expresses umbrage that Sheldon hacked his Facebook account, Sheldon defends himself: "Oh, it's hardly hacking when you use the same password for everything."

Kama Sutra • This classic work of Indian erotic literature, which has 1250 verses in 36 chapters, is known for its practical advice regarding coitus. It's generically referred to as the Indian book of love.

In "The Prestidigitation Approximation" (4-18), Leonard tells Priya that he wants to try out some positions from the book, and she calls it "crazy positions from an ancient Indian love manual."

Kandor • When Superman's home planet of Krypton exploded, Kal-El (his birth name), who later assumed the name of Clark Kent, thought he was the sole survivor, when in fact the entire population of the planet's capital city, Kandor, had been miniaturized by an android named Brainiac. As recounted in *Action Comics* #242 (July 1958), Superman rescues the Kandorians and keeps them at the Fortress of Solitude until he can figure out a way to restore them to normal size. As recounted in *Superman* #338 (August 1970), Superman later relocated them to another world that had a red sun, similar to what they had on Krypton. The former inhabitants of Krypton named the new world Rokyn ("gift from God" in Kryptonian).

In "The Bath Item Gift Hypothesis" (2-11), the boys have a spirited discussion about Kandor, under the pretense that they're having a scientific debate. The debate devolves into a discussion about Kryptonian mustard stains and sweat, and eventually Raj opines, "I give up. You can't have a rational argument with [Sheldon]."

Kegel exercises • Named after Dr. Arnold Kegel, this involves muscle contractions in the pelvic region. Among other benefits, doing the exercises can "increase sexual gratification and aid in reducing premature ejaculation," according to Wikipedia.

In "The Love Car Displacement" (4-13), Raj whispers to Howard about his Kegel exercises.

Khan • From the Star Trek film *The Wrath of Khan* (1982), Khan Noonien Singh, brilliantly portrayed by Ricardo Montalban, pits himself against his nemesis, Captain James T. Kirk. Khan takes over command of the U.S.S. *Reliant* and goes into battle against the U.S.S. *Enterprise*, helmed by Kirk.

In "The Creepy Candy Coating Corollary" (3-5), Khan figures prominently. Quoting Khan in the context of taking revenge on Wil Wheaton, Sheldon blusters and fulminates about destroying Wheaton, who wins a card tournament, because where's there's a Wil, there's a way. Wheaton lies and causes Sheldon to drop his shields. "From hell's heart, I stab at thee," said Khan. Apt words for Wheaton, who engineered a victory over certain defeat.

Klingon • From the Star Trek universe, this guttural speech, spoken by a warrior race, is "the galaxy's fastest-growing language," according to the Klingon Language Institute (which can be found on the World Wide Web at kli.org). "Here you can find information about the sound and look of Klingon, and even learn a few useful phrases in the Warrior's Tongue . . . Klingon was invented by Marc Okrand for use in some of the Star Trek movies. He invented not just a few words to make the Klingons sound alien, but a

SHEDDING LIGHT ON DARK MATTER | 273 |

complete language with its own vocabulary, grammar, and usage." For the Klingon-impaired, a useful resource is *The Klingon Dictionary*, written by Okrand.

Note: When meeting a Klingon for the first time, a proper greeting is always in order: "Heghlu 'meH QaQ jajvam," which translates to: "Today is a good day to die!" Klingons figure prominently as a regular reference point in discussions among the boys, who all speak fluent Klingon. Hence, instead of playing the unimaginative and unchallenging word game of Boggle, they spice it up by playing Klingon Boggle ("Pilot," 1-1). For those playing, I wish you *Qapla'*.

Kneeling before Zod • General Zod, or more accurately, General Dru-Zod, is a character in the DC Comics universe. He was trapped in the Phantom Zone (a kind of interstellar limbo), but occasionally escapes to bedevil his nemesis and fellow Kryptonian, Superman. The expression was popularized in the second Superman movie, in which a superpowered Zod, accompanied by Ursa and Non, are on Earth and force the U.S. president to surrender. "When the President pleads for Superman to save the Earth, Zod demands that Superman come and kneel before Zod!"

In "The Bat Jar Conjecture" (1-13), Howard exults when he discovers that "Fishman, Chen, Chowdry, and McNair aren't fielding a team in the university physics bowl this year," which gives the boys their opportunity to enter the fray relatively unopposed. Their opponents will, as Leonard asserts, "kneel before Zod," or, metaphorically, kneel before themselves.

Knight Rider • This popular television series, which aired from 1982 to 1986, featured Michael Knight riding around in a Pontiac Trans Am called KITT (Knight Industries Two Thousand), an extensively modified car enhanced with crime-fighting capabilities.

In "The Cruciferous Vegetable Amplification" (4-2), Sheldon (as a mobile virtual presence device) rides shotgun in Leonard's car as they head to work. "Together, in this car, with my enhanced capabilities, we're like Knight Rider," he exclaims.

Kobayashi Maru **scenario** • From the Star Trek universe, this is a battle simulation specifically designed to test a Starfleet Academy cadet's leadership skills. It's a no-win scenario in which the computer is programmed to force a favorable outcome for itself. In the history of Starfleet, no cadet has won in this battle simulation—except James T. Kirk, who reprogrammed it so he could win.

In "The Apology Insufficiency" (4-7), Sheldon is in a funk because he screwed up Howard's chances for a higher security clearance and a better job. Sheldon uncharacteristically finds solace in conversation with a sympathetic bartender—Penny. He likens his situation to the *Kobayashi Maru* scenario, to which Penny replies, "Exactly. Sometimes you can't win."

Though Sheldon cites Kirk as having won, Penny points out that Kirk cheated. Her point, of course, is that in the situation he inadvertently created with Howard, he's not going to "win" by cheating. Sheldon will have to actually apologize and make amends.

Kohlinar • From the Star Trek universe, as defined by Star Trek Freedom Wiki (www.startrekfreedom.com/wiki/index.php/Main_Page), "*Kohlinar*, as a word, describes both the Vulcan ritual by which all remaining vestigial emotions are demonstrated as purged, and the mental discipline whereby this state is subsequently maintained. After rigorous training in the *kahs-wan* during childhood, a mature Vulcan is prepared to make this final journey to pure logic, the duration of which can vary from two to six years (or longer)." It is not to be confused with *pon farr* (which it does sound like).

In "The Alien Parasite Hypothesis" (4-10), Sheldon explains to Amy the value of *Kohlinar*. She devalues it until she must purge her vestigial feelings for Zack, to whom she was initially attracted.

Koko the gorilla • According to Wikipedia, this Western Lowland gorilla "is able to understand more than one thousand signs based on American Sign Language, and understand approximately two thousand words of spoken English."

In "The Gorilla Experiment" (3-10), Sheldon hopes to teach Penny enough about physics that she can appreciate, if not understand, what Leonard, whom she is then dating, does for a living. Sheldon likens it to the Koko experiments, because he soon realizes the inherent futility of the task. Penny is no more capable of understanding physics than Koko is capable of piloting the Space Shuttle.

L

LaForge, Geordi • A character from *Star Trek: The Next Generation*. Lieutenant Commander Geordi LaForge was the helmsman of the USS *Enterprise-D* and, later, its chief engineering officer. Played by LeVar Burton, LaForge is blind but uses a custom-designed visor to "see."

In "The Toast Derivation" (4-17), Sheldon invites Geordi LaForge, via Twitter, to a get-together of acquaintances at his apartment. Toward the end of the episode, LaForge does indeed appear and, seeing Sheldon's friends bellowing in unison at karaoke, quickly leaves, saying, "I am so done with Twitter."

Large Hadron Collider (LHC) • CERN, or the European Organization for Nuclear Research, is the builder of the Large Hadron Collider. The collider, located near Geneva, is the world's largest and highest-energy particle accelerator.

In "The Large Hadron Collision" (3-15), it's a war of words when Leonard lucks out and is headed to Switzerland to attend a conference, where he will also get to see the CERN supercollider. The collision occurs when Leonard makes it clear that he has no intention of taking Sheldon along; instead, he plans to take Penny there for a romantic getaway—they'd be there on Valentine's Day.

Lee, Stan • Stan "The Man" Lee (born Stanley Martin Leiber) is a comic book icon. He is best known for creating, in the Silver Age of comics, some of its most enduring characters for Marvel Comics. (See the Stan Lee box on page 131 for more information.)

In "The Excelsior Acquisition" (3-16), Sheldon misses out on meeting Lee at Stuart's comic book store, but meets him later that day at his personal residence. The result? "I saw the inside of his house and got an autographed application for a restraining order," says Sheldon.

Rather than diminish Sheldon's ardor for Lee, that increases it. Sheldon is jazzed: "I get to hang out with him again at the hearing. This is going to look great hanging next to my restraining order from Leonard Nimoy."

Legoland • The amusement park in Carlsbad, California, encompasses 128 acres and, states legoland.com, is "geared specifically toward youngsters two through 12. With over 50 family rides, 'hands-on' attractions and shows, LEGOLAND California provides education, adventure and fun in this first park of its kind in the U.S." (There's now one in Florida, too.)

In "The Zarnecki Incursion" (4-9), the boys hit the road on a mission of death, destruction, mutilation, and devastation, to wreak vengeance on the unfortunate Todd Zarnecki, for having stolen Sheldor of Azaroth's virtual possessions. Raj suggests they visit Legoland while in the San Diego area because it's "more interactive" than Seaworld, which is Sheldon's suggestion.

Legolas • From the Lord of the Rings universe's race of elves, Legolas is chosen to be a member of the Fellowship that accompanies Frodo Baggins on his quest to take the One Ring to Mount Doom to destroy it. Legolas was played by Orlando Bloom in the Peter Jackson film adaptation.

In "The Monopolar Expedition" (2-23), as a test run for their trip to the

North Pole, Sheldon and the boys are in the freezer at the Cheesecake Factory, and Sheldon assigns them various tasks. Raj has to paint sideburns and a Van Dyke on an action figure of Legolas.

Elves can be perplexing for muggles like Kurt, Penny's ex-boyfriend, who confuses them with hobbits (or halflings). In "The Middle Earth Paradigm" (1-6) Leonard explains the difference: "A hobbit is a mortal halfling inhabitant of Middle-earth, whereas an elf is an immortal tall warrior." Even that description isn't sufficient—Kurt has the sensibilities of an orc.

LOLcats • A website (lolcats.com) with photographs of cats "speaking" ungrammatically.

In "The Panty Pinata Polarization" (2-7), Penny defends sending Sheldon a LOLcat link because the cats are so cute. Sheldon, however, feels otherwise: it earns a strike on her record—the first of three—and she's banned from the group (at least until she plays her trump card given to her by Leonard: the phone number to Sheldon's mother in Texas).

Lollipop Guild • In the 1939 film adaptation of *The Wizard of Oz*, when the residents of Munchkinland welcome Dorothy Gale, three munchkins greet her by singing, "We represent the Lollipop Guild . . . and in the name of the Lollipop Guild, we wish to welcome you to Munchkin Land."

In "The Vengeance Formulation" (3-9), after Sheldon is punk'd by Barry Kripke, Raj mocks him in a squeaky voice, citing dialogue by the Lollipop Guild.

The Lord of the Rings • An epic fantasy trilogy from British philologist and University of Oxford professor J.R.R. Tolkien. It is preceded by *The Hobbit* (1937). *The Fellowship of the Ring* (1954), *The Two Towers* (1954), and *The Return of the King* (1955) comprise The Lord of the Rings trilogy.

Each of the Peter Jackson film adaptations (released in 2001, 2002, and 2003, respectively) was a critical and financial success. Gross revenues totaled nearly $3 billion for the trilogy, paving the way for the long-anticipated release of the film adaptation of *The Hobbit* in 2012. *The Return of the King*, nominated for eleven Oscars, enjoyed a clean sweep, receiving the same number of Oscars won by *Ben-Hur* and *Titanic*.

The boys of *The Big Bang Theory* often cite Tolkien's epic, a favorite book and movie series, in their discussions of pop culture. In "The Precious Fragmentation" (3-17), they fight to possess the errant One Ring replica, which in turn possesses each of them.

When *The Lord of the Rings* were released on Blu-ray, New Line decided to release only the theatrical versions, to be followed at some point in the future by the extended versions, which forced fans to buy two more sets on top of the existing DVD sets they already own. Fans damned New Line's triple-dipping at their expense. Sheldon owns a copy of the theatrical edition, and he's distressed because Howard borrowed it and "damaged plastic retention hub number three" in "The Apology Insufficiency" (4-7).

M

Manga • A $3.6 billion industry in Japan, *manga* (from the Japanese word meaning "whimsical drawings") refers to comics in all forms with a wide range of subject matter. Imported into the United States, *manga* accounted for $175 million in sales in 2008. Subsets include *Shonen manga* (for boys) and *Shojo manga* (for girls). Popular titles include *Astro Boy* and *Sailor Moon*.

In "The Middle Earth Paradigm" (1-6), Sheldon is not sure what to dress up as for Penny's Halloween party and suggests several options, including some characters from *manga*. (He finally chooses to show up not as a character but as a scientific principle, the Doppler Effect.)

Manhattan Project • Under the command of Major General Leslie R. Groves Jr., this top-secret project began in 1939 and involved one hundred and thirty thousand people working at thirty sites around the United States, Canada, and the United Kingdom. The goal? To produce the world's first atomic bomb, a weapon that, it was hoped, would put an end to the long, bloody war against Japan.

In "The Classified Materials Turbulence" (2-22), when the boys meet to help Howard fix his space toilet problem, Stuart consults Leonard on a personal issue regarding Penny and sees a model of the toilet in the living room of Sheldon's apartment. Howard reminds him that it's classified, to which Leonard responds, "Yeah, it's a regular Manhattan Project."

Mars Rover • To date, there have been five rovers sent to Mars. One of them, *Spirit*, traveled a little under five miles before getting stuck in sand, and thus became a permanent, stationary object. In contrast, the 2004 rover *Opportunity* is still rolling across the red planet, setting a new record for longevity. Three more Mars Rovers are in the works, all from NASA's Jet Propulsion Laboratory near Caltech.

In "The Lizard-Spock Expansion" (2-8), Howard commits a no-no: he breaches security protocol by allowing a civilian without proper clearance to enter the nerve center of JPL where the Mars Rover is controlled, in an attempt to impress her. After driving the rover into a ditch, he covers up his tracks, but Sheldon exposes them two years later to an FBI agent in "The

Apology Insufficiency" (4-7), which results in Howard being denied a higher-level security clearance, handicapping his career possibilities.

The Matrix • A trilogy of movies—*The Matrix* (1999), *The Matrix Reloaded* (2003), and *The Matrix Revolutions* (2003)—starring Keanu Reeves as a computer programmer/hacker named Neo who, in fact, is the chosen "One" who pits himself against the Agents, who have abducted Morpheus. The first film in the series is generally considered the best. The *Matrix* films were noteworthy for their eye-popping special effects, then-groundbreaking techniques that have since become cliché: a stationary object shot with multiple cameras with a freeze-frame technique, accompanied by panning and rotation.

In "The Jerusalem Duality" (1-12), Sheldon is forced to admit that he must live in the shadow of a boy genius named Kim. Sheldon tells him, "The oracle told us little Neo was the One. You can see the Matrix, can't you?"

The third film, *The Matrix Revolutions*, is considered to be the weakest and most confusing. In "The Einstein Approximation" (3-14), when Sheldon is suffering the equivalent of writer's block, Leonard tells Howard, "I haven't seen him this stuck since he tried to figure out the third Matrix movie."

McRib • Sold periodically at McDonald's for a limited time, the McRib is a large ground pork patty with barbecue sauce and onions on a six-inch roll. Devotees swear by it and take frequent trips to the nearest McDonald's when the chain offers it for sale; others swear *at* it, saying it's about as palatable as abandoned shoe leather soaked with motor oil.

In "The Thespian Catalyst" (4-14), when Penny defends *Cat on a Hot Tin Roof* as an "American classic," Sheldon retorts that the McRib is also an American classic, but "I don't care for that either."

Meme • Coined by Richard Dawkins in his 1976 book, *The Selfish Gene*, and socially compared to the ability of a gene to self-replicate, a meme is "an idea, behavior, or style that spreads from person to person within a culture." Examples of memes given in Dawkins' book include melodies, catchphrases, fashion, and the technology of building arches. To which I'd add: rumors.

In "The Herb Garden Germination" (4-20), Sheldon and Amy decide to use their circle of mutual friends to plant competing memes—one mundane, the other potentially explosive—to see which one propogates. Meme #1: Amy is thinking of planting an herb garden, and she's had sex with Sheldon. Meme #2: Amy is thinking of getting orthodics, and she's pregnant by Sheldon. (None of those things is actually true, but they do get the rumor mill cranking.)

Milk Duds • Made by Hershey, this scrumptious chocolate-coated caramel is a perennial favorite.

Sheldon considers it to be "the most apologetic of the boxed candies" and, in exchange for his part in insulting Zack ("The Justice League Recombination," 4-11), offers him some, which Zack accepts. (He also accepts the boys' collective apology.)

Millennium Falcon • From the Star Wars universe, the Millennium Falcon is a spaceship that Han Solo won from Lando Calrissian; Han pilots it through the galaxy with Chewbacca, his tall, muscular, hirsute friend who can't speak English.

In "The Loobenfeld Decay" (1-10), when Leonard makes up an imaginary lecture to attend in order to get out of seeing Penny in a local theater production, Howard mistakenly believes the lecture is real, and tells him, "No, it's okay, it's your Millennium Falcon; you and Chewbacca do whatever you want to do. Me and Princess Leia [i.e., Raj] will find some other way to spend the evening."

"The Miller's Tale" • Using a pilgrimage as a framing device, Geoffrey Chaucer's *Canterbury Tales* recounts the various stories told by the pilgrims to pass the time as they travel to the shrine of Saint Thomas à Becket. Modern readers are usually surprised at how ribald the tales are, especially "The Miller's Tale," which is about a young suitor who, in the dark of night, kisses a beautiful young woman on "hir nether yea." As with Shakespeare, which is best appreciated in the original Klingon (or so says Chancellor Gorkon), Chaucer is best read in the original Middle English.

In "The 21 Second Excitation" (4-8), at a slumber party at Penny's, Amy Farrah Fowler is challenged to tell a dirty story, and she tells "The Miller's Tale." Penny is confused because Amy tells it in the original Middle English, but Bernadette gets it and thinks it's "pretty spicy."

Monopoly • One of the world's most popular board games, it is available in both electronic and "original board" configurations in a wide variety of themes.

In "The Boyfriend Complexity" (4-9), Sheldon states his preference for the original game, as opposed to any of the "novelty editions."

Morrisette, Alanis • A Canadian singer and songwriter who has sold more than 40 million albums worldwide. Her music is classified as alternative rock, pop rock, and post-grunge.

In "The Wheaton Recurrence" (3-19), in the throes of love for Penny, Leonard is putting himself through an emotional ringer. Sheldon tells Penny that it's affecting Leonard's sleep—and his own. "Let me tell you, sleep did not come easily with Leonard in the next room singing along with Alanis Morrisette."

Mumbai • The capital of India, formerly known as Bombay.

In "The Toast Derivation" (4-17), Amy characterizes the exotic-looking Priya as the "fiery jewel of Mumbai."

Muppet Babies • Also known as *Jim Henson's Muppet Babies* (after their creator), this animated series recounts the Muppets' adventures when living in a nursery, cared for by a woman known only as Nanny. The babies' active imaginations take them far afield, but Nanny's return pulls them back to the real world.

In "The Justice League Recombination" (4-11), when Sheldon opines that he and his friends can't collectively go to a Halloween party as the Justice League of America, he says that the default option is to go in "our Muppet Baby costumes."

N

Nadoolman, Deborah • A Hollywood costume designer whose work appeared in *The Blues Brothers* (1980), *Animal House* (1978), and *Indiana Jones and the Raiders of the Lost Ark* (1981).

In "The 21 Second Excitation" (4-8), Sheldon points out to Penny that not only was Nadoolman the costume designer for *Raiders*, but she also "designed the iconic red and black jacket in Michael Jackson's *Thriller* video."

Neutral Zone • A term from the Star Trek universe. Per Wikipedia: "A neutral zone was a sort of buffer zone between the territories of two different powers. If either party entered a neutral zone, it was an aggressive move and usually considered an act of war. The Federation had two Neutral Zones: one with the Klingon Empire and one with the Romulan Star Empire. Used on its own, the Neutral Zone generally refers to the Romulan Neutral Zone. A Neutral Zone in all but name also existed between the Federation and the Cardassians."

In "The Love Car Displacement" (4-13), when Penny and Leonard, who are no longer dating, are forced to share a bed during an out-of-town trip to Big Sur for a science conference, Penny explains that from the waist down, her shields are up. Later, though, she tells him, "You know, maybe it wouldn't be the worst idea in the world to violate the Neutral Zone for just one night."

Nimoy, Leonard • An American actor best known for his portrayal of Spock in *Star Trek: The Original Series* and the movie adaptations that followed. Now retired from the movie business after six decades as an actor, he currently spends a lot of time behind the lens as a still photographer.

Spock is frequently mentioned in *The Big Bang Theory* because of Sheldon's close identification and association with him. In adulthood, Sheldon's reverence for Spock (and, by extension, Nimoy) is such that when Penny gives him an inscribed cloth napkin from Nimoy, which he also wiped his mouth on, Sheldon is overcome with emotion ("The Bath Item Gift Hypothesis," 2-12).

That aside, the relationship Sheldon has with Nimoy is strained. In "The Excelsior Acquisition" (3-16), we learn that, in addition to the recent restraining order from Stan Lee, Sheldon also has one from Nimoy.

Nintendo 64 • The fourth generation of a video game console on which games like *Super Mario Bros.* are played. It was superseded by Nintendo GameCube and, later, Wii.

Sheldon is a big fan of Nintendo; he has classic Nintendo, Super Nintendo, and Nintendo 64, in addition to a handheld Nintendo DS3, which he surreptitiously used in his bathroom ("The Cooper-Nowitzski Theorem," 2-6) with the hope that Ramona Nowitzski wouldn't catch him red-handed, although she does. (She's vigilant.)

Norris, Chuck • An American martial arts expert best known for appearing in the chopsocky movie *Way of the Dragon* (1972), which also starred Bruce Lee, who knew his way around a pair of nunchucks. Norris went on to star in a television series called *Walker, Texas Ranger* (1993–2001). He's also the founder of a martial art called Chun Kuk Do, the precepts of which are his own Ten Commandments.

In "The Alien Parasite Hypothesis" (4-10), Sheldon is enamored with the number "73." Leonard calls it "the Chuck Norris of numbers," an opinion Sheldon dismisses. (For a full explanation of why it, like Chuck Norris, is impressive, at least according to Leonard, see www.walkingrandomly.com/?p=3024.)

The Notebook • A 2004 movie based on the bestselling short novel by Nicholas Sparks. This was the first in a long string of Sparks' *Bridges of Madison County*–styled tales, which are best read with a box of Kleenex in arm's reach (or not read at all).

In "The Boyfriend Complexity" (4-9), Howard admits to having rented the movie, and Raj admits to having enjoyed it.

O

O'Neill, Eugene • An American playwright and a Nobel Laureate in Literature. His first published play, *Beyond the Horizon* (1920), won the Pulitzer Prize for Drama. Among the dozens of plays he's penned, his best known is *The Iceman Cometh* (1939).

In "The Hot Troll Deviation" (4-4), Howard has to come to grips with his fantasy/obsession for Hollywood beauties. And in a fantasy sequence, *Star Trek*'s George Takei, *Battlestar Galatica*'s Katee Sackhoff, and Howard's girlfriend Bernadette triple-team him to bring his flights of fancy to the ground. Takei, discussing typecasting, laments, "You try and stretch as an actor, do Strindberg, O'Neill, but all they want is 'Course laid in, Captain.'"

One Ring • From the *Lord of the Rings* universe. Gollum also refers to it as "My Precious," as it is his raison d'être. Once Gollum got a hold of the ring, it in turn got a hold on Gollum. Exerting its tremendous power, it held Gollum captive and, in the end, cost him his miserable life, but also helped saved Middle-earth from Sauron.

The boys want it, too. And in "The Precious Fragmentation" (3-17), Leonard gets it—his own *precious* . . .

Orion slave girl • From the Star Trek universe, Orions are a green-skinned race from the planet Orion. The first slave girl to appear was Marta, played by Yvonne Craig, in *Star Trek: The Original Series*.

In "The Codpiece Topology" (2-2), we learn a deep, dark secret about Raj: once, while in San Diego at a Comic-Con, he had a dalliance with an Orion slave girl who turned out to be a man.

P

Paintball • A war-gaming sport involving mock battles using specially designed guns that fire paint pellets. The "military" objectives vary, but are generally holding or capturing terrain, and capturing or wiping out the enemy. Unlike, say, a computer video game, paintball takes place in the real world, and thus offers different challenges. Teamwork is essential, and leadership skills come to the forefront.

In "The Middle Earth Paradigm" (1-6), as the boys return from paintball, uniforms splattered with blue paint, Raj reluctantly admits, "We really suck at paintball." Nonetheless, it's one of their favorite weekend activities. And, as

Howard finds out, paintball does have its fringe benefits. In "The Cushion Saturation" (2-16), he's abandoned by his friends during a match and left alone in a shed with Leslie, who decides they should "make every moment count." And so they do: they have coitus.

In the same episode, Penny accidentally discharges three paintball shots into Sheldon's sofa seat cushion. A creature of habit who firmly believes that everything must be in its proper place, Sheldon comes unglued when he discovers that the cushion has been sent off for restoration.

Penis envy • *Time* magazine (Jan. 17, 1977), in "The Sexes: Liberating Women from Freud," explains: "As Freud saw it, female identity grows from an infant girl's shocking discovery that she lacks a penis. Later, in about the third year of her life, she carries this sense of castration and inferiority into the Oedipal cycle, blaming the mother for the loss of the penis, turning to the father as a love object, and converting the wish for a penis into a wish for a child. Child-bearing and most of women's aspirations are, thus, per Freud, attempts to compensate for the missing male organ, and penis envy becomes 'the bedrock' of women's unconscious frustrations throughout life."

In "The Love Car Displacement" (4-13), the subject of penises arises during a science conference at a panel Sheldon is chairing. As it turns out, neither Penny, Amy, or Bernadette have penis envy—but shorthanded Howard does.

Peppermint Patty • From the *Peanuts* universe, created by newspaper cartoonist Charles M. Schultz. Patricia "Peppermint Patty" Reichardt's main attribute is, as Wikipedia notes, "profoundly misunderstanding basic concepts and ideas that most people would consider obvious, leading to ulti-mately embarrassing situations." For instance, she at first thought the dog Snoopy was simply a "funny-looking kid with the big nose."

In "The Barbarian Sublimation" (2-3), the boys talk about what Raj calls a "weird comic book crossover." Howard suggests, "Like if Hulk were dating Peppermint Patty."

Periodic Table • Published in 1869 by Dmitri Mendeleev, the Periodic Table is a chart of chemical elements grouped by kind: metals, metalloids, and nonmetals, with further subdivisions within each.

In "The Love Car Displacement" (4-13), Leonard, Sheldon, Amy, and Penny play the game 20 Questions to pass the time. Sheldon's identity is one of the chemical elements on the period table—a notion that confuses Penny, who suggests "food" because, "Well, it's a table, right? I mean, why can't there be food on it?"

Phantom Zone • From the DC Comics universe, this is a form of interstellar limbo that served as a prison on Krypton. One of its more famous inmates is General Zod, who in *Superman II* came to Earth and, with fellow criminals Ursa and Non, began to terrorize the world until Superman stopped them.

In "The Bozeman Reaction" (3-13), Sheldon, playing charades with Penny and Leonard, gives the Phantom Zone as a clue, which is supposed to lead them to conclude "Higgs Boson Particle. How could you not get that?"

It may be obvious to Sheldon and Leonard, but to Penny it's about as clear as particulate soil on a colloidal suspension—i.e., mud. (Perhaps Penny needs to engage the superior colliculus of her brain?)

Picard, Jean-Luc • The commander of the starship U.S.S. *Enterprise* in the Star Trek universe. He's the kind of commander who thinks his way through problems before taking action, the kind of leader who inspires confidence and loyalty. Between William Shatner's Captain Kirk and Patrick Stewart's Jean-Luc Picard, anecdotal evidence suggests that fans prefer Stewart, who comes across as an exceptionally capable commander whom one would *willingly* follow into combat.

In "The Staircase Implementation" (3-22), Sheldon quizzes prospective roommates, including Leonard, who correctly answers that given a choice between Captains Kirk and Picard, the preferred choice is Picard. Given Sheldon's admiration for Mr. Spock, it's no surprise that he'd prefer the starship captain who is more cerebral.

Picasso, Pablo • Robert Hughes, an art critic for *Time* magazine, wrote, "To say that Pablo Picasso dominated Western art in the 20th century is, by now, the merest commonplace. Before his 50th birthday, the little Spaniard from Malaga had become the very prototype of the modern artist as public figure. No painter before him had a mass audience in his own lifetime." The late painter's website is at picasso.com. In 2010, his "Nude, Green Leaves and Bust" sold for an eye-popping $106.5 million at Christie's in New York.

In "The Bat Jar Conjecture" (1-13), Sheldon feels that being in a physics bowl competition is beneath him, given his intellect; he compares it to having Picasso play Pictionary, Noah Webster (who wrote a dictionary) play Boggle, or Jacques Cousteau (an underwater pioneer) play Go Fish.

Pillsbury Doughboy • The mascot for the Pillsbury Company is a small white figure with a scarf and a chef's hat. Pleasantly plump, the doughboy is also known as Poppin' Fresh, to suggest how he pops out of a can of Crescent Rolls and then into the oven.

In "The Hot Troll Deviation" (4-4), Howard's mother tells him that she left her girdle in the dryer too long, so of course it shrank. The visual effect, she says, is that she's "spilling out like the Pillsbury Doughboy!"

Planet of the Apes • The 1963 novel by Pierre Boulle was made into a film in 1968, starring former NRA head Charlton Heston ("Get your hands off my assault rifle, you damned dirty democrat!"). A remake with the same title, starring Mark Wahlberg, was made in 2001, and a reboot, *Rise of the Planet of the Apes*, came out in 2011. TV also aped the original movie, with a fourteen-episode series in 1974.

The most quoted line is by Charlton Heston, who, on a planet where humans don't talk because they lack a working vocabulary, astounds his gorilla captors by speaking. Heston, who plays an astronaut named Taylor, yells, "Take your stinking paws off me, you damn dirty ape!" At which point the apes go ape.

In "The Pancake Batter Anomaly" (1-11), Sheldon gets sick and the other boys run for cover, hiding out at a *Planet of the Apes* movie marathon at the New Art Theater, wearing ape masks. And naturally, when Raj is caught stealing some of Howard's popcorn, Howard cries, "Take your stinking paws off my popcorn, you damn dirty ape!"

Pon farr • From the Start Trek universe, this is nature's way of insuring the propagation of the Vulcan species. Says Wikipedia, it's "a psychophysical condition affecting Vulcans, in which Vulcan males and females go into heat every seven years, going into a blood fever, becoming violent, and finally dying if they do not mate with someone with whom they are empathically bonded."

In the 2006 pilot (unaired), a female colleague named Gilda has sex with Sheldon, who is costumed as Mr. Spock, at a *Star Trek* convention. She cannot resist him because he so accurately portrays a Vulcan undergoing *pon farr*.

Pope Paul V • Pope Paul V (1550–1621) forbade Galileo from publicly supporting the Copernican theory of the universe on the grounds that it was heretical. In response, Galileo went to Rome to defend the theory, which got him a prison sentence and religious penalties.

In "The Wheaton Recurrence" (3-19), Sheldon likens his archnemesis, Wil Wheaton, to Pope Paul V and himself to Galileo.

Power Rangers • An American entertainment and merchandising franchise inspired by Japan's Super Sentai franchise, the Power Rangers are humans that morph into superheroes. The normal battle configuration is five team members wearing color-coded battle suits.

In "The Guitarist Amplification" (3-7), Sheldon expresses concerns about getting to the theater on time, but Penny's in the hallway, and that brings everything to a halt as she and Leonard share an awkward encounter. Sheldon's urgings to his friends ("Go, go, Power Rangers, go!") go unheeded.

Q

Quiznos • A fast-food retail chain specializing in toasted submarine sandwiches. There are over four thousand shops domestically, with hundreds more around the world. Its main competitor is Subway, the industry leader.

In "The Alien Parasite Hypothesis" (4-10), Amy Farrah Fowler is slicing brain tissue, and when Sheldon—no biologist he—asks whether she's slicing it "too thin," she replies, "It's too thin if I were making a foot-long brain sandwich at Quiznos."

R

R2-D2 • This astromech droid appears in all six of the Star Wars movies, most often as a companion to C-3PO. R2-D2's name is said to have originated in a conversation between George Lucas and a coworker; they were editing *American Graffiti* (1973), and the coworker asked for "Reel Two, Dialog Two," which was abbreviated "R2-D2."

In "The Cruciferous Vegetable Amplification" (4-2), Sheldon appears in the guise of a mobile virtual presence device, making him a target for ridicule. Stealing a line from Raj, Howard says, "Oh, look, it's Leonard and R2-D-Bag."

Radiohead • An English alternative rock band formed in 1985, popular with fans and highly regarded by music critics, they have sold more than 30 million albums. In a ranking compiled by *Rolling Stone* magazine, they are counted among the top 100 bands of all time. The band, nominated for dozens of awards, has won the coveted Grammy three times.

In "The Work Song Nanocluster" (2-18), Sheldon loftily asserts, "I have a working knowledge of the entire universe and everything it contains." Attempting to put things in perspective, Penny asks, "Who's Radiohead?" Sheldon clarifies, "I have a working knowledge of the *important* things in the universe."

Raiders of the Lost Ark • A film and entertainment franchise from George Lucas. It has since been retitled *Indiana Jones and the Raiders of the Lost Ark*, to keep it consistent with the other films that followed. In the title role, Harrison Ford is a teacher, archaeologist, and adventurer. In this film, at the behest of the U.S. government, Indy goes up against the Nazis, who are anxious to find the Ark of the Covenant for use as a military weapon. Directed by Steven Spielberg, *Raiders* is a Saturday matinee, the ultimate popcorn movie, and great fun from start to finish. It inspired the Lara Croft game/movies, among other franchises.

This movie is the subject of "The 21 Second Excitation" (4-8), in which twenty-one seconds are restored in the original movie footage, thus providing the impetus for fans to see it again. (In actuality, there's no such restoration. What you see with the first movie is what you get. No director's cuts, no expanded or extended editions. Nada.)

Rebel Alliance • From the Star Wars universe, this resistance movement fought the Galactic Empire. One of its founding members was Princess Leia Organa.

In "The Zazzy Substitution" (4-3), Leonard has misgivings about Sheldon's new friend Amy, and tells him, "I'm not sure she's the best fit for our little—how should we call it—Rebel Alliance." To which Sheldon replies, "I never identified with the Rebel Alliance. Despite their tendency to build Death Stars, I've always been more of an Empire man."

"Red Leader"; "Red Five" • In *Star Wars IV (A New Hope)*, the climactic scene is an assault on the first Death Star with X-wing starfighters from the Rebel Alliance based on a moon, Yavin IV. Both code names are radio call signs: "Red Five" is Luke Skywalker, and "Red Leader" is Garven Dreis, his squadron commander.

In "The Love Car Displacement" (4-13), Sheldon is in the lead car and, as travel supervisor, is using a walkie-talkie to keep in communication with Howard in the rear car. Of course, to Sheldon, it makes perfect sense to use these two references from *Star Wars*, one of their favorite movies, as their call signs.

Red Vines • Manufactured by American Licorice, this red candy comes in long strings approximately six inches in length. It's described by its manufacturer as having "a distinctive, rich taste, soft and chewy texture, and desirable appearance."

In "The Hot Troll Deviation" (4-4), we learn that Sheldon keeps a bag of Red Vines in a drawer in his office. This distresses Raj because he wants a desk, but Sheldon maintains there's no budget for it—yet there's money for Sheldon's treats.

Renaissance Faire • Originally started in Southern California, these fairs are a step back in time to the Elizabethan Age. Attendees are encouraged to dress in period clothing, and merchants and actors are required to be in costume and role-play accordingly.

In "The Codpiece Topology" (2-2), the boys return from a Renaissance Faire symbolically dressed: Sheldon as a medieval monk, Howard as a court jester with a hand puppet, Raj as a nobleman, and Leonard as a knight in shining armor.

Sheldon—who is unhappy because it was the "worst Renaissance Faire ever . . . It was rife with historical inaccuracies"—later returns in a different guise, as Mr. Spock, which of course would violate *Star Trek*'s Prime Directive.

Road Runner • From the Warner Bros. universe, created by Chuck Jones, this superfast bird always eludes the conniving Wile E. Coyote. Road Runner's trademark is a distinctive "*Beep, Beep!*" sound he makes before rocketing off and leaving Coyote in the dust, usually holding a bag containing an anvil or explosive device.

In "The Cruciferous Vegetable Amplification" (4-2), Leonard sees Sheldon writing on whiteboards in their apartment and asks, "Working on a new plan to catch the Road Runner?" Sheldon replies, "The humorous implication being that I am Wile E. Coyote?"

Robin • A sidekick to Batman, from the DC Comics universe. Dick Grayson was the first Robin, who then became Nightwing and went on to star in *The New Teen Titans*. Jason Todd was the second Robin.

In "The Hofstadter Isotope" (2-20), Stuart and Sheldon debate whether Dick Grayson or Jason Todd should be the next Batman. Sheldon states, "I am asserting, in the event that Batman's death proves permanent, that original Robin, Dick Grayson, is the logical successor to the Bat Cowl."

Rock Band • A video game from Harmonix Music Systems, available on multiple devices, that allows players to simulate playing their favorite instruments as members of a rock band.

In "The Bath Item Gift Hypothesis" (2-11), the boys meet their match in Dr. David Underhill, who is smart, funny, tall, handsome, and personable. In other words, he's everything they want to be. Naturally, comparisons are made, and when Leonard, who is quite taken with him, tells Howard and

Sheldon that David's "in a rock band," Howard is unimpressed. "So? We're in a rock band." Leonard points out the difference: David is in a *real* rock band, whereas the boys merely play a computerized version.

In "The Psychic Vortex" (3-12), when Raj and Sheldon score at a university mixer, they bring the girls to Sheldon's apartment and they all play *Rock Band*.

Romulans • From the Star Trek universe. Hailing from the planets Romulus and Remus, this race began as a dissenting group of Vulcans who rejected the teachings of Vulcan philosopher Surak, who preached the suppression of emotions.

In "The Love Car Displacement" (4-13), *Star Trek*'s Neutral Zone, a buffer between the Federation and the Romulans, is discussed in the context of sexual politics—sharing a bed.

Ross, Alex • Nelson Alexander "Alex" Ross is a comic book artist whose distinctive painting style is a fan favorite—so much so that *Comic Buyer's Guide* had to retire the "Favorite Painter Fan Award" because Ross quickly came to dominate the category. His style makes his work a natural for covers, posters, and licensed products. Working with writer Paul Dini, he created *War on Crime*, an oversized graphic novel/album featuring Batman, in 1999.

In "The Peanut Reaction" (1-16), as the boys ponder what to get Leonard for his first ever birthday party, Raj buys him (as Howard tells it) "an awesome limited-edition Dark Knight sculpture based on Alex Ross' definitive Batman."

Rowlands, Gena • An American actress who has won two Emmys and two Golden Globes. She acted in *The Notebook*, which was directed by her son, Nick Cassavetes.

In "The Boyfriend Complexity" (4-9), Howard agrees with Raj that in *The Notebook*, Rowlands is "a treasure."

S

Sackhoff, Katee • A blonde American actress best known for her role as Captain Kara "Starbuck" Thrace on *Battlestar Galactica*. Sackhoff joined the cast of *CSI: Crime Scene Investigation* in 2010.

In "The Vengeance Formulation" (3-9), Sackhoff lectures Howard on the difference between fantasy and reality, as it pertains to him being with her or being with a real woman like Bernadette.

Later, Sackhoff again serves as Howard's conscience, in "The Hot Troll

Deviation" (4-4), teaming up with *Star Trek*'s George Takei to help Howard woo Bernadette.

Saturn 3 • Released in 1980, this derivative, unimaginative, lackluster "sci-fi" (a derogatory term among science-fiction fans) film starred Kirk Douglas, Farrah Fawcett, and Harvey Keitel. The story centers around a moon called Saturn 3 orbiting the planet of the same name, and a berserk robot named Hector.

In "The Lizard-Spock Expansion" (2-8), when Sheldon notes that *Saturn 3* is on, Raj protests: "I don't want to watch *Saturn 3*. *Deep Space Nine* is better."

Raj is right. It's clearly better. In fact, watching static on the screen is better.

Schumacher, Joel • The director of *Batman Forever* (1995), which featured Val Kilmer as Batman, Chris O'Donnell as Robin, Nicole Kidman as Dr. Chase Meridian, Tommy Lee Jones as Two-Face, and Jim Carrey as the Riddler.

In "The Creepy Candy Coating Corollary" (3-5), Sheldon cites Schumacher as being fifth on his list of all-time enemies, because he's the one "who nearly destroyed the Batman movie franchise."

Seaworld • With locations in San Diego, Orlando, and San Antonio, this is a watery wonderland where, among attractions too numerous to mention, you can see Atlantic Bottlenose dolphins, sea lions, and sting rays. Aquatic-oriented children and adults alike will find their porpoise—er, purpose—in coming is simply to have fun.

In "The Zarnecki Incursion" (4-19), Sheldon suggests a trip to Seaworld rather than Raj's suggestion of Legoland.

Second Life • An online virtual world populated by 20 million user accounts worldwide whose online personas, or avatars, interact with others: socializing, shopping, selling, etc. The sense of reality is heightened by its realistic look and feel.

In "The Fuzzy Boots Corollary" (1-3), Sheldon suggests that, to cool off, his friends join him for a swim in Second Life, as he "just built a virtual pool."

Semiotics • "The study of cultural sign processes, analogy, metaphor, signification and communication, signs and symbols," according to Wikipedia.

In "The Hamburger Postulate" (1-5), befuddled by the symbolism of a tie on Leonard's bedroom's doorknob, Sheldon solicits Penny's input: "I need your opinion on a matter of semiotics." Penny tells him it means that "someone doesn't want to be disturbed because they're, you know, getting busy." In short, Sheldon, coitus.

Shatner, William • Known and loved by science-fiction fans everywhere, Shatner had a long career in film and television before appearing as Captain James Tiberius Kirk in the original television series *Star Trek* (1966–1969), his best-known role. Trekkers (they hate to be called Trekkies) like to debate who, among the various commanders, is the best of the best. (Most salute Captain Jean Luc Picard.)

Sheldon has a strong appreciation for Shatner. In "The Bat Jar Conjecture" (1-13), when Penny asks a trivia question about who holds the record for the most appearances on the cover of *People* magazine as "Sexiest Man of the Year," Sheldon immediately responds, "William Shatner."

In "The Pants Alternative" (3-18), Sheldon muses, "Why wasn't William Shatner in the new *Star Trek* movie?" (Abrams and his staff of writers say they tried but couldn't figure out a plot point where Captain Kirk could be logically inserted, as they had done with Leonard Nimoy's Mr. Spock.) But in the same episode, perhaps realizing that Shatner was becoming a fading star, Sheldon says that he is the William Shatner of theoretical physics.

She-Hulk • From the Marvel Comics universe, Jennifer Susan Walters is a female version of the Hulk. A lawyer by profession, she's the cousin of Bruce Banner, the Incredible Hulk.

In "The Boyfriend Complexity" (4-9), Raj asserts that the "bravest person in the Marvel Universe . . . [is] whoever has to give She-Hulk a bikini wax."

"Shields up" • From the Star Trek universe, the act of extending an artificially created force field around a starship, other craft, or planetary body to protect it against all manners of hazards, especially ship-to-ship attacks.

In "The Love Car Displacement" (4-13), Penny tells Leonard, who is sharing a bed with her in Big Sur during a science conference, that insofar as she's concerned, from the waist down, her shields are up. Not too long after that, though, Penny lowers said shields.

Engage. Thrusters on half-impulse power . . .

Shiksa • The Yiddish word for an attractive girl or woman who is a Gentile (a non-Israelite) and would be a temptation for a Jewish boy or man.

Penny. Summer Glau. Sheldon's fraternal twin sister, Missy. Katee Sackhoff. All *shiksas*. Every woman that Howard has lusted after and never known (in the biblical sense). But he's now engaged to a blonde *shiksa*, so his tale ends well. *Shalom!*

Short Round • From the Indiana Jones universe, this character, whose real name is Kennon Wong, is a young orphan who becomes Indy's sidekick. He first appeared in *Indiana Jones and the Temple of Doom*, a relentlessly grim film that, by general consensus, is the worst of the series.

In "The 21 Second Excitation" (3-23), after Sheldon sneaks into the theater to steal two reels of film (footage from *Indiana Jones and the Raiders of the Lost Ark*), he calls Leonard "Short Round" to identify him as his sidekick.

Shuttlecraft • From the Star Trek universe. Notes Wikipedia, it's "a smaller type of ship, usually capable of atmospheric transport, detachable from a larger starship's shuttle bay."

In "The Maternal Congruence" (3-11), when Leonard's mother comes to visit, Sheldon knocks on Leonard's door and offers solace. When asked what he wants, Sheldon replies, "What I want is to be departing the Starship *Enterprise* in a one-man shuttlecraft headed to the planetoid I rule known as Sheldon Alpha Five."

Shyamalan, M. Night • An American filmmaker and screenwriter of Asian Indian heritage whose contemporary, paranormal movies often employ twist endings, he came to prominence with his 1999 movie *The Sixth Sense*, which was nominated for six Academy Awards.

In "The Terminator Decoupling" (2-17), Leonard observes that, with one beer in him, Raj mysteriously turns into M. Night Shyamalan.

Silence of the Lambs • Directed by Jonathan Demme, this 1991 movie, based on Thomas Harris' novel of the same name, is the story of brilliant psychiatrist/serial killer Dr. Hannibal Lecter (Anthony Hopkins) and FBI trainee Clarice Starling (Jodie Foster). The movie won five Academy Awards for "Best Picture," "Best Actress" (Foster), "Best Actor" (Hopkins), "Best Director" (Demme), and "Best Adapted Screenplay" (Ted Tally).

In "The Jiminy Conjecture" (3-2), Sheldon, Howard, and Raj descend into the darkened depths of the Entomology Department to ask Professor "Creepy" Crawley to settle a bet. Its oppressive, dark atmosphere prompts Raj to say, "Holy crap. It's like *Silence of the Lambs* down here."

Silver Bullet • Coors light beer packaged in a silver can.

In "The Zazzy Substitution" (4-3), Penny's refrigerator is stocked with

Silver Bullets, which an inebriated Raj is sucking down, one after another, changing his behavior from civilized to obnoxious.

Silver Surfer • From the Marvel Comics universe, a superhero and tragic figure who first appeared in *Fantastic Four* #48. Astronomer Norrin Radd strikes a deal with Galactus to spare his home planet from destruction by agreeing to serve as an advance scout to locate other planets for his insatiable life-form consumption. Galactus gives Radd a small portion of his power, transforming him into a silver-colored man who uses a silver surfboard that flies faster than the speed of light (299,792,458 meters per second, to be exact) to travel through interstellar space.

In "The Jiminy Conjecture" (3-2), for a bet, Howard puts up his issue of *The Fantastic Four* with the first appearance of the Silver Surfer.

SimCity • Designed by Will Wright, this city-building simulation game, like a giant coral reef, keeps adding to itself. It runs on all the popular computer and gaming platforms. As Wikipedia notes, "The inspiration for *SimCity* came from a feature of the game *Raid on Bungeling Bay* that allowed Wright to create his own maps during development. Wright soon found he enjoyed creating maps more than playing the actual game, and *SimCity* was born."

In "The Pants Alternative" (3-18), Sheldon needs to prepare, physically and mentally, to overcome his stage fright. So he immerses himself in a fantasy construct he enjoys, where he feels "most at home," as Raj puts it. The place is SimCity. "More specifically, the SimCity I designed: Sheldonopolis." (Its name was obviously inspired by Superman's city of Metropolis.)

The Simpsons • An animated feature created by cartoonist Matt Groening in 1989 about a working-class family in the fictional suburb Springfield. It's a satire of contemporary America and a major pop culture franchise, and it's the longest-running entertainment series on American television. Hard-core fans will want (or might already have) *Simpsons World, The Ultimate Episode Guide: Seasons 1–20*, a massive twelve hundred-page illustrated explication of every episode. D'oh!

In "The Griffin Equivalency" (2-4), Howard makes an allusion to Leonard that Raj is Doctor Apu from the Kwik-E-Mart on *The Simpsons*. Dr. Nahasapeemapetilon Apu is an Indian who holds a PhD in computer science, and who also attended Caltech (Calcutta Technical Institute).

Slumdog Millionaire • Directed by Danny Boyle, this 2008 film was adapted from the novel *Q&A* by Vikas Swarup. The winner of eight Academy Awards, it's about an eighteen-year-old street-smart orphan named Jamal Malik from the slums of Mumbai who goes on India's television show *Who Wants to be a Millionaire?* Convinced that he's somehow cheating, on the grounds that no "slumdog" could possibly know so much, he's arrested by the police and, while recounting his life, proves how he legitimately came to know the answer to each of the questions posed by the show's host.

In "The Terminator Decoupling" (2-17), actress Summer Glau is on the same train as the boys, heading down to San Francisco to attend a symposium. Raj, who is known to stretch the truth to further his own ends, tells Glau that *Slumdog Millionaire*, a movie she "loved," was based on his own life.

Smurf Rescue • A vintage ColecoVision video game from 1982 that ran on the Atari 2600. In the game, Smurfette is held at Gargamel's castle, and the player will encounter, and overcome, a series of obstacles to rescue her.

In "The Toast Derivation" (4-17), Sheldon offers this, along with Atari's *Cookie Monster Munch* and a text adventure called *Zork*, as possible choices for play at a get-together at his apartment. Barry Kripke speaks for the other two guests when he suggests karaoke and beer instead.

Snoopy Sno Cone Maker • Manufactured by Sababa Toys starting in 1979, this children's toy transforms ice cubes into shavings, which are then flavored, to create "snow" cones. (Snoopy is an anthropomorphic dog in Charles Schultz's newspaper strip, *Peanuts*.)

In "The Irish Pub Formulation" (4-6), Leonard mentions that Raj had given Sheldon one as a Thanksgiving gift.

Spider-Man • The most popular character in the Marvel Comics universe, Spider-Man is the alter ego of high school nerd Peter Parker, who was bitten by a radioactive spider, giving him superpowers consistent with a spider's abilities. Created by Stan Lee and artist Steve Ditko, Spider-Man's endearing quality is that even though he was blessed (or cursed, depending on your perspective) with superpowers, he still had to live in the real world, with all its attendant frustrations.

In "The Hofstadter Isotope" (2-20), Sheldon confuses Penny when she is shopping for a comic for a nephew at Stuart's comic book store. She suggests Spider-Man but is bewildered by all the different comic books in which he's appeared in and thus unable to make a decision.

More than any other character in the superhero universe, the boys recall Peter Parker. Parker, the archetypical nerd, is tall and thin, and with distinct features, and, like all the boys, he is fiercely smart, though shy and unsure of himself around girls.

Spider-Man 2 • From the Marvel Comics universe, this 2004 movie, the second in the series, was directed by Sam Raimi and stars Tobey Maguire as Spider-Man/Peter Parker and Kirsten Dunst as Mary Jane. The film pits Spider-Man against Doc Ock, played by Alfred Molina.

In "The Creepy Candy Coating Corollary" (3-5), Sheldon, who has an eidetic memory, says that June 30, 2004, was the opening day of *Spider-Man 2* at the AMC Pasadena (which has since closed).

"Splash Zone" • In David Cronenberg's 1981 movie, *Scanners*, the character Revok can cause another person's head to explode merely by imagining it.

In "The Cooper-Hofstadter Polarization" (1-9), Sheldon is dealing with the ongoing frustration of Leonard's swollen ego as they try to give a talk together on a jointly written paper. Sheldon warns the audience, "Heads up, you people in the front row, this is a splash zone." Then he concentrates intently in the hope that he will cause Leonard's head to explode.

Spock • A character from the Star Trek universe who first appeared on television in *Star Trek: The Original Series*, played by Leonard Nimoy. Originally, it was assumed by the network that Captain James T. Kirk, commander of the starship *Enterprise*, would be the standout character, but not so. Spock—half Vulcan, half human—proved to be the most enduring and fascinating character in the franchise. Spock's most recent appearance was in J.J. Abrams' reboot, *Star Trek* (2009).

As mentioned in *Nimoy, Leonard*, Spock is frequently mentioned in *The Big Bang Theory* because of Sheldon's close identification and association with him. In "The Codpiece Topology" (2-2), Sheldon takes a trip to a Renaissance Faire dressed as Mr. Spock, complete with pointy ears and a Tricorder in hand. In "The Adhesive Duck Deficiency" (3-8), Sheldon explains to Penny that Spock was not the head engineer of the *Enterprise* but its science officer, and they have a discussion about maintenance matters. Most significantly, in "The Thespian Catalyst" (4-14), we see Sheldon's deep-rooted attachment to his mother when he acts out a work of fan fiction he wrote as a child, "Where No Sheldon Has Gone Before," which centers around Spock taking him from East Texas into the future to help save "a troubled galaxy." He breaks down in front of Penny and, on the phone, tells his mother, "I love you. Don't let Spock take me to the future!"

Stadium Pal • A plastic bag for men to strap to their lower leg to collect their piss, allowing them to drink like a fish and not worry about getting up and going to the men's room. The product's official website (stadiumpal.com) states that it's "the ultimate portable urinal" and cites its popularity among long-distance motorcycle riders, paragliders, and those attending events like Oktoberfest, Mardi Gras, and New Year's Eve at Times Square.

In "The 21 Second Excitation" (4-8), Howard straps one on while he's standing in line to get into a midnight showing of *Raiders of the Lost Ark*. Of course, using one is all well and good until you have to run with it sloshing around your leg.

Starfleet Academy • From the Star Trek universe, Starfleet's motto is "From the stars, knowledge." Modeled, presumably, after a naval military academy like Annapolis, Starfleet Academy is located near San Francisco, and its cadets come from all over the galaxy, all members of the United Federation of Planets. Upon graduation, Starfleet's cadets are commissioned as ensigns and assigned to their first duty station, which they hope will be in a Federation starship.

In "The Creepy Candy Coating Corollary" (3-5), Sheldon, who identified with the character of Wesley Crusher on *Star Trek: The Next Generation*, wore his Starfleet Academy cadet uniform and traveled by bus to a convention in Mississippi, hoping to get Wil Wheaton's signature on his "mint-in-package Wesley Crusher action figure."

Starfleet General Order 104 • In the Star Trek universe, Order 104, Section C addresses the issue of "fitness of duty," stating that it "grants to the Chief Medical Officer the right to relieve the commander on duty if the CMO can demonstrate the commanding officer is physically or mentally unfit. The CMO must log in his medical records the test results that led to this conclusion," according to *Star Trek Role Playing Game: Player's Guide*.

In "The White Asparagus Triangulation" (2-9), Sheldon cites this as Section A of this General Order to Leonard, who refuses to accept it. When pressed to explain why, Leonard says, "General Order 104, Section A, does not apply in this situation . . . Because this is not *Star Trek*."

In point of fact, there *is* no "General Order 104, Section A," so Leonard could have responded: "It does not apply in this situation because it doesn't exist in the Star Trek universe; and, besides, this is not *Star Trek.*"

Star Trek films • To date there have been eleven films based on the Star Trek universe, with a much-needed, *long* overdue reboot in 2009 called, simply, *Star Trek*, from director J.J. Abrams (not to be confused with *Star Trek: The Motion Picture* [1979], the first film in the franchise). He will again take the conn for the next film in this series.

A frequent point of reference on the show, the *Star Trek* television universe, from the original television series to the 2009 movie reboot by J.J. Abrams, is often referred to on *The Big Bang Theory*.

The following entries are arranged chronologically by date of movie release.

Star Trek: The Motion Picture • After waiting for a decade to see the original cast on the silver screen, Star Trek fans were finally rewarded on December 7, 1979, with the release of this movie. The plot: the *Enterprise* rushes into deep space to confront V'ger, which turns out to be an alien-modified *Voyager 6*. The result: it failed to please critics and the fans, who agreed that it was a cosmic bore. It grossed—an appropriate word in this case—$139 million worldwide, but on the strength of the franchise, not on its own (de)merits.

In "The Alien Parasite Hypothesis" (4-10), Sheldon tells Amy Farrah Fowler that this movie is, in a word, "terrible."

Star Trek IV: The Voyage Home • Directed by Leonard Nimoy, this 1986 movie broke the Star Trek film franchise mold. Set largely on Earth circa the mid-eighties, in and around San Francisco, it's a story in which the crew must fly back to present-day Earth to save its future. Earth is threatened by extinction from an orbiting massive alien artifact that sends out a signal only humpback whales can answer. *The Voyage Home* is a fan favorite, in part because it's the only film set on an Earth we recognize, whereas the other movies all take place in outer space.

In "The Lizard-Spock Expansion" (2-8), Sheldon asserts that this movie is "unarguably the best," though Raj, who favors *Wrath of Khan*, disagrees.

Star Trek V • Directed by William Shatner, this 1989 movie is generally considered to be the worst Star Trek movie of all time. The blame can be laid on its banal plot involving a renegade Vulcan who hijacks the U.S.S. *Enterprise* to travel to the planet Sha Ka Ree, where he expects to come face-to-face with God. (Set phasers on stunned disbelief.)

In "The Lizard-Spock Expansion" (2-8), Sheldon and Raj have a heated discussion on which is the worst Star Trek movie of all time. Raj cites *Star Trek V*, but Sheldon logically articulates why the first Star Trek movie is overwhelmingly worse.

Star Trek Nemesis • Directed by Stuart Baird, this 2002 film was the tenth in the Star Trek franchise. Neither a critical or financial success, it is notable for being the last film that featured a legacy crew, that of *The Next Generation*.

In "The 21 Second Excitation" (4-8), Leonard and Sheldon contextually discuss this movie in relation to waiting to see *Raiders of the Lost Ark* with footage restored.

Star Wars • Released on May 25, 1977, the first in a series of seven movies in the Star Wars film franchise. It was later updated with new special effects and the addition of new scenes, and retitled *Star Wars Episode IV: A New Hope*. Most baby boomers strongly prefer the first three films in the series because of their emphases on story value; today's audience, used to more sophisticated special effects and eye candy, tends to prefer the more current films. For fans who want to know more about *Star Wars*, a handy resource is the "Wookiepedia: The Star Wars Wiki" (http://starwars.wikia.com/wiki/Main_Page).

Though the boys are bigger fans of *Star Trek* than *Star Wars*, George Lucas' space fantasy provides plenty of reference points throughout *The Big Bang Theory*, especially in terms of trivia questions. The boys have seen all six of the theatrical releases, and through dating Leonard, even Penny's knowledge of *Star Wars* is impressive.

Star Wars: The Empire Strikes Back • Directed by Irvin Kershner, *Star Wars Episode V* is a fan favorite for many reasons: the battle on the ice planet Hoth, Luke undergoing training under the Jedi master Yoda, the floating gas mining colony over Bespin where Han Solo sees his old friend Lando Calrissian, Han getting the deep-freeze treatment (carbon freezing), Luke and Darth Vader in mortal combat, Leia professing her love for Han, and more. A fun movie to watch and rewatch, this is. (*Note:* To convert speech to Yoda-talk, check out the Yoda-Speak Generator at yodaskeap.co.uk/index/php.)

In "The Wheaton Recurrence" (3-19), after a bout of coitus, Penny quotes Yoda: "Do or do not. There is no try." Leonard is suitably impressed. Now, if he can only get her to wear that metal bikini Princess Leia wore in *Star Wars: The Return of the Jedi* . . . (There are actually websites devoted to that bikini. Check out leiasmetalbikini.com for some eye-popping photos.)

Star Wars: The Phantom Menace • Directed by George Lucas, released on May 19, 1999, this is *Star Wars Episode 1*. It's the story of Anakin Skywalker as a young slave on the planet Tatooine, and introduces us to Queen Amidala, whom he later marries. The movie is visually stunning, with first-rate special effects, but unfortunately the story does not rise to a similar level. As a result, fans and critics alike lambasted it.

In "The Hot Troll Deviation" (4-4), during a heated discussion between Raj and Sheldon at the Cheesecake Factory, Sheldon cites a number of impossibilities, including *The Phantom Menace* being "a timeless classic." He's right: *The Phantom Menace* is a triumph of spectacle over story, a video game on steroids. Even Wil Wheaton, on Twitter, wrote, "True fact: doing the Jar-Jar voice was a challenge, because I'd blocked out the entire memory of suffering through *Phantom Menace*." Ouch!

Strindberg, August • A prolific Swedish playwright (1849–1912). From Wikipedia: "A bold experimenter and iconoclast throughout, he explored a wide range of dramatic methods and purposes, from naturalistic tragedy, monodrama and history plays, to his anticipations of expressionist and surrealist dramatic techniques."

In "The Hot Troll Deviation" (4-4), during an imaginary discussion between actors George Takei and Katee Sackhoff, they commiserate about typecasting. Takei says, "You try and stretch as an actor, do Strindberg, O'Neill, but all they want is: 'Course laid in, Captain.'"

Superman movies • A franchise from DC Comics, the original 1978 movie featured Christopher Reeve as Superman, Margot Kidder as Lois Lane, Marlon Brando as Superman's dad, and Gene Hackman as Lex Luthor.

The creators of Superman the comic, writer Jerry Siegel and artist Joe Schuster, had a difficult time selling the idea to a publisher. After six years, National Allied Publications published *Action Comics* #1 in June 1938. The creators were paid a total of $130 ($10 a page) for their work, and lost all rights. It was a pretty bad deal, since the Superman franchise became a super-property, valued at $1 billion according to attorney Marc Toberoff. But just as Superman stands for "truth, justice, and the American way," justice eventually prevailed, and the lucrative rights to Superman will soon revert to Siegel and Schuster's heirs.

In "The Big Brain Hypothesis" (1-2), the boys invite Penny out for dinner and a Superman movie marathon. As is often the case, they get into a discussion about the scientific accuracies and inaccuracies in those movies, which are rife with both. As Sheldon points out, a falling Lois Lane traveling at 120 miles per hour would be killed if she struck Superman's open hands. Leonard, though, maintains that Superman would match her velocity and thus prevent any damage to Lois.

Super Mario Bros. • A video game created by Japanese Shigeru Miyamoto and Takashi Tezuka for Nintendo in 1985. Super Mario is a "short, pudgy, Italian-American plumber who lives in the Mushroom Kingdom. He repeatedly stops the turtle-like villain Bowser's numerous plans to kidnap Princess Peach and subjugate the Mushroom Kingdom," states Wikipedia.

Kicked out of his own apartment in "The Codpiece Topology" (2-2), Sheldon is on the stairs balancing his laptop on his lap, playing "*Super Mario* on a poorly coded Nintendo 64 emulator."

SyFy • A ghastly rename for the television station that used to be called the SCI FI Channel, which hard-core fans derisively pronounced "skiffy," an allusion to the peanut butter named Skippy, because it sticks to the roof of your mouth. Longtime fans prefer, simply, "SF" or "science fiction" for the genre. The term "sci-fi" was coined by Forrest "Forry" J. Ackerman, who liked the sound of the abbreviation "hi-fi." Calling it "sci-fi" in print or in conversation brands you, among hard-core fans, as a muggle. So don't.

In "The Thespian Catalyst" (4-14), Leonard tells Raj that he hasn't adjusted to the change in the TV station's name, which he pronounces as "siffy," a silly-sounding name.

T

Takei, George • An American actor of Japanese descent, George Hosato Takei is best known as Hikaru Sulu, the Helmsman on U.S.S. *Enterprise* in the original series of *Star Trek*. He went on to command his own starship, U.S.S. *Excelsior*, in *Star Trek VI: The Undiscovered Country*.

As Howard wrestles with his conscience in "The Hot Troll Deviation" (4-4), his doubt manifests itself as two actors, George Takei and Katee Sackhoff, who team up to dish out dating advice. Though Takei appeared in seventy-nine episodes of *Star Trek: The Original Series*, he rarely got a chance to demonstrate his acting skills, particularly his great sense of comic timing. Now open about his homosexuality, Takei takes a good-natured ribbing from Sackhoff, who questions what he could possibly know about women, given his sexual orientation. Takei drolly replies that he reads.

The Taming of the Shrew • A play by William Shakespeare that is categorized as a comedy, but it's no laughing matter for women's libbers, who consider it misogynistic: the main plot is that Petruchio "tames" Katherina until she becomes tractable.

In "The Cohabitation Formulation" (4-16), Priya and Leonard both are very familiar with this play: she acted in it at Cambridge, and he wrote a paper on it in college.

Teleportation • Popularized by Star Trek as a means of transportation, usually from ship to shore, teleportation involves a process called "energizing," which is essentially a way of "faxing" people or objects. Often associated with the famous line, "Beam me up, Scotty"—which has *never* been uttered in any of the Star Trek movies or television shows—theoretical physicist Stephen Hawking told the *New York Times'* Deborah Solomon that "the *Star Trek* version is bogus, but there's a sense in which Hawking radiation—the light and particles that come out of black holes—escapes by teleportation."

In "The Jerusalem Duality" (1-12), Sheldon, though he's a big *Star Trek* fan, tells Leonard, "I would never use a transporter." The idea of having one's atoms disassembled and then reassembled elsewhere is a problematic proposition: the likelihood of human and mechanical errors logically leads Sheldon to the conclusion that it is not yet ready for prime time.

Terminator • A popular franchise that has spawned movies, books, and television series, in which various versions of Terminators travel back in time to change the past, in order to prevent the future from happening. The first movie, *The Terminator* (1984), starred Arnold Schwarzenegger, who reprised his role in *Terminator 2: Judgment Day* (1991), and *Terminator 3: Rise of the Machines* (2003).

In "The Terminator Decoupling" (2-17), the boys have a close encounter with a Terminator, in the guise of Summer Glau, who terminates Howard and Leonard's attempts to pick her up.

Tetris • A puzzle video game invented by Alexey Pajitnov and released in 1984, which has sold over 70 million video-based copies, and more than 100 million copies for play on cell phones.

In "The Peanut Reaction" (1-16), the boys are at the Cheesecake Factory playing a variation of Tetris—Trestling, which combines Tetris with arm wrestling—to the annoyance of the restaurant staff.

"There are more things . . ." • From *Hamlet* (Act 1, scene 5) by William Shakespeare. "There are more things in heaven and earth, Horatio, / Than are dreamt of in your philosophy."

In "The Gothowitz Deviation" (3-3), in which Sheldon successfully modifies Penny's behavior with the use of positive reinforcement by giving her chocolate treats, he dismisses Leonard's assessment of the proceedings. Sheldon responds with this quote.

Theremin • This eerie-sounding musical instrument was invented by Leon Theremin in 1928. Because of its unusual and distinctive sound, it's been used in many movie soundtracks, including the original *The Day the Earth Stood Still* (1951), *The Lost Weekend* (1945), and *Spellbound* (1945). Its sound was simulated by soprano Loulie Jean Norman for the original *Star Trek* television show that first aired in 1966.

What makes it unusual is that the Theremin is played without touching the actual instrument. From Wikipedia: "The controlling section usually consists of two metal antennas which sense the position of the player's hands and control oscillators for the frequency with one hand, and amplitude (volume) with the other, so it can be played without being touched. The electric signals are amplified and sent to a loudspeaker."

In "The Bus Pants Utilization" (4-12), Sheldon uses a Theremin to distract the other boys. Leonard, who is at the end of his rope, yells out, "We're working here!" Sheldon serenely replies, "That's all right. I can barely hear you over my Theremin." Leonard's response: he pulls its plug.

Nerd note: Sheldon says that he's always loved the Theremin after hearing it as part of the original *Star Trek* television theme music in 1966. One might reasonably ask: In what universe did he hear the Theremin played on *Star Trek*? Because on planet Earth, what he heard was not the musical instrument itself but the voice of a famous coloratura soprano named Loulie Jean Norman.

The Thing • From the Marvel Comics universe, he is one of the members of the Fantastic Four. First appearing in *The Fantastic Four* #1 (November 1961), Benjamin Grimm as the Thing certainly looks grim, with his lumpy, orange-colored skin. With a quick temper and superhuman strength, he's a formidable one-man army.

In "The Boyfriend Complexity" (4-9), the boys discuss who's the bravest person in the Marvel Comics universe. Leonard suggests that the person who goes into a bathroom after the Thing deserves that honor.

The Thing • Not to be confused with the Marvel Comics character of the same name, this 1982 science-fiction/horror film was directed by John Carpenter. From Wikipedia: "The film's title refers to its primary antagonist: a parasitic extraterrestrial life form that assimilates other organisms and in turn imitates them. It infiltrates an Antarctic research station, taking the appearance of the researchers that it kills, and paranoia occurs within the group."

In "The Monopolar Expedition" (2-23), when the boys are in the North Pole at a remote testing facility, Howard suggests they all watch this movie.

The Time Machine • A 1960 film based on the H.G. Wells book of the same name, in which a time traveler goes thousands of years into Earth's future to find two races: the warring subterranean Morlocks and the peaceful surface-dwelling Eloi. The film depicts a curious-looking time machine with a large circular disk positioned behind the time traveler, who mans a dashboard resembling a slot machine. The movie was remade in 2002, but lacked the charm of the original.

In "The Nerdvana Annihilation" (1-14), the boys chip in to buy a movie prop, the Time Machine, which takes Sheldon on a flight of imagination: he sleeps, but not soundly, because he's in a nightmare in which the Morlocks attack him.

Thomas the Tank Engine • A toy train manufactured by Gullane (Thomas) Limited. Says its official website (thomasandfriends.com): "Thomas is the No. 1 blue engine. He is a cheeky little engine who often gets into scraps, usually by being over-eager to do things best left to bigger and more sensible engines."

In "The Irish Pub Formulation" (4-6), Raj mentions that he got Sheldon one as a Thanksgiving gift.

Thor • "A hammer-wielding god associated with thunder, lightning, storms, oak trees, strength, destruction, fertility, healing, and the protection of mankind," says Wikipedia. This Norse god was the inspiration for a character of the same name created by comic book legend Stan Lee, who in his autobiography wrote, "How do you make someone stronger than the strongest person? It finally came to me: Don't make him human—make him a god." The character of Thor first appeared in *Journey Into Mystery* #83 (August 1962). In March 1966, *Journey Into Mystery*, with issue #126, was retitled *The Mighty Thor*. In April 2011, simultaneously released with the Thor movie (directed by Kenneth Branagh and starring Chris Hemsworth), The Mighty Thor #1 was published. The first *Thor* movie, directed by Kenneth Branagh and starring Chris Hemsworth, was released in May 2011.

In "The Middle Earth Paradigm" (1-6), Raj dresses up as Thor for Penny's Halloween party.

Total Recall • Based on the Philip K. Dick short story "We Can Remember It for You Wholesale," this 1990 film stars Arnold Schwarzenegger as Doug Quaid, who is confused about his identity. His mission to find out who he really is takes him to Mars, where he searches for Martian rebels, especially a mutant named Kuato, to help him combat Cohaagen, who rules the colonists with an iron fist. As is always the case with a Dick story, reality gets bent, folded, twisted, and mutilated.

In "The Vengeance Formulation" (3-9), Howard admits to Penny and Leonard that when he settles down into a relationship, he'd want it to be with a movie star like Megan Fox or Katee Sackhoff. Astonished, Leonard exclaims, "You'd have a better shot with the three-breasted Martian hooker from *Total Recall*!"

Toy Story 3 • In Pixar's final film in this beloved series, Andy, the little boy, is now grown. As he gets ready to go off to college, he symbolically leaves his childhood, and his associated toys, behind. A critical and financial success, the film was nominated for an Academy Award for "Best Picture." Alas, it didn't win in that category, but it did take home two gold statuettes for "Best Animated Short Film" and "Best Animated Feature Film."

In "The Apology Insufficiency" (4-7), when Sheldon atones for his sin of blurting out Howard's Mars Rover incident to an FBI agent, which costs Howard the security clearance and a better job, Raj witnesses the exchange and says, "I haven't cried like this since *Toy Story 3*."

Travel Town • Located at Zoo Drive in Los Angeles, this is a museum "preserving and celebrating the rich railroad heritage of Los Angeles," according to its official website, traveltown.org.

Given Sheldon's love for trains, it's not surprising that this is one of his favorite destinations, which he suggests as a tour stop for Raj's sister Priya in "The Irish Pub Formulation" (4-6). She's not a big train enthusiast, though, except for perhaps the sleeping compartment if Leonard's around.

Tribbles: "The Trouble with Tribbles" • Episode 44 from the original *Star Trek* television series, which aired on December 29, 1967. This episode, one of the most popular, and humorous, episodes in Star Trek history, was written by David Gerrold, then an undergraduate. The plot: a small, furry, sentient creature called a Tribble is brought about the Enterprise as a pet, but reproduces so fast Tribbles soon overrun the ship.

In "The Hofstadter Isotope" (2-20), Sheldon chides Leonard for turning off the TV, which is showing "the classic *Deep Space Nine/Star Trek: The Original Series* 'Trouble with Tribbles' crossover episode."

Tri-D chess • For chess fans who like a challenge, Tri-D (tri-dimensional) Chess is a favorite game onboard the U.S.S. *Enterprise* in *Star Trek: The Original Series*.

"The Pancake Batter Anomaly" (1-11) opens with Sheldon easily besting Leonard at this game. Sheldon then taunts, "It must be humbling to suck on so many different levels."

Truth or Dare • A party game in which one must truthfully answer a question ("truth") or perform a challenge ("dare"). In both cases, it's usually embarrassing.

In "The 21 Second Excitation" (4-8), it's a girl's night in: Penny, Bernadette, and Amy are having a slumber party at Penny's apartment. As is traditional slumber party fare, they play a game of Truth or Dare, and Bernadette asks a truthful question that visibly upsets Penny: "Why are you still hanging out with Leonard so much, even though you broke up with him?"

Twitter • A popular social networking site that restricts "small bursts of information," or "tweets," to 140 characters in length.

In "The 21 Second Excitation" (4-8), Wil Wheaton tweets in the movie theater while Sheldon and his friends are standing outside, waiting to get in. The act raises Sheldon's ire because, as Sheldon says, Wheaton knows full well that Sheldon is reading his tweets.

Though the tweeting on the show is obviously fictional, Wil Wheaton does tweet in real life, at @wilw.

U

Uhura, Lieutenant • A character from the Star Trek universe, hailing from the original series. She was played by Nichelle Nichols, who was the first African American in a major TV role. (Nichols also gave William Shatner an interracial snog on TV—another first.) Frustrated by the perfunctory lines she was given, Nichols was ready to resign from *Star Trek*, but she was forced to reconsider when another African American lauded her performance and cited her as an inspiration—Dr. Martin Luther King, Jr. She chose to stay on the job, but unfortunately, her lines never improved. She spent most of her time saying, "Hailing frequencies are open, Captain," as the good lines invariably went to Captain Kirk or Mr. Spock. Nonetheless, Nichols played the role for the duration of the series and reprised it in *Star Trek: The Motion Picture*, which writer Harlan Ellison acidly but accurately termed "The Motionless Picture."

In "The Prestidigitation Approximation" (4-18), we learn that Raj has a Lieutenant Uhura uniform, which Leonard wants Priya to wear. But she dispels his Star Trek fantasy: "Leonard, it is a source of great pain to me and my family that my brother has that outfit in his wardrobe. Can we not discuss it?"

In "The Roommate Transmogrification" (4-24), though, Priya finally acquiesces and, in Raj's bedroom, Leonard has what Raj tells Sheldon is "astronomically inaccurate *Star Trek* sex with my sister." (It's astronomically inaccurate because Leonard postulates that they're having sex in outer space on the U.S.S. *Enterprise*, ten miles above Earth. NASA, however, cites fifty miles as a minimum distance for being termed an astronaut.)

U.S.S. *Enterprise* (NCC-1701) • From the Star Trek universe, we first see this legendary starship in the original television series. It was twice refitted, for

Star Trek: The Motion Picture and *Star Trek II: The Wrath of Khan*, and finally destroyed in *Star Trek III: The Search for Spock*. (*Note:* There are numerous other starships named *Enterprise*, distinguished by different registry numbers.)

Sheldon's imaginary home away from home, the *Enterprise* is where he would like to be stationed as a science officer. In "The Thespian Catalyst" (4-14), he and Penny do a dramatic reading of an early piece of fan fiction he wrote, in which Spock teleports to Sheldon's East Texas home. Penny, in the role of Spock, says, "Spock to *Enterprise*. Transport successful."

V

Vulcan nerve-pinch • This pressure-point technique is principally used to immobilize people, but it also works on other life forms, including, in one case, a horse-like creature. Spock favors this technique, but he uses it only in emergencies. One such instance was in *Star Trek IV: The Voyage Home*, in which they travel back in time to the 1980s. They are on a public bus in San Francisco and a punk rocker with a ghetto blaster is playing music at full volume, and when politely asked to turn it down, he defiantly turns it *up*. Spock then performs the Vulcan nerve-pinch, causing the punk to lose consciousness and earning Spock a grateful round of applause from the others on the bus.

In "The Cooper-Hofstadter Polarization" (1-9), the roommates are literally at each other's throats because Sheldon is unhappy that Leonard plans to present their joint paper with or without him. As Howard records the physicists gone wild on his cell phone, he cries out, "Vulcan nerve-pinch!"

W

Watchmen • From the DC Comics universe, this twelve-issue limited series was published from 1986 to 1987. The creative team includes writer Alan Moore, artist Dave Gibbons, and colorist John Higgins. From Wikipedia: "Moore used the story as a means to reflect contemporary anxieties and to critique the superhero concept. *Watchmen* depicts an alternate history where superheroes emerged in the 1940s and 1960s, helping the United States to win the Vietnam War. The country is edging towards a nuclear war with the Soviet Union, freelance costumed vigilantes have been outlawed, and most costumed superheroes are in retirement or working for the government."

Directed by Zack Snyder, this 2009 movie received mixed reviews by film critics.

Its length (2 hours, 43 minutes), its rating (R), and the necessity of pleasing fans by sticking closely to the original story line proved to be insurmountable handicaps. Costing $130 million to film, it grossed only $107 million domestically, though foreign receipts brought the total up to $185 million worldwide.

In "The Psychic Vortex" (3-12), Raj arrives at Sheldon's apartment with the four-hour edition of *Watchmen*, thinking that the others will want to watch it. But he's wrong: Leonard's got it, Howard's seen it, and Sheldon's already posted a detailed analysis online.

West, Adam • The actor best known for playing Batman in a TV series and a related movie. The show, which aired from 1966 to 1968, was a missed opportunity. Instead of playing it straight, this campy interpretation showed little of the dark side of the Dark Knight. He is much more accurately portrayed in the Frank Miller comic book interpretations and the movies, which are deliciously dark, just as Batman's creator intended.

In "The Precious Fragmentation" (3-17), the boys detour from a trip to the Chinese restaurant to follow Adam West, and have to explain to Penny who he is. Incredulous, Sheldon asks Leonard, "What do the two of you talk about after the coitus?"

Earth to Sheldon: Clearly not popular culture.

Wii • This Nintendo video game console has sold over 76 million units in its various versions. It replaced the Nintendo GameCube.

Sedulously avoiding real physical activities, the boys enjoy their sports electronically, playing Wii boxing, racing, archery, and fishing. They also play Wii bowling, though they actually do bowl in real life as well. (Penny and Sheldon are particularly good.)

In "The Boyfriend Complexity" (4-9), Leonard bonds with Penny's father, Wyatt, during a session of Wii fishing, which spares them a rocking boat, mosquitoes, squirming bait, and possibly getting a finger or thumb accidentally perforated with a hook. In other words, for these boys, Wii is just the safer way to go: the real world has barbs.

Windows Vista • Released on January 30, 2007, this operating system for PCs garnered heavy criticism.

In "The Toast Derivation," (4-17), Sheldon went up to Bill Gates after he gave a speech at Caltech to point out his dissatisfaction with Vista. Give 'em hell, Sheldon; Microsoft Word for Mac sucks worse than Aquaman.

Winter, Johnny • John Dawson "Johnny" Winter III is a rock guitarist who has won two Grammys for albums by Muddy Waters (*Hard Again* and *I'm*

Ready). He performed a nine-song set at Woodstock in 1969. In 1988 he was inducted into the Blues Foundation Hall of Fame.

In "The Terminator Decoupling" (2-17), Howard shows off his sparkling wit to Summer Glau by telling her that if she were to marry the bluesman, her name would be—insert drum roll—"Summer Winter."

Wolverine • From the Marvel Comics universe, he's "a mutant possessing animal-keen senses, enhanced physical capabilities, three retracting bone claws on each hand, and a healing factor that allows him to recover from virtually any wound, disease, or toxin at an accelerated rate," per Wikipedia.

In "The Jiminy Conjecture" (3-2), the boys contend that Wolverine, Sheldon's second-favorite X-Man, was born with bone claws. Sheldon chides them: "If you people spent less time thinking about sex and more time concentrating on comic books, we'd have far fewer of these embarrassing moments."

Wonder Woman • From the DC Comics universe, this popular superheroine originally appeared in *All Star Comics* #8 (December 1941). Her principal means of transportation is an invisible jet plane. States Wikipedia, "Her powers include superhuman strength, flight, super-speed, super-stamina, and super-agility. She is highly proficient in hand-to-hand combat and in the art of tactical warfare."

In "The Vengeance Formulation (3-9)", Howard is on the horns of a dilemma. Bernadette's attracted to him, but what he really wants, or thinks he wants, is a relationship with a dream woman, like Scarlett Johansson or Wonder Woman, neither of whom are within his grasp, as Penny points out when she sees him looking for Bernadette at the Cheesecake Factory. She sarcastically says, "Oh, gee, you're too late. Scarlett Johansson and Wonder Woman were just in here trolling around for neurotic little weasels."

Both Penny and Sheldon have dressed up as Wonder Woman over the course of the show: Penny succumbed to peer pressure ("The Justice League Recombination," 4-11), and Sheldon lost a bet ("The Wheaton Recurrence," 3-19).

Wozniak, Steve (Woz) • A gifted engineer and one of three founders of Apple Computers (the other two being Steve Jobs and Ron Wayne). The "geek" face of Apple, Woz has a large following among engineers, who identify with him and not Jobs.

In "The Cruciferous Vegetable Amplification" (4-2), Sheldon meets Woz. Impressed, Sheldon rushes home to get his Apple II computer, which Woz designed, for an autograph.

X

Xavier, Professor • From the Marvel Comics universe, Xavier, familiarly known as Professor X, is the founder and leader of the superheroes known collectively as the X-Men. To foster the education of his fellow mutants, he founded Xavier's School for Gifted Youngsters.

In "The Pants Alternative" (3-18), Sheldon suffers from stage fright and Penny and the boys rally around him to offer advice. The boys suggest they could be his X-Men, though Sheldon maintains that C-Men (for "Cooper") would be more appropriate. (Naturally, he doesn't see the obvious problem with that suggestion.)

Xbox • A video game console manufactured by Microsoft. It comes with a central box and a hand-operated controller. It plays a long list of games, notably *Halo*.

As with sports (with the exception of bowling), the boys aren't interested in forming a real rock band, but they enjoy *pretending* to be in one. In "The Bath Item Gift Hypothesis" (2-11), when Howard says they're in a band, Leonard corrects him: "No, we *play* Rock Band on our Xbox."

In "The Bozeman Reaction" (3-13), their Xbox and Xbox 360 are stolen during a break-in.

Y

"You have the conn" • From the Star Trek universe, an expression frequently used by a bridge officer, usually the ship's captain, to pass over control of the bridge to a subordinate. According to an entry in the Star Trek Freedom Wiki by Daniel Greene: "In the Star Trek universe, the term 'Conn' is used to refer to the control of the ship as well as the navigation and/or helm station located on the bridge."

In "The Euclid Affair" (2-5), as Penny drives Sheldon to work, he reluctantly concedes that she's driving and is thus in control. She decides to drive on Euclid Avenue, and though he prefers a different, more efficient route, he tells her, "But you have the conn."

In "The Bus Pants Utilization" (4-12), after Sheldon fruitlessly lobbies to run an app project Leonard is in charge of, Sheldon, conceding reluctantly once again, says, "Sheldon Cooper is nothing if not a team player. Dr. Hofstadter, you have the conn."

Young Sherlock Holmes • Directed by Barry Levinson, this 1985 mystery/ adventure film features two teenagers attending the Brompton Academy— Sherlock Holmes and John Watson. It's one of three Chris Columbus movies the boys watch on Columbus Day, in "The Pirate Solution" (3-4).

Z

Zork • One of the first interactive fiction computer games from Infocom. States Wikipedia, "*Zork* is set in a sprawling underground labyrinth which occupies a portion of the 'Great Underground Empire.'" The player is a nameless adventurer whose goal is to find the treasures hidden in the caves and return alive with them, ultimately inheriting the title of Dungeon Master.

In "The Hofstadter Isotope" (2-20), Penny drops by Sheldon's apartment and sees Leonard and Sheldon. It's Friday night, so it's traditionally the time they eat Chinese food and play video games. The selection that night is *Zork*, the "buggy beta version" of the 1980 interactive text adventure. Sheldon is a big fan of the interactive text adventures, probably because, as he puts it, they run "on the world's most powerful graphics chip—imagination."

AFTERWORD

"All Good Things . . ."

In the Darwinian world of television sitcoms, in which the survival of the fittest is the rule of the jungle, the key to longevity is the blessed word "renewal." It means the show is being picked up for at least one season, and hopefully more.

On the heels of Jim Parsons winning the Golden Globe, on January 16, 2011, the news broke that CBS was renewing *The Big Bang Theory* for an additional three seasons of twenty-two episodes each, guaranteeing (so far) a seven-season run, with the option of additional renewals if the show continues to rank high in the ratings.

CBS Entertainment President Nina Tassler broke the news after the deal closed, saying, "It doesn't take a theoretical physicist to see why this show is a *big* part of our comedy future. From ratings to critical acclaim to pop culture buzz, it's struck a chord on all levels."

As it was for other long-running shows—*Mash, Cheers, Frasier, Seinfeld, Friends,* and *Star Trek* to name the most obvious standouts—the challenge will be for *The Big Bang Theory* to maintain its high level of quality and keep viewers interested in the years to come, up until its final episode airs.

Will *The Big Bang Theory* End with a Bang or a Whimper?

The penultimate and final episode of *Star Trek: The Next Generation*, which aired in 1994, brought the story line back to its beginning. A two-parter (episodes 25 and 26), we once again saw the mercurial entity Q, who put Captain Picard on trial in the first episode, "Encounter at Farpoint" (air date 1987). After all the years, Q put Picard to a final test—and he passed it with flying colors. He solved the puzzle of how to destroy an interstellar anomaly, which Q took as proof that humanity, for which he'd had a dim view, showed potential and had earned its right to expand throughout the universe.

In the last scene of the last episode, we saw the officers of the bridge playing poker. Picard entered the room and asked to join them, which was a first. As the commander, he'd never fraternized with his subordinates in such fashion, but they were happy to see him join in. As he took a seat and dealt out the cards, Picard said, "And the sky's the limit . . ."

What might be the limit for Penny, Leonard, Howard, Raj, and Sheldon? Will the last episode be simply another day in their lives, or will the characters, having learned from their experiences, boldly go somewhere they have not gone before?

It's far too early to tell. But one thing is for sure: until that day comes, every Thursday night at 8:00 P.M., Eastern Standard Time, millions of loyal fans will tune out of the real world to tune in to a show that has educated as much as it has entertained us. It celebrates not only those with beautiful minds, but also those who are beautiful in many ways.

But all good things really must come to an end. After seven years—or more, if we're fortunate—of personal and professional growth for all of them, the sky will indeed be their limit.

May they live long and prosper.

ACKNOWLEDGMENTS

Tim Kirk: Thanks for the conceptual artwork and many textual and illustrative suggestions that were instrumental in shaping this book, especially the fact-checking on the travel section. As a former Disney Imagineer, your ideas are always thought-provoking and illuminating, and challenge me to think as creatively as possible.

Ned Brooks: As a bona fide rocket scientist, your comments about the science section proved invaluable. Thank you for shedding light on dark matters for me, and for having done so for more years than I can remember.

Scott Mendel: Your unflinching honesty turned an unworkable book proposal into a workable one. Thank you for respecting me and my work enough to tell me what I need to know.

Glenn Yeffeth: As my publisher, your enthusiasm from the beginning on this book, and the editing/design/production team you tasked to turn the manuscript into a book, made a world of difference: the finished book reflects your shared sensibilities, and it's obviously the better for it.

Leah Wilson and Heather Butterfield: The best editors work with the writer toward a common cause: to make the book as good as it can possibly be. This book is a testament to your attention to detail, with an eye toward constantly seeking improvement of the end result. I am indebted to both of you.

Oriana Leckert: Your eagle eyes spotted what I missed, time and again. Thanks for looking over my shoulder and, when necessary, suggesting I take another look when it was needed.

Jennifer Canzoneri: My thanks for all the work expended on my behalf to tirelessly promote and market the book, especially at Comic-Con, to insure it reaches the widest possible readership. I am forever grateful.

Kirsten Cairns: Thanks for taking time out of your busy schedule to write a sidebar of convention tips for newbies.

Mary: As always, you're my sounding board on every book in every possible way, from the first to the last page. In the course of this project, the unexpected happened: you, too, became a fan of *The Big Bang Theory*. That's the best compliment you could have given me. Thank you.

ABOUT THE AUTHOR

George Beahm frequently writes about popular culture. His thirty-two books have explored, among other topics, the fictional worlds of Stephen King, Patricia Cornwell, J.K. Rowling, C.S. Lewis, J.R.R. Tolkien, and Philip Pullman.

He resides in southeast Virginia with his wife, Mary.

His website is at www.georgebeahm.com.